From Fulham 1
20 years of Rugby L(

G000153327

Edited by Dave Farrar and Peter Lush

London League Publications Ltd

From Fulham to Wembley
20 years of Rugby League in London

Front cover photos:
Top: Fulham players on lap of honour after beating Wigan 24-5 on 14 September 1980. (Photo: Ken Coton)
Bottom: London Broncos players after beating Castleford 33-27 in the 1999 Challenge Cup semi-final. (Photo: Gerald Webster & the *Rugby Leaguer*)
Back cover photos:
Top: London Broncos team 2000 season (Photo: Peter Lush)
Middle: Buck - the London Broncos' mascot (Photo: Peter Lush)
Bottom: Supporters on the bus trip to Wembley 1999 (See chapter 4).
(Photo: Barry & Gwen Warren)

A CIP catalogue record for this book is available from the British Library.

First published in Great Britain in May 2000 by:
London League Publications Ltd.
P.O. Box 10441, London E14 0SB

ISBN: 0-9526064-4-5

Cover design by: Stephen McCarthy Graphic Design
                      46, Clarence Road London N15 5BB
Layout by: Peter Lush
Printed and bound by: Catford Print Centre, PO Box 563, Catford,
                      London SE6 4PY

About the editors

Dave Farrar has been watching Rugby League for nearly 40 years. He was born in Salford and his parents watched the original Red Devils (Salford RLFC) in the 1930s. He moved to London in 1980 and started watching Fulham. He has now followed Rugby League in London for 20 years and is a committed supporter of the London Broncos. Apart from the books listed below, he has also written *The Right to Vote* (with Yve Amor). He has also written regularly for *London Calling!* and is vice-chairman of the London Broncos supporters club. He works as a manager in local government. His favourite London Rugby League players are Mark Riley, Tulsen Tollett and Steele Retchless.

Peter Lush was introduced to Rugby League by Dave Farrar in October 1980, when having nothing better to do on a Sunday afternoon, he went to watch Fulham play York at Craven Cottage. 20 years later he is still enthusiastic about the game. He also has a season ticket for West Ham United FC, has a soft spot for Brentford FC, and is a member of Middlesex County Cricket Club. Apart from the books listed below, he also co-wrote *The Employment Handbook - a guide for housing co-operatives*. He writes regularly for *London Calling!* and *The Greatest Game* and once wrote a match report for *League Express* (see chapter 4). When not writing about or watching sport, he works as a housing and personnel consultant. His favourite London Rugby League players are Chris Wilkinson, John Gallagher and Shaun Edwards.

Previous publications:
Touch and Go - A History of Professional Rugby League in London
by Dave Farrar and Peter Lush with Michael O'Hare
I Wouldn't Start from Here by Peter Lush and Dave Farrar
The Sin Bin by Steve Spencer, Peter Hardy and Dave Farrar
From Arundel to Zimbabwe by Robin Osmond, Peter Lush and
Dave Farrar
Tries in the Valleys edited by Peter Lush and Dave Farrar
Going to the Cricket by Robin Osmond and Peter Lush
Our Game edited by Peter Lush and Dave Farrar

Editorial note: Except where a piece is attributed to a particular writer, all the pieces in the book were written by Dave Farrar and Peter Lush. Most of the interviews were by Peter Lush.

Foreword

My introduction to Rugby League in London was Christmas 1994. I signed for the Broncos a week before Christmas and flew over to join the club, who were pressing for promotion from the Second Division. At home, Christmas Day would be spent playing cricket on the beach. Instead, I had bacon and eggs with scrum-half Kevin Langer for breakfast and then got on the coach to go to the hotel at Haydock where we were staying before playing at Leigh on Boxing Day.

It was so cold at Leigh, there was horizontal sleet. The water in the shower afterwards was a hot drip so we could not get clean properly. And we lost. "This is what England is always like" I thought, but things got better. John Ribot had convinced me that helping build Rugby League in London was important for the game. I also knew Steve Rosolen and he'd been here for a long time.

As well as playing, I was involved when we started some of the work in the schools at that time. We learnt some important lessons that helped the club develop this very important area of work.

The club was given a place in the top division in the last winter season before Super League started. We had struggled and then a month before Super League started in March 1996 we were beaten at Dewsbury in the cup. However, the first season in Super League was very important and helped establish the club at the top. It taught us what pioneering was all about, from the first game at Halifax, which we won, to the 56-0 win against Castleford at the end of the season. The first game at the Valley against Paris was fantastic - a very successful night for London. Then the game we drew at Wigan was an enormous result. We played a stalling game which was controversial, but Terry Matterson's great touchline kick at the end got us a draw. Players such as Peter Gill, Greg Barwick, Kevin Langer and Terry Matterson all made a great contribution to that team. Maybe we could have even finished higher. We lost at St Helens in the play-offs - I was sin-binned in my last game! But there was a great sense of achievement about that season.

We also bought in some younger players to the first team. At the start of the season I had gone with Dave Rotheram to put our case to the League that our Academy team should play in the Super League Academy. We now have players coming through and challenging for first team places from the Academy. We have made great progress in that area and now have under-16 and under-13 teams in place as well.

I was bitten by the bug of London Rugby League and was delighted to be offered the Chief Executive post when I retired from playing in 1996. Sometimes having that role has been hard - I have had to negotiate with players who were team mates. But I am confident that we can continue to build a strong structure for the club. 20 years history as a club means that we are not a "young club" any more, just young compared to the others. Playing five years in Super League is also an achievement.

We still face a massive challenge to establish ourselves in the community. The staff and the players work very hard for the club so that our support will grow. With their commitment and that of our supporters, we deserve a full stadium and a successful team. Sir Richard Branson and David Hughes also give us important financial backing and support.

There is no better group of supporters in Rugby League than ours. They must be the most travelled in the game - both for home and away games. They deserve all the success we can get. The Wembley final was very special and I was very pleased that the London supporters had a chance to see their team play at Wembley. I find our supporters very easy to relate to. Sometimes they give me a hard time, but I would worry if they didn't - it would mean that no one cares.

Tony Rea

Tony made 47 appearances for the club (46 games plus 1 as substitute), scored 11 tries and 44 points. Since 1997 he has been the club's Chief Executive.

Tony Rea (left)
with Les Kiss
at Sheffield in
August 1999.
(Photo: Peter Lush)

Introduction

20 years! When Fulham beat Wigan 24-5 before nearly 10,000 people at Craven Cottage in September 1980, there were sceptics who believed that Rugby League in London would be a nine-day wonder and not last. If nothing else, the game has shown great tenacity to survive and at times even prosper in London. We're still here and proud of it!

This book is not intended to be a season by season history of the last 20 years of professional Rugby League in the capital. We covered that ground up to 1995 in our previous book, *Touch and Go*. Rather, this is a celebration of the club's twentieth anniversary - a landmark in the history of Rugby League - by far the longest lasting club outside the game's heartlands in Britain or in Australia.

Most of this book features people involved in the club, who have worked with great dedication to keep the club alive. The players, coaches and club officials featured are a representative selection. Choosing who to include was a nightmare task. An original list of over 50 players was slowly cut to 30, while trying to ensure that all periods of the club's history were fairly covered. We hope that readers will appreciate the problem - please don't write indignant letters to us if your particular favourite is not here.

From the beginning, the club's supporters have always been a central part of the London Rugby League scene. Fulham's inspirational first player-coach Reg Bowden recalls the supporters in the first matches at Craven Cottage being very keen but not always understanding the rules and "even cheering the knock-ons". Since then, supporters have travelled vast distances to the north of England every other week to support their team - even at times when they were at the wrong end of the Second Division. Supporters such as Bob Evans, Ron Snares and Harry Stammers became known throughout the north for their passionate commitment to the game.

Huw Richards's marvellous account of the 1985-6 season in *XIII Winters* described the supporters' enthusiasm at the famous match at Huddersfield in March 1986, when the club's closure had been announced and despair would have been understandable. A Huddersfield match steward said: "What the' eck are you closing for? We could do with some of this." The piece is entitled "Getting worked up watching *Bambi*" -

another comment on the Fulham fans' capacity for enthusiasm, based on the idea that some coaches were showing the film *Rambo* to their players for motivation.

The supporters club has been an important part of the club since the early days. To avoid repetition from *Touch and Go*, we have not included interviews in this book with the Snares family, or with Barry and Gwen Warren who all played a vital role in sustaining the supporters club and much more. We hope that the memories and reflections in chapter 4 of the book will suffice.

Nor have we interviewed people such as Tim Lamb and Richard Lawton, club directors in the Chiswick period, again because we featured them in *Touch and Go*. Their involvement, along with many others in a voluntary capacity, kept the club alive then, when the idea of marketing budgets and a team of full-time staff and development workers was a distant dream. Stephen Froggatt's piece in chapter 4 recalls the spirit of those times.

Finally, we look forward with confidence to the future of Rugby League in London in the new millennium and to the club celebrating more anniversaries in the future.

Dave Farrar and Peter Lush

Thank You

We would like to thank everyone who wrote pieces for the book, lent us photographs and scrapbooks or gave up time to be interviewed. Michael O'Hare patiently spent time beyond the call of duty sub-editing, although of course any mistakes are down to us. In particular, our thanks to:

Ken Coton	Barry and Gwen Warren
Stephen Froggatt	Nigel Waters
Harold Genders	Sue Webber
Frank Levy	Gerald Webster and the *Rugby*
Huw Richards	*Leaguer*
David Stevens	Tim Wood
Barry Taylor	Craig Wilson
Neil Tunnicliffe	

We would also like to thank everyone who ordered the book in advance.

Key Dates in London Rugby League

Internationals:
1908:   First international in London. Great Britain 6 New Zealand 18 at
        Chelsea FC's Stamford Bridge
1930:   First international at Wembley. Wales 10 Australia 26
1990 : Great Britain 19 Australia 12 at Wembley
1992:   World Cup Final at Wembley - Great Britain 6 Australia 10
1994:   Great Britain 8 Australia 4

Clubs:
The Challenge Cup Final was first played at Wembley in 1929. Wigan beat
Dewsbury 13-2.
In the 1930s, there were three short-lived attempts to start clubs in London:
1933-4: London Highfield (Played at White City Stadium)
1935-6: Acton & Willesden
1935-7: Streatham & Mitcham
The famous Maori New Zealand Rugby Union All-Black, George Nepia, played
for Streatham and Mitcham from December 1935 to December 1936.

In 1955, Independent Television organised a tournament in London, with
matches played mid-week under floodlights at football grounds and shown on
television. Warrington beat Leigh in the final 43-15, with the famous
Australian winger Brian Bevan scoring two tries for Warrington.

In 1965, as part of a festival of sport at Crystal Palace, a seven-a-aside Rugby
League tournament was held. This tournament provided the impetus for the
relaunch of amateur Rugby League in the south, which had not existed since the
early 1950s.

In 1980, Fulham RLFC was formed, based at Fulham Football Club. In the first
season, 9,554 saw their victory over Wigan 24-5 in the first game at Craven
Cottage. The modern-day record crowd for a club match in London, apart from
the Challenge Cup Final, was set when 15,103 saw Fulham lose 9-5 to
Wakefield in the Challenge Cup

1981   Fulham finished third in the Second Division and thus were promoted
        to the First Division
1982   Fulham relegated from the First Division

1983	Fulham won the Second Division Championship and were promoted to the First Division.
1984	Fulham relegated from the First Division. The original club was liquidated and Fulham RLFC (1984) formed by Roy and Barbara Close. Played at Crystal Palace National Sports Centre.
1985	Fulham moved to the Polytechnic Stadium, Chiswick
1989	Australian Ross Strudwick appointed as coach
1990	Fulham moved back to Crystal Palace National Sports Centre
1991	Fulham and Ryedale-York tour the Soviet Union, the first British clubs to tour there.
1991	Club name changed to London Crusaders
1993	London Crusaders moved to Barnet Copthall Stadium. Famous former New Zealand Rugby Union All-Black full-back John Gallagher signed.
1994	London Crusaders finish third in the Second Division, and reached the Premiership Final at Old Trafford
1994	The club was purchased by the Brisbane Broncos, and renamed London Broncos
1995	The Super League was formed, to start in March 1996, including the London Broncos. The Broncos were put into the Stones Bitter Championship (i.e. the top division) for the 1995-6 centenary season.
1996	London Broncos played at Charlton FC's The Valley for the first Super League season. Over 9,000 people saw Paris St. Germain beaten in the first match. Tony Currie becomes coach. Finished fourth in Super League. Barry Maranta becomes chairman and majority shareholder
1996	Martin Offiah joined the club from Wigan
1997	The club moved to Harlequins RFC's The Stoop. Shaun Edwards joined the club. Finished second in Super League and beat Canberra Raiders in a World Club Championship match.
1998	Reached the Challenge Cup semi-final for the first time, losing to Wigan. Sir Richard Branson becomes chairman and majority shareholder.
1999	Reached the Challenge Cup Final for the first time, losing 52-16 to Leeds in the last final to be played at the old Wembley Stadium.
1999	Appointed Australian John Monie as coach.
2000	Moved back to Charlton FC's The Valley. Shaun Edwards retires.

Showbiz supporters: Two genuine Rugby League enthusiasts.
Top: The late Brian Glover (right) with Liam Bushell.
Brian Glover's last film was *Up and Under* - the big screen version of
John Godber's play about Rugby League.
Below: Actor, writer and Rugby League enthusiast Colin Welland, who was a
club director at Craven Cottage and supported the club at Chiswick.

(Both photos: Barry & Gwen Warren)

Contents

The Flatcappers cartoon by Nigel Wilde.
Originally published in *The Greatest Game* and *The Sin Bin*

Bob Evans

Rugby League lost one of its biggest enthusiasts when Bob Evans died on 1 May 1999, a few hours before the London Broncos played in the Challenge Cup Final. He had a ticket for the match, to support the club that had introduced him to the game he loved.

Bob started watching Rugby League at Fulham in 1980, attending a match out of curiosity because Fulham were playing York, where he lived as a young child. He soon developed a passion for the game. In 1983, with Mike Geen he launched the *Rugby League Diary*, produced to keep southern based fans up to date with the game's news. The first edition said that: "We have watched RUGBY LEAGUE for three seasons and have become increasingly frustrated with the poor coverage of this sport in southern newspapers. We have therefore decided to start an information sheet to help people like ourselves, to keep in touch with RUGBY LEAGUE and not have to play or watch this game in a vacuum." Barry and Gwen Warren, for many years bastions of the Supporters Club, remember Bob standing outside Craven Cottage selling the *Diary*, which usually had six A4 pages of accurate, detailed information on the game.

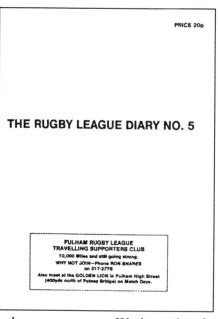

Along with other volunteers, Bob helped Fulham in a number of capacities in the mid-1980s, including match manager, amateur liaison officer and team administrator. With other supporters, Bob was involved in the work of restoring the Polytechnic Stadium at Chiswick for use by Fulham. Barry Warren remembers Bob "hiring a JCB for the weekend and

Bob Evans with Fulham player Huw Rees in front of the main stand at the
Polytechnic Stadium, Chiswick. (Photo courtesy Sarah Marshall)

digging out the path that ran along the perimeter fence". In 1987 he played a key role in setting up the first Fulham Colts team, despite the fact that he was living in the north-west at the time, because he had moved there for work reasons. His partner Sarah Marshall remembers them making sandwiches for the players on Saturday mornings before the colts matches.

Roy Lester has many memories of him. "I first got to know Bob when we played at Craven Cottage. All the players knew him. Then when the club moved, and I became coach, he was very supportive, very helpful and nothing was too much trouble. He helped pull the club through that period, as did a lot of other people. He was very charismatic, intelligent and dedicated to the game. He had so much enthusiasm for anything he did, not just Rugby League."

When Bob moved to the north-west in 1987, he linked up with Roy again, who by now was coach at Carlisle. Roy recalls that "Bob did the player match stats for me and anything else I asked him to do. He would drive up from Wigan to training twice a week. He always wanted to be totally involved. Once, we were playing Swinton, and Frank Low, one of our directors and our main financial backer, had been away and asked me to meet him at Manchester airport and take him to the game at Carlisle. But the flight was going to be late so I asked Bob to meet him. Bob was not very pleased - he didn't want to miss the game, but he agreed to do this for me. Frank still remembers that trip up the M6 - he had never been driven so fast, because Bob was determined to get to the game on time."

Bob developed systems for analysing players' performances through statistics that were respected wherever he used them. Roy Lester recalls that: "I trusted his stats. I never heard anyone dispute his figures. The players totally believed them."

In 1987, Bob was chosen as Traveleads Rugby League Fan of the Year, winning a holiday in Canada. As part of the award ceremony in Leeds, Sarah recalls him being photographed on a horse held by a Canadian mountie with Bob wearing a bowler hat and umbrella (because he worked at the stock exchange). There was also a photo of Bob receiving the award included in the 1988 Challenge Cup Final programme. Roy Lester says that it was "a massive achievement to become Fan of the Year from London. I can see him now sitting on the horse. The photo was in all the national and Rugby League papers."

But Sarah also remembers that "at first Bob was disappointed with the prize - there was no Rugby League in Canada. But we went anyway and had a wonderful holiday, a week in the Rockies and then a week visiting cities - Vancouver, Toronto and Calgary. It was in Canada that Bob discovered baseball, which became another passion for him. A later holiday to America included visits to baseball games in Boston, where we spent a week, Seattle and Cooperstown, to see the Baseball Hall of Fame."

Tony Barrow, now Swinton's chief executive, remembers meeting Bob at Fulham and then getting to know him on the 1988 Lions tour to Australia. Tony was coach at Oldham and got Bob involved there. He recalls: "He did some scouting for me and the match stats. He came to all the training sessions and loved every minute of it. He had the best stats system I have ever seen. He became a close friend of mine and came with me when I went to Swinton as coach. He loved Rugby League and studied the game. I used to send him videos to watch and he would analyse them. He was very knowledgeable. If he had played the game when he was younger he could have become a very good coach. When we were in Australia he met Wayne Bennett and Tim Sheens, two of the leading Australian coaches, and listened to them. He studied the Australian game and was hungry for information.

Our players would go to him after the game for their figures - tackles, yards made, how many balls they caught and how many they dropped. He still worked with us when he moved back to London [in April 1989]. He was a great man to have on the staff, someone I always liked to have with me. I taught him about coaching and he took his grade one and grade two coaching certificates."

Barry Warren also remembers how Bob could analyse a game. "He could see things in a game that I could not see - he could talk through the moves. He had a deep understanding of it. He kept records of all the matches he attended. His handwriting was impeccable and he would make notes and keep the stats."

Barry and Gwen also remember how Bob loved talking about the game. "The time he missed the supporters' coaches and was left behind in Featherstone in 1983 it was because he was talking to people in the bar about the match. When he realised what had happened he got a lift to Leeds, got the train, arrived before us in London and met the coaches at

Hammersmith." Barry remembers: "Once, we were staying with Bob and Sarah in Wigan. Bob and I went out to buy a paper on the Sunday morning at the local garage. We met Alan McInnes, the former Wigan coach. Half an hour later we were still there, talking about Rugby League. Another time we were with Bob and met Maurice Lindsay in Billy Boston's pub near Central Park." Sarah also recalls that when they lived in Wigan: "We used to drink in the Boar's Head and Maurice Lindsay used to drink there. He called us his 'little friends from London'. "

She also remembers trips with Barry and Gwen to the Isle of Man in the 1980s to watch the Charity Shield games and meeting leading Rugby League officials David Howes and David Oxley there, both of whom knew Bob.

For a time Bob did the match statistics for Sky television, working with Ian Proctor. He was invited by Phil Larder to do the stats on a Great Britain tour to New Zealand. He flew out and got as far as Bangkok, but his trip was stopped there. Because of an oversight he did not have the necessary transit visa for Australia, so had to return home. Another disappointment was not getting the job as a London Development Officer, his lack of experience in the professional game going against him, although he was pleased that his friend John Cain did get the job. Bob later assisted the Surrey Heath amateur club when he was back in London.

He had many other interests apart from Rugby League, including football, (where he supported Aldershot Town), cricket and steam trains. He worked in the stock exchange and finance industry, where his understanding of statistics and figures was very useful. After being made redundant for the second time in 1994, he took courses in writing and developed an interest in the arts, writing and the theatre.

Bob was 47 when he died. The week before the Cup Final, Bob attended his last game of Rugby League at The Stoop, when the London Broncos organised a reunion before the match against Warrington. There he saw many old friends from the Fulham days, including former coach Roy Lester.

Bob had spoken to Tony Barrow, a few days before the final, and had said that he planned to attend the game. Friends who heard the news on Cup Final morning were stunned and sad. Bob's funeral at Mortlake crematorium was packed with mourners, including many people from all

The Bob Evans Memorial Trophy - presented to the club in London that has made most progress with junior development, chosen by the Broncos' development staff. Kingston were the first winners in 1999.
(Photo: Peter Lush)

over Rugby League. Both weekly Rugby League papers and the London Broncos programme had tributes to him and there was a minute's silence in his memory before the next Broncos home game.

People throughout Rugby League miss Bob - he had friends throughout the game. Huw Richards remembers: "Visiting Sydney in 1987, I was introduced to every League person I met as 'a friend of Bob Evans'. Nobody needed any further explanation."

In 1996, Dave Farrar and I were at Halifax for the first London Broncos Super League game. A Halifax supporter came over to us and without a word of introduction, asked: "Is Bob Evans with you today?" This was years after Bob had stopped watching the club regularly because of his work with Roy Lester and Tony Barrow. Tony says that: "There are not enough people like him in the game. I still miss him." Roy remembers him as "a lovely man, really nice. He always had time for you and would always help out".

Peter Lush

With thanks to:
Sarah Marshall
Barry and Gwen Warren
Tony Barrow

Roy Lester
Huw Richards

1. The Players

The Craven Cottage heroes
Adrian Cambriani	10
Tony Gourley	11
Ian van Bellen	14
Martin Herdman	16
Steve Diamond	20
Hussain M'Barki	21
Steve Mills and	
Charlie Jones	25

Crystal Palace and Chiswick
Chris Wilkinson	31
Frank Feighan	33
Colin Fenn	35
Dave Gillan	38
Russ Bridge	39
Dave Rotheram	
and Darryl Pitt	42
Mick Taylor	48

A London Crusade
Steve Rosolen	49
Scott Roskell	50
Mark Riley	52
Mark Johnson	54
Abi Ekoku	58
John Gallagher	60
Sam Stewart	63
Leo Dynevor	65

The Bucking Broncos
Kevin Langer	67
Peter Gill	68
Terry Matterson	71
Tulsen Tollett	75
Martin Offiah	77
Shaun Edwards	81

Steve Mills's Fulham shirt - the original club strip
(Photo: Peter Lush)

Trying to select the players to include in this chapter was a nightmare. Due to the turnover in players over the years there is a vast selection to choose from. For example, the first season provided so many highlights, who on earth could you leave out? We decided to have some players from each era of the club's existence and long service has counted for more than, say, a brilliant period of one or two seasons - with some exceptions, such as Ian van Bellen - the crowd's first hero, who played just a single season. However, from the Craven Cottage period David Eckersley, John Risman, Mal Aspey, Dave Allen, Harry Beverley, Tony Kinsey, Joe Doherty and Chris Ganley were all vital parts of the team, as was Tony Karalius in the first season. Steve Bayliss's try scoring also made an impact. It was a difficult decision to exclude them. Reg Bowden and Roy Lester, both key players at that time, are covered in chapter 2 of this book.

Other players had to be left out as well. Harold Henney held the pack together for two seasons as new coach Roy Lester rebuilt the side from 1984 to 1986. Alan Platt was also a high quality signing at that time. At Chiswick, Australians Michael Davis, Don Duffy, Peter White, Craig Taylor, Glen Haggath and Pat O'Doherty all helped strengthen inexperienced teams, while British players Steve Guyett, Kieron Murphy, Nick Grimoldby and Mick Hutchinson all developed when the team became southern based from 1986. Greg Pearce contributed much and his transfer fee helped keep the club alive for another year. Chris Smith, a recruit from Rugby Union, was a high quality forward and goal-kicker.

Shane Buckley was a regular try scorer for Ross Strudwick's Crystal Palace based team and Nick Halafihi added quality to the pack. Under Tony Gordon, apart from the players covered, Logan Campbell, Neville Ramsey and Andre Stoop all contributed to the marvellous 1993-4 team. Sadly, there just wasn't enough room to include them all.

For the Broncos, Steele Retchless has been a marvellous example of a tackling machine and will go down in history for his winning try in the 1999 Challenge Cup semi-final. Tony Rea played an important role as hooker for two seasons before retiring to become chief executive. Justin Bryant was the last of the Australian "backpackers" to turn up for a trial and become a valuable first team player. Tony Mestrov, Tony Martin, Greg Barwick and Rusty Bawden all made valuable contributions to the 1996 and 1997 teams. Darren Shaw and Ikram Butt also played an important role in establishing the Broncos at the top level. These too were all left out of our final selection.

Another key player is Karle Hammond, who was an inspired choice as captain in 1999 and held the team together through some hard times as well as showing skills in all aspects of the game. Many Broncos fans were stunned when he was not included in the Great Britain squad for the 1999 Tri-Series in Australasia.

Early hero - Adrian Cambriani. Supporters' club chairman Ron Snares is on the right. (Photo: Barry & Gwen Warren)

Modern day hero - Karle Hammond
(Photo: Peter Lush)

The Craven Cottage heroes

Adrian Cambriani

Adrian Cambriani, Fulham's "Golden Boy" and star winger, has three claims to fame. He was Fulham's first Rugby Union signing, he scored the club's first try and he was the club's first international, together with Martin Herdman. Such was his impact that after his first game of Rugby League he was *The Observer's* Sports Personality of the Week. An article by Gill Martin in October 1980 described him as "the new blond, blue-eyed Adonis of Rugby".

Adrian was signed from Swansea as a Welsh Rugby Union youth international for a signing-on fee believed to be £16,000. He was spotted by Harold Genders who attended the Welsh Rugby Union junior international matches seeking potential Rugby League talent. Before joining Fulham he had toured South Africa with the Wales youth team.

The fee a lot of money for an 18 year-old, but the Fulham experiment was nothing initially if not bold. His two tries against Wigan in that memorable debut seemed to repay a large part of that faith, but from then on his career was dogged by a series of injuries. Yet Adrian was quick to learn and provided pace to a back line which otherwise had a veteran look to it in the early seasons.

The fact that Cambriani managed over 100 appearances for the club shows that he did establish himself in League and his 42 tries in this period showed what a finisher he could be on his day. At the demise of the original Fulham, as with a majority of the squad, Cambriani left the club with a view to playing elsewhere, after the players had been declared "free agents" in a court case, but his plans did not work out. He was eventually welcomed back by the coach, Roy Lester, with the comment "He was never a ringleader as the free agents were concerned, I am delighted to have him back".

His worth was proved at a Lancashire Cup match at Wigan in 1985 when he scored a try and made another for Steve Garner in a 13-24 defeat, at a time when the club were rebuilding from nothing and gave their famous opponents a fright, leading with 15 minutes to go. In some ways that later season was more impressive than the first when he scored 13 tries, as the 10 he scored in that season was in a side that only slowly knitted together.

Adrian's high point was appearing for Wales in the club's first season. His final appearance was for Fulham against Papua New Guinea in 1987, soon after he retired due to recurring injuries. His seven years spent at the club is one of the longest in terms of years playing for the first team, a record only beaten by Dave Rotheram and Darryl Pitt. And he was also the first Fulham player to appear on the catwalk as a male model, a trend followed by some Broncos players in the 1990s.

119 appearances plus 2 as substitute
42 tries
146 points

Tony Gourley

Managing Director Harold Genders's recruitment policy for the forwards to play in the first Fulham team was very clear - he wanted them big and experienced. Other words, like fierce and ferocious come to mind. At that time, scrums were a place to fight for the ball, not just a means of restarting the game. These forwards could look after themselves. Not dirty - sending offs were relatively rare - but certainly hard.

Tony Gourley was not only a key member of the pack in the first season, but for the first five. He stayed loyal to the club when other players left in 1984, was club captain for his last three seasons and vice captain in 1981-2.

Until he was 18, he played football and Rugby Union, joining Old Rochdalians RUFC after leaving school. A friend arranged for him to go training at Rochdale Hornets and he turned professional at 20. He says he was "very green". In his first match, a friendly, he dived on a loose ball and was kicked in the head and shoulder. Welcome to Rugby League!

He enjoyed his nine years with Rochdale and was also selected for Lancashire, winning two caps. In 1978, Hornets played Salford on a Friday night and Tony got the man-of-the-match after having an outstanding game. He was then pursued by Salford coach Alex Murphy and signed for them. Salford's great team of the 1970s was coming to an end, although he says "it was nice to play with a better class of player. It

Tony Gourley -
a model made
by a supporter

(Photo: Peter Lush)

made my job easier and I was scoring tries". By the end of his second season, Salford were in transition and Fulham came in for him. He remembers there were only 12 players at his first training session and he was introduced to other new team mates at the first game against Wigan.

He recalls the "come on Fulham" shouts in raucous cockney accents, and says "we built up a good rapport with the supporters." Surprisingly he did not see joining Fulham as a gamble. "I knew the people I was playing with - some world beaters in their own right who commanded respect throughout the game. Our pack could create gaps for the backs to run off us. It was a pleasure to play with those players."

The first game, not surprisingly, was a highlight for him. "Against all the odds we gave Wigan a stuffing. And beating Bradford in the Wembley eve friendly. They were the best team in the country and we gave them a lesson. And we beat Leeds 9-3 in the John Player Trophy, winning the scrums 3-1 against the Great Britain hooker." Also very memorable was the match against Australia in 1982, when he captained Fulham, although the result was disappointing as the Kangaroos secured victory in the last 10 minutes.

He also remembers the club holiday in Portugal at the end of the first season: 76 players, wives and children staying at Ernie Clay's hotel.

Tony was one of the stars of the "Grillsteaks" television commercial the players made at the start of the second season. Sadly the commercial was not shown in the south, so most Fulham fans never saw it.

Immediately after filming, three players walked out on the club before the match at home to Warrington, seeking transfers or better terms. Tony had just had a cartilage operation and had not been expecting to play. He says he had been out "socialising" for three day before the match when he was called up in an emergency. Reg Bowden remembers him playing the match with strapping "everywhere, looking like an Egyptian Mummy!"

Reg Bowden describes Tony as: "the best tackler we had. He had great enthusiasm and never took a backward step. He would always take the ball up, and is a tremendous character as well."

Tony believes that with a couple more squad players, Fulham could have stayed in the first division in 1981-2 and established the club there, instead of the "yo-yo" existence it experienced in the first four seasons.

He recalls: "There was a strong camaraderie for the players - travelling down for home matches and staying in the hotels." Of the crisis period of 1984, he says that: "All I wanted to do was play Rugby League and help Fulham through a traumatic time. But some of the players we had at the start of the 1984-5 season were trialists and not up to professional standard which left us struggling against seasoned professionals."

A laceration of the eyeball against Bridgend in March 1985 forced Tony to retire from playing professionally. A possible comeback with Rochdale was blocked when Fulham wanted a fee for him.

Since then, he has been involved in coaching in the amateur game, recently at Littleborough in the Pennine League. Until a couple of years ago (in his mid 40s) he was still playing occasionally and played in touch rugby tournaments.

Outside Rugby League, Tony runs a successful fish and chip business in Rochdale. He keeps in contact with some of the players from his Fulham days and still enjoys his involvement with the game.

Interview in June 1999

125 appearances plus 6 as substitute
2 tries
6 points

Ian van Bellen

To the new Rugby League fans at Craven Cottage in 1980, Ian van Bellen was the first hero. Although he only played one season at Fulham, he is fondly remembered to this day. He was 18 stone and six foot tall, running into the other team, not looking very athletic, but clearly being very effective. Ian says that the best part of his game was "carrying the ball and attracting players around me, then slipping the ball out of the tackle to our backs" and it clearly worked.

He played football at school and recalls that his older brother Victor "talked me into having a go" at Rugby - first Union at Huddersfield RUFC, where he was in the first team at 15, and then League. Soon scouts were after him, and both brothers were offered terms by Wigan. But Victor did not want to leave Huddersfield (this was before the M62 linking Yorkshire with Lancashire across the Pennines was built), so they joined Huddersfield instead in 1963. However, Ian still has the contract that Wigan offered him.

After eight years at Huddersfield he went to Castleford, but returned two years later. In 1978, Neil Fox was Huddersfield's coach, and it was he who sold Ian to Bradford Northern. This was - in terms of medals - the most successful period of Ian's career, as he won everything except a Challenge Cup final medal, and enjoyed playing alongside his younger brother Gary.

In 1980, Harold Genders asked him to join Fulham. He recalls: "When he told me who he was signing, I realised he really meant business. These were quality players. When I first went training at Golborne, there were only seven or eight players and I was the first Yorkshireman. More came each week and Reg really pushed us at training. I had never trained so hard and felt really fit.

"My season at Fulham was superb. The enjoyment of going down for the weekend, training down there and meeting the London fans. It was so exciting to come out for the Wigan match, and the team were ready for it. We took them apart. The Bradford Northern game was a real highlight as well, when we took them on in the friendly, and the Wakefield game in the Cup, when we lost 5-9. Getting promotion was the icing on the cake - and then we had a tremendous holiday in Portugal."

Ian still has one of the tee-shirts the club produced with a drawing of him on it, saying "Fabulous Fulham". He says that: "The supporters were part of the team. There was a contingent of prison officers from Brixton, and they met us regularly at the games. I was very pleased to be invited to present the Supporters' Club awards for the 1981-2 season."

Occasionally things went astray. Ian remembers playing against Doncaster when he and John Wood tried a crossing move, got it wrong and ran into each other, knocking themselves out. He says "there were no drinks after that." And earlier in the season, Reg Bowden had told Ian he should not have the Sunday dinners his mother was making for him before playing in away matches. Reg had to explain this to Ian's mother as well when she was concerned about him keeping his strength up without his Sunday dinner.

Ian was sorry to leave Fulham and the supporters were devastated by the club's decision to release him. Managing Director Harold Genders believed that Ian would be too slow for the First Division. Looking back, Reg Bowden now believes that he should have kept Ian as a squad player for the second season, when Fulham faced a dreadful injury crisis. Ian joined Blackpool, then played for Halifax in the First Division, before joining Kent Invicta. His career finished at Keighley in 1984-5, when he retired after 21 seasons in the professional game.

Ian then became coach at amateur club Underbank for three seasons,

Ian van Bellen on a Fulham tee-shirt (Photo: Peter Lush)

15

before playing veteran Rugby Union back at Huddersfield RUFC. He remembers playing against Headingley, before 1995 when union officially went "open" and allowed Rugby League professionals back into the sport, when an England Rugby Union player was playing for the Leeds based club, returning from injury. He was asked afterwards what it was like playing against Huddersfield's three former League professionals, which split the beans. The whole team was suspended for a fortnight. After that, Ian carried on playing as before, finally retiring in 1998.

He still watches the Huddersfield Giants and now works as a builder, which keeps him fit.

A profile in *Open Rugby* in 1981 said that "it was obvious that van Bellen was the man the crowds loved most of all" and that Ian "is a gentleman of League, one of the game's nice guys. He will also go down in the history books as London's first real Rugby League hero. Fulham owe him a big debt and so does the game."

As two Fulham supporters, an elderly couple, said during one of the more miserable home defeats of the second season, "it hasn't been the same since the Dutchman left" and they were right.

Interview in June 1999

20 appearances plus 2 as substitute
4 tries
12 points

Martin Herdman

Martin Herdman was the first Londoner to play for the Fulham team. However, his first sporting love was boxing and was training as a super-heavyweight for the 1980 Moscow Olympic squad, but was very disappointed when it was decided not to take a super-heavyweight. "I was disillusioned with boxing because of that, although later I did fight a few times as a professional, at the same time as playing Rugby League. Once we played Hull KR on the Sunday and I was boxing on the Tuesday. Our coach Reg Bowden wasn't very happy with me boxing." As an amateur, Martin boxed for England and was London ABA heavyweight champion and South West London ABA heavyweight champion.

16

Martin's introduction to Rugby came through playing union at the age of 14. "I was never a great Rugby Union player although I did play for Middlesex, but I never played for a first class club. I went to watch Fulham at Craven Cottage and wrote to Reg for a trial. He asked me to play for Peckham against London Colonials. He was concerned about my lack of League experience, and asked me to play another six games for Peckham. I was disappointed - I thought I would get signed straight away. Then I heard that York were interested in signing me. Reg and Bill Goodwin - the Peckham coach - heard this and Fulham quickly offered me a trial against Batley. Then Harold Genders signed me."

Martin adapted quickly to Rugby League. "It suited my temperament and style - I enjoyed running with the ball. I got a lot of help from the other forwards - Tony Gourley, Harry Beverley, John Wood and David Hull all knew their way round a Rugby League pitch, they were good teachers and helped me learn."

"I had a great time. For the first two seasons I would travel up north on the Friday night for training, stay there, and travel back with the team on Saturday for home games. We would stay at Watford. For away games I would travel back on the Sunday night."

Soon, Martin was selected for the Welsh team. He qualified for them through his father. "After six games I was a Welsh International. I was getting paid for a sport I loved - I would happily have done it for nothing. It was fantastic for me and my family - my son Luke was a year old, I had been out of work and we had been struggling. Within three months I had become an international Rugby League player. It was difficult to grasp how quickly it had happened." Martin played twice against the 1982 Australian tourists - arguably the best touring team ever seen here - for Fulham and Wales. "Fulham gave them a tough game," he remembers.

In 1983-4, Martin spent a short time on loan at Leigh before that summer trying his hand at American football with the Kansas City Chiefs. "I had never played American football, but their coach saw me play Rugby League and figured I would be a good back. They took me to their mini-camp in the USA, for a week of weight and agility tests and medicals. That went fine so I went to their summer camp. But they had a playbook the size of a telephone directory with all the plays - their set moves. It was impossible to learn it in that time. Players were cut from the squad every day. It was very tough - and players from the squad also went to hospital every day. I was never cut but I saw the coach John Macovick and said I needed more time to learn. But he could not give me the time, so we parted company on good terms. It was a fantastic experience. I was interviewed about my time there by Nicky Horne for Channel 4's *Touchdown* programme".

Martin Herdman as Charles in *As You Like It* at the Globe Theatre
(Photo: Nigel Norrington)

On his return to England, Martin found the Fulham club had changed hands and he became caught up in the "free agents" dispute over the players' status with the new club. His involvement effectively ended his League career. "When it was decided we were free agents I wrote to every club in the League with a poster 'Biggest, strongest, fastest Rugby League forward in the world. Would be interested in signing. Sensible offers only'." Martin believes that he was blacklisted - no clubs contacted him. "I was 28 and totally out of the sport I loved." He did play a handful of games in 1986 for Fulham at Chiswick, but found it very different from the set up he had been used to at Craven Cottage.

Martin's career then moved in a completely new direction, as he established himself as an actor. "As one door closes, another opens. I went on a one-year post-graduate acting course. I got an agent and have been working steadily ever since. I have been in every soap going, including seven episodes of *Coronation Street*, three series of *Soldier, Soldier* and *The Bill*. In that I usually get parts as villains because of my size. I prefer live theatre but it is very hard work with little reward." In the last year, Martin has been on tour in *The Ladykillers* and before that was in *As You Like It* at the Globe Theatre on London's South Bank. That production also went on tour to Japan. He also plays and sings in a band.

Golf is now his main sporting interest, where he plays in matches for SPARKS, the children's charity. He coaches Rugby Union at Staines RUFC and watches Rugby League on television. Both his sons follow his interest in sport, with Luke playing Rugby Union and Jacob aiming to become a professional golfer.

Looking back, he has fond memories of his time playing for Fulham. "I was immensely proud to have been involved at Craven Cottage. It was one of the best sporting periods of my life - a fantastic time. It was a unique experience for a lot of people."

Interview in November 1999

71 appearances plus 21 as substitute
14 tries
1 drop goal
45 points

Steve Diamond

Steve Diamond has for a long time held two of the club records - the most goals in a career and most points in a career. These records are even more meritorious when you consider he only played for three seasons and two of those were in the top flight with a side that was relegated on both occasions. He is also one of a select band of players who have made more than a hundred appearances for the club.

Steve was born in South Wales and played for Newbridge and Newport at Rugby Union before moving to Rugby League with Wakefield Trinity. Steve was signed by Fulham from Wakefield in August 1981 for a big fee at that time of £12,000. Paradoxically, one of his first games for Fulham was against Wakefield and it was Steve's goals which made the difference in a narrow 13-12 victory. A flexible player, Steve was forced to play in several places in the back line due to the small Fulham squad and the inordinate number of injuries the side seemed to pick up while playing in the First Division.

Despite Fulham being relegated in his first season Steve managed to score 92 goals and 203 points. In his second season, when Fulham were promoted as Second Division Champions, he topped the Rugby League scoring charts. These remained club records until John Gallagher topped them in 1993-4. Steve's consistency was all the more remarkable as the club's training ground at Golborne in Lancashire had no goal posts and Steve had to supplement his training with shots at posts in a local park.

Steve Diamond kicking another goal! Fulham versus Leeds
25 April 1982 (Photo: Barry Taylor)

20

In his final season Steve scored 77 goals in an horrendous year when Fulham were narrowly relegated but which saw the club struggle to field teams on occasions and gates drop to dangerously low levels. Steve's club record of 691 points is not likely to be challenged in the near future with the nearest player some 200 points behind.

Although Steve played for his native Wales at League this was not during his Fulham period. However, he played in Fulham's tour match against Australia in 1982 scoring a goal in a 5-22 defeat. Steve Diamond left the club as part of the "free agents" dispute in the 1984-5 season, joining former Fulham coach Reg Bowden at Warrington. A few months later he returned to Yorkshire, joining Hunslet. A spell at Castleford followed before he returned to Wakefield to finish his Rugby League career in the 1986-7 season.

109 appearances
24 tries
305 goals
4 drop goals
691 points

Hussain M'Barki

Truth, especially in sport, is usually stranger, and more interesting, than fiction. So it should not be any great surprise that, in the history of Rugby League in London, Fulham's first star not to come from the Rugby League heartlands was a Moroccan, Hussain M'Barki, that country's first professional Rugby League player.

Well, perhaps that's not entirely correct. Londoner Martin Herdman had joined the club nine months before Hussain first played under the unlikely pseudonym "A. Smith", to avoid detection by the Rugby Union authorities, against Featherstone in September 1981. Martin was a valuable addition to the squad, a powerful, quick forward and the team's first Londoner. But Hussain's speed, side-step and try-scoring added genuine star quality and a touch of the exotic to a team that was often struggling to hold its own in the First Division at that time.

Hussain's first sports were football and athletics, where he was a sprinter. A coaching clinic at school introduced him to Rugby Union. "I was picked at full-back and was told it was like being a goalkeeper - catch the ball and run with it. A week later I was picked for a trial for the school under-16 team. Then I played for the Academy team, the college and the town. By the age of 16 I was picked for a cup match for the town team. I had a good game and scored a penalty and a drop goal. It was on television." Selection for the national under-18 team followed with an appearance against Romania in Bucharest. By 1975, at the age of 19, Hussain was in the full national Morocco Rugby Union team. He scored two tries against Belgium "and my career really took off. I was the first choice full-back for Morocco until I switched to Rugby League in 1981".

An invitation to play in a testimonial match in France saw him get the chance to play in Narbonne. "I went from a small club in Morocco to playing with the big stars in France. It was the highlight of my Rugby Union career. He moved to Cahors, but a problem with his playing licence restricted his appearances to only cup games for the first season there. But then, the problem resolved, he could concentrate on developing his rugby. In 1980, he played against France for Morocco and "I scored our first try against the French for 60 years, a run from our dead ball line to score".

Hussain had been approached by French Rugby League clubs to switch codes, and there was also an approach from Carlisle before he joined Fulham. "It was a gamble - I had a good job in France." When he arrived at Heathrow, the immigration authorities were suspicious of his reasons for coming to Britain. "Playing Rugby League? For Fulham?" They seemed to think this was unlikely. "But in the end everything was all right. Harold Genders was there to meet me, and the airport police chief

Hussain M'Barki scoring against Dewsbury at Craven Cottage
3 October 1982 (Photo: Barry Taylor)

22

was a Fulham supporter and asked for my autograph. I played three games on trial, everyone kept my cover as a Rugby Union player, and everything promised to me was done."

Because the team were based in Lancashire, Hussain stayed in Widnes, lodging with player-coach Reg Bowden's aunt. His English, first learnt at school, now developed with a Widnes twang. "The people in Widnes were brilliant and were good supporters of Rugby League. And I really learnt about Rugby League in those first three years at Fulham."

Fulham supporters soon came to appreciate his pace and eye for a scoring chance as he settled down and adapted to his new code. In 1982, previewing a big cup match, journalist Philip Shaw described the chants of "Hoo-sane!" at Craven Cottage for the crowd's new hero.

"Reg Bowden looked after me and showed me how to play. I went to watch games with him to learn. The players were like a family to me. And Harold Genders was the boss - he did everything for the club. He was a tremendous gentleman."

As well as playing on the wing, Hussain played some games at centre. "In 1982 I played at centre against Hunslet in the cup and won man-of-the-match. But Reg mainly saw me as a winger." Later, when he returned to the club in 1988, he played at full-back as well.

Encouraged by his experiences with Fulham, Hussain tried to bring other Moroccan Rugby Union players over. "There was a forward playing for Nice in France in 1983. He would have been ideal, fast and big. But he crushed a ligament in his knee and never played again."

In 1984, when the club moved out of Craven Cottage and the Closes becoming the new owners, Hussain became caught up in the "free agents" dispute. He could not reach agreement with the new club and eventually joined former Fulham coach Reg Bowden at Warrington. Of all the players who left at that time, the loss of Hussain was most keenly felt by the supporters. He was considered "one of ours", who learnt his Rugby League in Fulham colours, different from the players the club had signed from other clubs in the north.

Hussain played a season for Warrington, then two for Oldham. In his first season there he was voted "Player of the Year" and the team reached the Challenge Cup semi-final, losing to eventual winners Castleford, as well as being runners up in the Lancashire Cup. The next season, Oldham narrowly lost 16-22 to the all-conquering Australian tourists and then in the Challenge Cup beat Wigan 10-8, the last Challenge Cup match Wigan lost until 1996. In 1987, Hussain moved again, to Hull. He remembers the 0-0 draw with Leeds in the Challenge Cup semi-final, and losing the replay 4-3 four days later.

But at the end of the 1987-8 season, Hussain was 32 and his wife wanted to come back to London, to find a suitable school for their children. He met Fulham director Tim Lamb and agreed to return to the club in September 1988. The club programme said that supporters were "pleased and thrilled" at his return. But he found it difficult at first to re-establish himself in the side, although within a couple of months his first-team spot was secure. He continued playing until 1992, often at full-back or in the centre as well as his original place on the wing. Within months of his return, he soon regained his position as the club's top try scorer, which he held until overtaken by Scott Roskell in 1997.

Hussain feels that the club in this period should have concentrated more on developing local talent. He became involved in development work in Rotherhithe, and bought talented youngsters such as Andrew Mighty and Roy Leslie to the club.

He also coached the London Select amateur team that played a nine-a-side game against Moscow Spartak as a curtain raiser at Wembley before the Great Britain versus Australia test match in 1990.

His development talents and enthusiasm came to the fore once he retired from playing and he turned to starting and developing Rugby League in his native Morocco. His efforts have seen a viable club competition develop and his country participate in the 1995 emerging nations World Cup and the qualifying matches for the 2000 tournament. He feels they need more international competition, sponsorship and resources for the game to reach its full potential. He was bitterly disappointed to have to play recent World Cup matches in France without some of the Moroccan players who play in France, because their French clubs had failed to release them. But he now intends to concentrate on developing the game in Morocco and use those players as the base for the international side.

When not in Morocco, Hussain lives with his family in east London. His four children all enjoy sport. His 13-year-old daughter plays Rugby

Union. One of his sons also enjoys Union, and has played at regional schools level. When not busy with Rugby League, Hussain works as a telecommunications consultant.

Neil Tunnicliffe, British Rugby League's former chief executive, wrote a piece on Morocco for Dave Hadfield's excellent book on international Rugby League, *XIII Worlds*. He said of Hussain: "M'Barki is a man whom it is difficult not to like and admire, a warm and courageous human being whose achievements on and off a hundred square miles' worth of fields of differing provenances and orientations weave a yarn which forms a unique weft in the multicoloured and variegated tapestry that is the 100-year history of our game. There can be few if any sports which can top Rugby League for the sheer larger-than-life, man-of-the-world, seen-it-all, designed-the-T-shirt singularity and vivacity of its characters...M'Barki's short, wiry frame stands, like Alan Ladd on an orange box, shoulder to shoulder with the best of them." That says it all, really.

Interview in January 2000

148 appearances plus 15 as substitute
74 tries
265 points

Steve Mills and Charlie Jones

Halfway through the 1982-3 season, Fulham looked certain to once again win promotion. But Reg Bowden's squad needed young blood if it was to face First Division Rugby League. So Reg returned to his home town team Widnes once again seeking players and signed Steve Mills and Charlie Jones on 11 March 1983, initially on loan and then for a joint transfer fee. Both players were to serve the club well during the mid 1980s.

Steve Mills had not played Rugby League until he signed for Widnes. At school he concentrated on cross-country running and track athletics. He then took up Rugby Union at West Park RUFC and, after starting in the colts team, won a place in the first team. Approached by Widnes, he played a trial game, and signed for them in 1980, at the age of 21.

But as a full-back he found it hard to establish himself at Widnes, and with Great Britain full-back Mick Burke in the first team there were few opportunities for him. He mainly played in the A team, covering most of the back positions. In 1981-2 he went to Leigh on loan and played a few first team games there. Then in March 1983 he was offered the chance to play for Fulham. He recalls: "I was quite excited about this. They were a good up- and-coming club. I had seen Reg Bowden play at Widnes although he had left by the time I joined. It was an honour to be approached by him."

He found it very different from A team life at Widnes. "Around 100 people would watch the A team games. Now I was playing in front of thousands at Craven Cottage. I remember the match against York when we won the championship and I scored a hat-trick".

Steve remembers finding it difficult in the First Division. "It was not a good season. We were relegated and I found it difficult to find my form." But he learnt a lot from the older players at the club. "They would give you advice and were always very encouraging."

At the end of that season many of the established players left the club, which was now back in the Second Division. For Steve, the highlights of the rest of his time at Fulham were cup matches against good opposition. "At Central Park we came close to beating Wigan in the Lancashire Cup. And against Castleford in the John Player Trophy at Chiswick I scored two interception tries from passes from John Joyner. We tended to play well against better opposition although we could fade towards the end of games. Our opponents frequently could not understand why we were near the bottom of the table."

From 1984-5 until he left Fulham at the end of the 1986-7 season, Steve was one of the key players in a time of constant change for the club. The last year he travelled from the north on the train with fellow players Charlie Jones and Chris Wilkinson for home games. He trained with Thatto Heath and on his own to keep fit. He was also working shifts and sometimes would do a Sunday night shift after playing.

He came close to joining Salford in 1987, and then joined Carlisle, where Roy Lester, the former Fulham coach, was now team manager. Fulham received a transfer fee similar to the one they paid in 1983. Steve had been the top try scorer for his last three seasons at the club and had

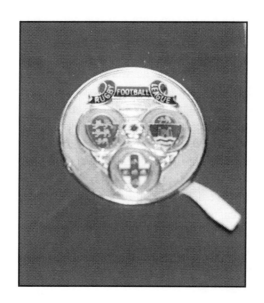

Steve Mills's Division Two championship medal (Photo: Peter Lush)

Home Player of the Year trophies won by Steve Mills 1986-7 and 1984-5
(Photo: Peter Lush)

also won two player-of-the-year awards. He has fond memories of
Fulham's fans. "They were always friendly and hospitable. I stayed with
Ron and Mo Snares after one of the end-of-season functions. They were
always very supportive."

He played just over a season with Carlisle before retiring from Rugby League. He returned - under an assumed name - to playing union at West Park in their veterans team for five years.

Steve believes that his strengths were "originally my speed. And to some degree skill - being able to go past a player. Also learning to read the game - especially when playing full-back. I enjoyed playing there, you could see the whole game in front of you. The only problem was, as the last line of defence, if you made a mistake the opposition scored. But looking back maybe I didn't have enough determination to succeed. I didn't like to lose, but I saw the game as a hobby - something I enjoyed."

Steve's only involvement in Rugby League now is to take his eight-year- old son to occasional matches at St Helens and try to convince him that it's better than watching football at Everton. He works at Pilkington Glass in St Helens in quality control in the automotive plant.

He enjoyed his four years at Fulham and was a quality player in teams that were often struggling.

100 appearances plus 8 as substitute
50 tries
3 goals
199 points

Charlie Jones started playing Rugby League at school at the age of seven. He played for the Widnes under-11 team and then joined local amateur side Widnes Tigers. He played for them at every level up to under-18 and also represented Lancashire and Great Britain at under-18 level.

When he was just 18, in October 1978, he signed for Widnes. He remembers: "Other clubs were interested but I was very keen to play for our town team." He stayed at Widnes for five years, but says of that time "It was very hard. You had little chance to prove yourself in a very successful first team, so after five years it was time to move on."

But he was surprised when approached by Fulham. "Reg Bowden came round to see me - I was working on my car. He said he wanted me to sign on loan for the rest of the season to strengthen his squad. Steve Mills and I made our debuts at Whitehaven, when we won 6-0."

They soon signed permanently. "It was a brilliant experience. We were treated like gods by the fans. They were fantastic."

Charlie Jones (photo: Peter Lush)

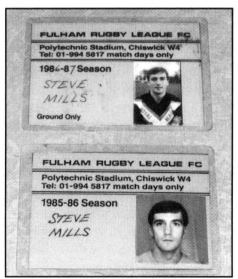

Steve Mills's player passes (Photo: Peter Lush)

The highlights of his time at Fulham were winning the Second Division Championship, "then the season after that we did the double over Widnes - my old team. It was great playing against the top sides like Wigan, St Helens and Hull KR. We often lost on stupid mistakes. If we could have stayed up we could have established ourselves in the First Division and given London the team they deserve."

Charlie says he learnt a lot from the older players when he joined Fulham. He played in different positions - at centre or on the wing, but preferred second-row "as you were more involved. But I was only 12½ stone - not really big enough for second row." Steve Mills remembers him as "always giving 100 per cent effort. Charlie would run through a brick wall for you". New coach Roy Lester said of him in 1984: "I can ask Charlie to do anything and play anywhere and I know he'll give everything...he even volunteered to be hooker last year when we were short of one."

Charlie stayed with Fulham when the club left Craven Cottage and enjoyed playing for Roy Lester. With Steve Mills and Chris Wilkinson he made up a small group of northern-based players who stayed with the club after the 1985-6 season. He recalls "We got the 8am train from Runcorn to Euston, were met at the station and taken to the ground by car. After the game we had to dash across London for the train home. During the week I trained with a local amateur club where Keith Elwell was coach".

During the 1987-8 season, Charlie was given a free transfer by Fulham, as the squad was now to be based completely in the south. After a period playing as an amateur he joined Runcorn Highfield. He played 50 games (plus 2 as substitute) for them before returning to the amateur game in 1991. Today (the summer of 1999) he is still playing at prop for his local side West Bank in the North West Counties League and works as a fork-lift truck driver for a building firm in Prescot.

Fulham fans remember Charlie for his drive and determination for a team that often weren't doing well. Charlie remembers the "fantastic spectators" the club had. "They were always there wherever we played. Even if we were 40-0 down they would be there cheering you on. I always enjoyed mixing with the fans after the game and talking to them. They pay the wages and players should always treat them right."

Interview in July 1999

94 appearances plus 22 as substitute
16 tries
63 points

Crystal Palace and Chiswick

Chris Wilkinson

Chris Wilkinson was the first young player to join the club permanently from a northern amateur club. To supporters, to suddenly go from the Boar's Head in Division Seven of the North West Counties League to Second Division professional Rugby League at Fulham seemed an enormous leap. But, in fact, Chris had been training with Fulham in the 1983-4 season, invited by Roy Lester. But he did not sign for the club until the start of the 1984-5 season, when many of the established players were leaving the club.

Chris first played Rugby League at junior school, then played for Leigh Juniors until, as an open age team they became the Boar's Head. He captained the Leigh town junior teams from under-11 to under-16 level. He also played for the Lancashire under-19 team and was selected for the Great Britain under-19 squad but injured his knee.

He had some experience of playing at a professional club at Oldham, but they were very strong at scrum-half, and he realised he could not progress beyond the A team there.

Chris remembers training at Fulham. "Roy Lester had seen me play in the Shaw Cup competition and invited me to training. But they had player-coach Reg Bowden at scrum-half and I didn't think Reg would pick me ahead of himself. Then when Reg and the others left Roy stopped me on my way home and got me to sign for Fulham." The next day Leigh approached him to join them, but he had already committed himself to Fulham and would not play for his home-town club until 1995. Roy Lester said about signing Chris: "We've bought someone into the league with fantastic potential... With all the troubles we've had someone like Chris is a joy to have at the club".

Chris recalls: "My first game was at Sheffield and Ken Green was the other half-back. Gary Hetherington was playing for them, but we won. That first season went so quickly. It was a big jump from a pub side to playing professionally. Roy Lester was a big help and looked after me."

Chris remembers the cup games against First Division teams as his highlights of his time with the club. "We played Hull at Crystal Palace.

31

We were winning 14-0 despite all their star players, but experience told in the end. Against Halifax it was freezing cold. We were winning 4-0 and I scored the only try, but we lost 4-17. At Wigan in the Lancashire Cup we were winning until close to the end. I scored a goal from near the half-way line that put us in front but their experience and fitness won it for them."

Chris found that the other players made him feel at home at the club. "Steve Mills was always consistent. Tony Kinsey had so much potential. Tony Gourley's loud voice petrified me! We used to play cards on the coach. Shaun Hoare was a good friend as well."

After the summer crisis of 1986, when the club nearly went out of business, Chris had a short loan period at Barrow. He returned to Fulham, playing home games by travelling down on the train from Runcorn early on Sunday mornings. He fell out with the club, but still went to watch the team play at Dewsbury, with the aim of sorting things out with them. Ironically, however, he ended up signing for the Yorkshire side.

Chris played a couple of seasons at Dewsbury, but got tired of travelling across the Pennines four or five times a week. A return to Lancashire at Swinton followed. He recalls: "I signed for Swinton - it was the biggest club I had joined. We got promoted and we played one season in the First Division. We had good players but could not always compete with the established teams in fitness and experience. We were relegated at the end of that season. But I remember kicking the winning goal against Warrington at Swinton which was special."

Chris then joined Leigh in 1995. He remembers a 24-0 victory at Hull KR in the Challenge Cup in 1996 as the highlight of his time there. "No one had given us a chance to win, but hundreds of Leigh fans came to support us. It was our Wembley."

In 1998, Chris played his final season in the professional game at Oldham. He now plays for local amateur side Leigh Miners Rangers. He played for them when they beat professional club Bramley in the Challenge Cup and won the man-of-the-match award, with Mike Ford as the opposing scrum-half.

Chris believes that the main strengths of his game are kicking, defence and passing. "I would like to play now with the 40/20 rule. It offers a lot of chances to create attacks."

Chris still lives in Leigh and works at ICL in stock control. In a professional career lasting 14 years he scored over 500 goals and more than 1,200 points. He served Fulham well at a time of transition and upheaval for the club.

69 appearances plus 4 as substitute
17 tries
141 goals
13 drop goals
363 points

Interview in July 1999

Frank Feighan

Frank Feighan's Rugby League career started on a building site. Not throwing a ball around in the lunch break, but through meeting London Rugby League stalwart and Fulham coach-to-be Bill Goodwin. Frank was goaded by Bill who told him he did not have the "bottle" to play Rugby League. To shut up Bill and his mates, he started training at Bill's amateur Rugby League club Peckham and soon made his debut. His lack of knowledge of the game soon showed. He recalls: "I ran around trying to trip everyone up and Bill had to pull me off after ten minutes... I liked what I saw and wanted more of it."

A successful amateur career led to trials with Reg Bowden's Fulham. Frank scored a try on his Fulham debut against Blackpool Borough, at Craven Cottage in October 1982. But, with the team still based in the north at that time, it was difficult for southern players to become established and Frank returned to the amateur game.

His professional career started properly at the age of 26 the following season at the ill-fated Kent Invicta, where Peckham coach Goodwin had taken charge. Bill was later to recruit Frank back to Fulham in 1985, this time at Chiswick.

Frank's great claim to fame was that he won the BBC's Try of the Year in 1983-4 with an amazing solo try for Kent Invicta against First Division Castleford in the Challenge Cup. However, the Kent club hit financial problems. Frank says that the collapse of the club after a promising start was a great disappointment. "It was a good set-up and then certain players went, and then Bill had to go and finally the whole team had fallen apart and we found ourselves at Southend - it was a great pity." After the season in Kent, the team moved to Southend, where it survived a season before very low crowds before finally pulling out of the league. At Kent Invicta, Frank made the most appearances for the club, playing 34 out of 36 games and scoring six tries. His team mates included former Fulham favourite Ian van Bellen. At Southend, Frank played 20 games, scoring eight tries. After the demise of Southend Invicta, Frank briefly returned to the amateur game before rejoining Fulham, now based at Chiswick.

In March 1986, he played in the historic game at Huddersfield which supporters believed was the end of the road for the club because the owners, Roy and Barbara Close had decided to put the club up for sale. When asked by coach Roy Lester if he would play at Huddersfield for nothing, he said: "I'd walk up the motorway to play." It is a comment that has since passed into legend. Frank scored at Huddersfield and his comments epitomised the spirit at the club at the time which ultimately led to its survival.

When new owner Paul Faires took over in April 1986, Frank was blessed with the title "Frank the Tank" as part of a new policy of giving the players nicknames. The team were christened the Fulham Bears. It was typical of those times at the club, which also saw disco music before matches and fire-eaters at half-time.

The next season, after another near-fatal collapse of the club, the first home game was a disastrous defeat against Sheffield Eagles. But morale was restored by Frank scoring a sensational interception try from his own line, racing 95 yards. Fulham were 32-0 down at the time and eventually lost 68-14. But supporters who were there still fondly remember that try.

As he got older, Frank played in the pack as well as his favoured position on the wing. He retired at the end of the 1987-8 season, but had played a significant role in establishing a largely southern-based team at the club. His performance in the professional game showed the potential there was among the London amateur Rugby League ranks for Fulham to find new players.

Frank has a final southern Rugby League claim to fame because he played for all three southern Rugby League professional teams: Fulham, Kent Invicta and Southend Invicta. He also made a considerable contribution to the amateur game in London. Frank Feighan was a true London Rugby League hero.

38 appearances plus 6 as substitute
10 tries
35 points

Colin Fenn

Colin Fenn still has the scars from his first game of professional Rugby League. The second-row forward, who played for Fulham between 1986 and 1989 recalls: "It was at Whitehaven and we lost 72-6. I spent most of the game on the bench, came on and made about 10 tackles in five minutes and then I made a tackle along with team-mate Martin Dean who accidentally butted me and opened a huge gash by my eye. They stitched me up in the changing room, six stitches, and I've still got the scar."

The team that went to Whitehaven was a makeshift one put together by coach Bill Goodwin. Fulham had gone under financially for the second time in six months, and were rescued by Tim Lamb and Richard Lawton, with financial backing from Roy Close, just before the 1986-7 season started. Some players in the makeshift teams Bill was forced to field were pure emergency cover and were gone within weeks. But for Colin, then 27, it was the launch of a professional career that would last three years and 58 matches, make him the club's first London-born captain and see him make his mark as one of the most accurate, if unorthodox, goal kickers of the club's first 20 years.

He'd been a fan before he was a player, travelling from his home in East Ham to watch the early Fulham teams at Craven Cottage: "That was a very important part of it for me. I cared passionately about making Rugby League work in London. It was a bond we all had in common, players and supporters. It was extremely important to making the club what it was."

Colin had played Rugby Union at Langdon School in East Ham, before joining the East London Rugby Union club: "I always fancied Rugby

35

League, not least because union was in one of its kicking phases and you never seemed to get the ball. I'd had northern friends who'd called me a 'southern softy' for playing union. Even so, the prospect of a life ban from union was something to think about. I joined the amateur South London Rugby League club, who were basically a New Zealand team, and really enjoyed it, then Bill Goodwin spotted me after only four or five games."

He was working as a careers officer in East Ham at this time: "I'd often go into work on Monday with scars and bruises on my face. It came in quite useful - I never seemed to have any trouble with the kids." Working and living in East London added to the burden of travel: "Twice a week I went straight from work to training and I'd often not get home until around 12.30 am. On Sunday you had to be up at six and might not be home until two or three in the morning. You had to want to do it - it was very arduous."

There were also enormous compensations. Like everyone who was there he has vivid memories of the 68-14 defeat by Sheffield in Fulham's first home game of the season: "We were flogged by Whitehaven and then by Sheffield, but we still got a fantastic reception. I kicked a couple of goals from the touchline which got the crowd on my side. There was a real buzz about the place. The fans were so passionate about it that you couldn't not give your all."

He also recalls a good spirit in the side, with home-grown players like himself, Steve Guyett, Mick Hutchinson and Nick Grimoldby fitting in well with Australians like Glen Haggath, Pat O'Doherty and Bob Knight: "They were good guys and they had their heart in the clubs. Glen wasn't everybody's favourite - he was very brash and could be quite abrasive, but he gave us a lot. He was one of the few experienced players who went out of his way to help the less experienced and I think the club might have done better if it had hung on to him."

He would have been worth his place simply as a hard-working second-row with a consistently good tackle count. But it was his goal kicking that made him stand out. His style, appearing to crouch over the ball, was rugby's answer to Lee Trevino's golf swing - while it looked unconvincing, it was consistently effective in putting the ball exactly where he wanted it. Colin remembers being slightly nonplussed by comments on his distinctive style: "I simply did what felt natural and I used to practice a lot," he remembers. Sixty-five goals in that first season and 107 in all testify to his effectiveness.

His second season should have been even better. He started it as Fulham captain: "Bill Goodwin in his understated way simply said 'you're in charge'." He felt that a team with considerable home-grown talent should have done well in the Second Division, but that the Australian imports were not as good as the previous year's: "We needed more backup from the Aussies. They were less committed than the previous season's imports and we rapidly broke into English and Australian factions."

His captaincy ended after a disagreement with the club board before the match against the Papua New Guinea tourists: "They wanted to bring in a system of fines for players and I was opposed to it. I was dropped from the Papua New Guinea match and lost the captaincy. I was devastated, but it was a point of principle."

Fulham never felt quite the same for Colin after that, although he stayed with the club for another year before going first to amateur Rugby League club Essex Scimitars then eventually back to union at East London, where at 41 he's still enjoying his rugby in Eastern Counties Division Two. He left the careers service to join insurance company Sun Alliance as management development consultant before setting up his own training consultancy in October 1994.

In spite of its disappointing conclusion, he looks back fondly on his League career, still follows the game and was at Wembley to see the Broncos in the 1999 Challenge Cup Final.

"To be a Londoner playing for a London team, to experience the buzz, the sense of unity and the way people cared so passionately was something I was very proud to be involved with."

50 appearances plus 8 as substitute
1 try
107 goals
218 points

Interview in November 1999 by Huw Richards

Dave Gillan

Not many players came to play professional Rugby League in London via Papakura New Zealand, Southend Invicta and the amateur London Colonials RLFC, but this was Dave Gillan's unlikely route to Rugby League at Fulham. He made his debut in September 1986 when the club was establishing a predominantly southern-based team. Dave was signed by Bill Goodwin for Southend Invicta and played with such Kiwi stars as Gary Freeman and Mark Elia there. At Fulham, he again teamed up with Bill Goodwin, who was now coaching the London club.

At 5 feet 10 inches and 13 stone, he was a useful half-back and was top scorer in 1987-8 with nine tries. Not your average Rugby League player, he studied to be a teacher while playing for Fulham and he also worked as a picture framer. This was not a strange occupation for a Rugby League player who listed one of his hobbies as wandering through art galleries! One of the more bizarre things to happen to Dave Gillan was that he was once sponsored for the season by the "Communist Party of Great Britain". At least that was what it said in the programme, though the truth was that it was a wind-up, but it certainly raised some eyebrows. It also surprised Dave. Despite the merry-go-round of players who graced the Fulham shirt in the 1980s, Dave Gillan was one player who stuck around, joining the very elite band who have played in more than a hundred games for the club. He also scored 38 tries.

A modest player, when asked if he had won any honours in the game, Dave replied, "you must be joking!" Dave also had a sharp sense of humour when asked on two separate occasions what were his biggest dislikes he replied: "Aussies, I can't stand them", a brave comment considering the Fulham Australian contingent. Dave was also one of those Kiwis that you immediately take to your heart, he was once reported as saying: "Although I was forced to play Rugby Union through out my schooldays, I started playing Rugby League in my own time when I was about nine, and stayed with it as it's simply a much better game."

Dave made his debut away at Mansfield Marksmen on 29 September 1986 and scored, but was on the losing side as Fulham went down 18-32. He also scored hat tricks against Huddersfield and Carlisle, both at Chiswick. He later converted to loose-forward to great effect and had the honour of being club captain and playing against the touring Papua New Guinea side for Fulham in their 1987 tour match at Chiswick.

97 appearances plus 4 as substitute
38 tries
152 points

Russ Bridge

The changes in management in 1986 saw a new policy applied to Fulham's players. Most of the team was to be based in the south, supplemented by some Australians and a few northerners. Of the players signed then, the one who made the most consistent contribution to the team was Russ Bridge.

Russ is from Bolton and played football at school until a Welsh teacher, Len "Taffy" Thomas, started a Rugby League team. He immediately took to League, played for the Bolton schools team and had a trial for the Lancashire schools. He also played Rugby Union for Rossendale RUFC.

Russ Bridge (Photo: Peter Lush)

He went to college at West London Institute of Higher Education, where Bev Risman, long involved in the London Rugby League scene, was a lecturer. In Russ's third year, Bev was involved in starting a college Rugby League team. Taking up League again, Russ was selected for the 1986 Great Britain Student World Cup squad. He says it was a "marvellous experience" to visit Australia and New Zealand. Kieron Murphy, who also later signed for Fulham, was also a member of the Great Britain squad.

Coach Bill Goodwin then invited him for a trial at Fulham. He made his debut in the first home match of the 1986-7 season, a 14-68 defeat against Sheffield. Despite the score, this game was fondly remembered by supporters who were relieved to have a team to watch at all after the club had nearly collapsed over the summer.

He soon signed for Fulham, and remembers that "it was amazing to be given the opportunity to play professionally, getting paid for playing the game I loved". He started for Fulham as a centre, with the odd game on the wing. But, in 1988, Bill Goodwin and Bev Risman said that, because tackling was the strongest part of his game, he should move to hooker, even though he had never played in the scrum before. He replaced Craig Taylor, who had returned to Australia. He won the Players' Player of the Year award after his first season in the pack. His progress was shown by his inclusion as a substitute in the *Open Rugby* Second Division Form Team of the Season for 1989-90.

Despite, as he accepts "not being the biggest player on the pitch", he soon adapted to this new role, and played the rest of his career in the pack.

He says that "virtually every game was a highlight for me. I had to pinch myself to remember that this was real. I've never lost that - nerves and adrenaline before a match". He particularly remembers the cup matches at Chiswick against Castleford and Halifax, with the chance to play against First Division players, and the Lancashire Cup game against Wigan at Hendon FC in 1989. He also enjoyed playing at Swinton and Rochdale where friends and family from the north-west would come and watch him.

In 1990, Russ and his wife Jayne decided to move back home to Lancashire, where they still live. He had been the first of the southern-based players to make both 50 and then 100 appearances for the club.

He was then shocked to be phoned by Bill Goodwin to hear that Wigan were interested in signing him. He played for them against Warrington in the pre-season Lockyer Cup, and then against Widnes at Swansea in the Charity Shield. He remembers training with the Wigan stars, but was disappointed when Wigan decided not to sign him. Instead, Leigh, then managed by Alex Murphy, signed him from Fulham. He stayed at Leigh for five years, and enjoyed his time there, which included one season in the First Division.

He was considering retirement, having been passed over as A team player-coach at Leigh, when he was contacted by Rugby League's perennial strugglers Highfield. Initially apprehensive, believing that "this is where people go to die", he went training with them and believed they could improve. He says that it was difficult with its run of continuous defeats, but "you can only give 100% yourself". By the end they were not getting heavily defeated every week, but at the end of 1998, the club, by then renamed the Prescott Panthers, suddenly folded, Russ says it was a "sad ending" for a club with over 70 years history.

His involvement in Rugby League now is as a member of the Disciplinary Panel, sitting in judgement on players' misdemeanours around every six weeks. He also plays Rugby Union for Rossendale RUFC in North West Division three, which he finds a "reasonable, competitive" standard.

At work he now manages a pupil referral unit, which aims to stop pupils being excluded from school, but misses the involvement in sport he had as a PE teacher.

He turned down a coaching opportunity at Rochdale Mayfield to play Union at Rossendale, but may well return to League in a coaching role in the future. And he has many fond memories of his time at Fulham, which gave him a start in an 11 year professional career in Rugby League.

Interview in June 1999

109 appearances plus 4 as substitute
12 tries
48 points

Dave Rotheram and Darryl Pitt

Only two players have played for Fulham, London Crusaders and London Broncos - Dave Rotheram and Darryl Pitt. Now both retired as players, until the end of the 1999 season they were joint coaches of the club's Alliance team.

Dave Rotheram's interest in Rugby League was through his father taking him to watch St Helens at Knowsley Road. "When I was seven, in 1976, Saints won the Challenge Cup. Saints's captain, Kel Coslett's daughter, was in my class at Bleak Hill Primary School and I remember him bringing the cup to show us." Dave continued to play Rugby League at Rainford High School. "But when I was 14 my family moved to Doncaster. The Dons were hopeless at that time and there was no junior Rugby League in the area. So I played Union, and played for Yorkshire under-16 and under-18 teams. In 1986, I started playing for the Armthorpe Plough in open-age amateur Rugby League."

Dave was introduced to Fulham by Bev Risman. "I went to college at West London Institute and Bev took me to Fulham to play for the under-19 team the club were starting. We played local amateur teams. In 1987-8 I played in the A team when my student commitments allowed me to. I was also captain-coach of the West London Institute team. In 1989 I played for England in the Student World Cup when we were runners up to Australia. That was a fantastic two weeks."

Dave's first team debut for Fulham came in a defeat - a 60-0 slaughter at Whitehaven in February 1989. "The conditions were appalling. And I got a bad knee injury and was out for a month. I played a few games the next season and when I finished at college in 1990 I broke into the first team." Russ Bridge's departure to Leigh meant that the team needed a new hooker. Dave filled the role very well, only missing one game that season.

Dave played in the historic tour to the Soviet Union in May 1991. "We played in huge stadiums. In Alma-Ata, 12,000 came to watch. It was a six hour flight east of Moscow. Then we played in Leningrad. This game against Ryedale-York was the last one played by Fulham. After that the club became London Crusaders. The match at the end of the tour in Moscow was the Soviet Union's first and only international in Rugby

League, as the nation then became the CIS and then Russia. The Great Britain Select XIII for that game contained 10 Fulham players".

Dave played as hooker or in the front row. "I preferred hooker - you were more involved and didn't get bashed so much. I was not quite big enough to play in the front row. I had all the basic skills to play hooker and until I got a knee injury in 1995 played consistently and was usually injury free. I enjoyed playing with Dave Cruickshank for Fulham when he was scrum-half. He was a good experienced player who bought the best out of me. I also learnt a lot from Paul Johnstone who worked tirelessly to get the A team established at the club. Coach Tony Gordon and former Kiwi international player Sam Stewart were very good - their 1993-4 team was the best I played in. We had great backs that could score tries from anywhere. That season was the highlight of my playing career."

Dave has fond memories of the Premiership semi-final win at Doncaster that season. "We knew Tony Gordon was leaving and we worked very hard to win that game for him. There was a big hostile crowd but we were elated to win through to the final at Old Trafford."

At the end of the 1994-5 season Dave ruptured his cruciate ligament playing for the A team in a friendly against the Fulham Travellers amateur team. "That was the time that Super League was announced and it was clear that to continue playing I would have had to have gone full-time. I

Three Crusaders - Scott Roskell, Dave Rotheram and Mark Johnson. Mark had just played for Salford in the Challenge Cup (Photo: Peter Lush)

would have had to give up teaching, so I decided instead to concentrate on coaching." In 1995-6 Dave coached the A team, who won the Alliance Second Division under his direction.

From 1996 to 1998, Dave was the Academy team coach. "In 1996 Robbie Moore bought over seven Australian kids to give us the nucleus of the team, and Tony Rea and I recruited London players. We had to apply for membership of the Academy and state our case at Red Hall [Rugby League's headquarters]. In the first season we finished sixth, which was a good result with many players who had never played league before. We found some good talent - Matt Salter was selected for the Great Britain Academy tour to New Zealand and Dominic Peters, Tony Martin and Wayne Sykes were in that team. During the three years I was academy coach, nine players went on to play for the first team."

In 1999, the club decided to enter the Alliance again, reforming an A team and, with Darryl Pitt, Dave became coach of the A team again. "We started from scratch. Injuries in the first team squad that took away our players meant we were relying on former Academy players and amateurs. For example, Dave Long joined us from a Rugby League Conference club and has now played for the first team. Another of our players, Ed Jennings scored 154 points in 21 games and has also played for the first team."

Towards the end of the season, Dave and Darryl suddenly found Martin Offiah and Shaun Edwards being given A team games. "Martin played three games and was great. He got stuck in and encouraged the other players. It was the first time Shaun had ever played an A team match and he was motivated for it."

Dave is a fully qualified Rugby League coach. In the summer of 1999, he was one of the coaches working with the best 64 under-15 players at a special training camp organised by the RFL at Ampleforth College. And in the autumn he was head coach of The South and Wales under-18 team against the Australian schoolboys. He is currently teaching two days a week and looking after his one-year-old daughter Rebecca for three days. For relaxation he plays Rugby Union at the Purley John Fisher club in Croydon. He wants to stay involved in the game in the future, although he is wary of going full-time in Rugby League, with the lack of security that coaches have. He hopes to continue to develop the club's young players and help them establish themselves with the Broncos. For the 2000 season Dave took over coaching the club's academy team.

Interview in October 1999

114 appearances plus 36 as substitute
14 tries
56 points

Darryl Pitt first played Rugby League at under-7 level. He worked his way through to the under-10s. Then his fledgling career suddenly stopped. "We played in bare feet until under-10 level. My mother stopped me playing because she didn't like me playing in boots." He started again at Banyo High School when he was 15 and then joined Fortitude Valleys in 1985, playing a few games in C grade. In 1986 he played for the North Banyo under-21s, winning the Brisbane sub-District Grand Final. He rejoined Valleys and in 1988 broke into the first grade team. Valleys were Brisbane Winfield Cup winners in 1988 and 1989.

Between those two victories, Darryl came to England to play for Carlisle. "It was Fulham supporter Bob Evans who suggested I try my luck in England. He was following the Lions tour in 1988 and came to the Valleys club because so many Fulham players were from there. He was doing the stats for Roy Lester at Carlisle and suggested Tony Catton and I went there. We went on a trial basis, but had an enjoyable six months. It was very different from the facilities at Valleys. The Rugby League Club had moved out of the Carlisle United football ground by then and training was in a floodlit area behind the stand. There were two lights on telegraph poles, with only a 50 metre by 10 metre area that was floodlit. It was a real culture shock compared to Brisbane, but the people in the town and the club were very good to us."

In 1989, Darryl returned to play in England, this time with Fulham. "I felt I had achieved what I wanted in Australia. I liked playing in England and preferred it to trying to play in Sydney. I had spent Christmas with Ross Strudwick when he was at Halifax and it was through him I joined Fulham. But Ross already had the eight imports he was allowed, so most of the time I played in the Alliance team with Bill Goodwin and Paul Johnstone." Darryl's first game in the first team was a 44-0 defeat at Hull

KR. But the next season he became established in the first team and was top try scorer, despite missing six weeks of the season with a knee injury. In 1991-2 he was the Lancashire Division Two Player of the Year and was included in the *League Express* Division Two Team of the Season. In 1992-3 his experience was recognised when he became the club captain.

One of the highlights of his time with Fulham, as with many other players, was the trip to the Soviet Union. "I played for the Great Britain Select in the last match. There were six Australians in that team. I still have the jersey - Fulham and York crests in Great Britain colours." The 30-0 victory against Wakefield is another fond memory, as is scoring the Club Try of the Year at Whitehaven in 1994-5, a length of the pitch run. "I'll never do that again."

Along with Dave Rotheram, Darryl has seen more changes at the club than any other player. "It's been a roller-coaster ride and I'm glad to have been part of it. Changes in names, ownership, grounds. I've developed a lot of friendships over the years with players I've met and played with. Often the Alliance games have been enjoyable, blokes playing for the love of the sport, putting their bodies on the line."

After three seasons as a first team regular, Darryl found himself out in the cold in the 1993-4 season, to the surprise of many supporters. "The club had moved to Barnet and I was working at Crystal Palace, 20 miles away. I had been in dispute with the club because I was owed money from the previous season. I felt that Tony Gordon wasn't prepared to support me which was disappointing because it could have been my best season with the club. My only option was to play Alliance and wait for a call up." Under Gordon's successor, Gary Greinke, Darryl returned to the first team, and then played at the top level in the Centenary season and the first Super League season. His versatility meant he was often on the bench, making 17 appearances as a substitute in each season. "I have played every position at some stage. I preferred centre, with the one-on-one defence and running into gaps. You can run the ball and use the open space out wide. But with the low numbers we had in the squad I had to play all over the place. If I came on as a sub I would aim to get involved as much as possible. Sometimes I was also a reluctant second-string goal kicker." In fact, Darryl made over 150 appearances, including ones from the bench and scored more than 50 tries.

46

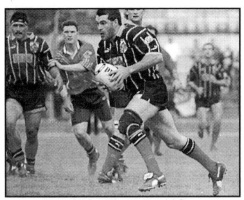
Darryl Pitt (Photo: David Stevens)

He was disappointed not to be offered a playing contract for 1997, but was offered the post of coach for the Alliance team. "I was settled in London and wanted to stay with the club. Development officer Dave Evans and I did the Level Three Coaching Certificate in Leeds. It was the last course that John Kear ran before becoming head coach of Sheffield Eagles. I had only done coaching with kids before, but I enjoyed it. I try to break things down and make them easy to understand, then build them up again. It is nice to see skills develop and young players progress." That season the Alliance side were runners up in the Second Division, despite using 52 players. The following season Darryl became assistant Academy coach and then in 1999, as the club relaunched the Alliance team, he became its coach along with Dave Rotheram.

Of the many players he has played with, Darryl recalls Mark Lee as being "very quiet off the field and very tough on it. Steve Rosolen was similar - really fierce and tough on the field. John Plath enjoyed himself off the field but was a very good competitor. Terry Matterson was very skilful and led by example, while Peter Gill was an inspirational figure. Darren Shaw was very tough, but a gentleman off the field."

Darryl now works as head caretaker at St Joseph's College in south London, a job that fits in well with his Rugby League commitments. Darryl recently coached the London and South East under-17s against an Australian schools team. He clearly enjoys working with young players, helping them develop in Rugby League. "To me Rugby League is the most exciting team game in sport, both for the athletes and the spectators. I hope we help the young players at the club develop and form a sporting career. We must put resources into the 16 to 19-year-olds - they are our future first team."

100 appearances plus 54 as substitute
52 tries
25 goals
1 drop goal
255 points

Interview in October 1999

Mick Taylor

Mick Taylor was a true stalwart of the club from when he signed in 1989 into the early 1990s. He arrived as Ross Strudwick was attempting to strengthen the team and had already He had played one season under Ross at Halifax. Mick was just the sort of player with northern experience who was essential to the London side composed as it was of the usual curious chemistry of Australians and southerners with only the thinnest veneer of players who had experienced the game in its northern heartlands. He was also one of the few signings from a northern club at that time to actually come and live in the south.

Mick was captain for a time at Crystal Palace when the side turned out worthy if uninspiring performances and held a creditable position in an intensive eight-team Second Division which was a half-way house between the elite and the lesser clubs of the Third Division. Mick scored on his debut against Ryedale-York in 1989 under the old Fulham banner and was voted home player of the year that season.

Mick had signed for then First Division Halifax from Oldham for £20,000 and then moved to Fulham for £7,000. His favoured position was in the centre, but he also played wing and in his latter days in the capital even played in the pack.

He was joint top scorer in his first season alongside Brett Daunt with 12 tries. One of the honours he gained was that he was picked for the Great Britain Select side that played the Soviet Union on the Russia tour.

Mick moved back north in November 1992, having been a consistent presence for the club for nearly four years. He moved onto Bradford Northern for the rest of that season and then joined Huddersfield in September 1994, playing against the London Broncos for them in January 1995, reviving memories for the London fans. He retired at the end of the 1995-6 Centenary season.

84 appearances plus 3 as sub
19 tries
76 points

A London Crusade

Steve Rosolen

Steve Rosolen had the longest career of all the Australian players who have played for London. This in itself says a lot about a player who oozed class at whatever level he played. Steve made his debut in the inauspicious surroundings of Crystal Palace National Sports Stadium against Oldham in a Second Division fixture.

Steve was to see the lows and the highs of Rugby League in the capital, playing in front of a few hundred but also playing in front of thousands at Old Trafford, Sydney and Brisbane. Steve grew up on Rugby League in the Queensland town of Bundaberg, a place more well known for it's beer than its sporting prowess, at least outside Australia.

Steve had played against the greats of Australian Rugby League, including Wally Lewis and Gene Miles in the Brisbane competition just one season before the Brisbane Broncos were to dominate Queensland. Steve came to Britain to try his luck but his luck lasted 50 minutes, when in his debut for Salford in a trial game against St Helens he broke his right arm and returned to Australia.

This was to be a recurring theme as Steve was to have a string of injuries, more a tribute to his uncompromising forward play than just bad luck. Back in Australia Steve had the honour of playing for North Sydney and winning the reserve grade grand final in front of 40,000 fans.

What a contrast 40,000 in Sydney, 600 at the Palace. The team that Tony Gordon constructed was remembered for its fine back line-up but it was the class of players such as Scott Carter, Sam Stewart and especially Steve Rosolen that really provided the basis for the expansive back play. Considering his achievements, it is a mark of respect for that team that he recalls playing in the Divisional Premiership final as his greatest memory.

In any attempt to pick an all-time London side, Steve Rosolen would be one of a handful of forwards who would be quick to be pencilled in. The strength of Steve was seen when he was badly injured at the start of the first Broncos season in 1994-5 and with his absence the side often struggled until he returned.

He was one of the few players to stay with the club as the Crusaders became the Broncos, and new coach Gary Greinke broke up the marvellous 1993-4 team. Steve's work-rate, skills and defensive ability were an asset to the club as it established itself as a force in Super League. Sadly, injuries got the better of him in the end and he retired in August 1998. Seven years' loyal service to the club was ended on medical advice after a serious arm injury.

158 appearances plus 13 as substitute
31 tries
124 points

Scott Roskell

One of the few players to survive the transition from London Crusaders to the Broncos in Super League was Australian winger or centre Scott Roskell. Of perhaps more significance is the fact that he still holds the try scoring record for the club, with 86 tries in six seasons.

Scott first played Rugby League for junior club Southport Tigers. Then, "after leaving school I took a year off from the game, then joined Runaway Bay. From there I played for Gold Coast for two seasons, before returning to Runaway Bay for another season. I was also selected for the New South Wales Country XIII against the City team. It was the first time the Country side won that game, and David Krause, a future Broncos team-mate, kicked the winning goal."

Andrew Zillman and Russell Browning had returned to Australia after playing for the Crusaders and it was they who encouraged Scott to sign for the club. "I came to London with Dave King. I did not know Ross Strudwick, but had seen him on television, playing for Valleys. I had never been to London before, and did not expect to be here seven years later."

Scott soon settled into Rugby League life in London. "There were about 20 of us living in a house, including Darryl Duncan, Paul Fisher and their girlfriends. Then four Russians joined us. It was quite cramped."

Scott has fond memories of the 1993-4 season with Tony Gordon. "There were some of the best players I played with in that team. And off the pitch they were a good bunch of blokes. We gelled well together. I remember the Premiership Final at Old Trafford - I was injured and could hardly run. We were 18 points down at half-time but recovered. Before that we had scored 66 against Keighley in the quarter-final game. Tony Gordon was a very good coach."

A new experience for Scott that season was the Regal Trophy game at York. "I had never played in the snow before and only seen it when I went skiing. In the second half we played with the blizzard behind us - the York players were covered in snow."

His other great season was in 1997 with the Broncos. "It was Tony Currie's second season. Terry Matterson, Peter Gill, Rusty Bawden and Tony Martin - formed a fine combination of young and old players." He remembers the fabulous World Club Championship victory over Canberra. "In Australia we conceded 66 points to them and their forwards were laughing at us. Then at The Stoop I got sin-binned in the first minute and two tries were scored on my side of the pitch. From 14-0 down we got back to 14 all and beat them 38-18. That was the best feeling I have ever had after a game."

Scott preferred playing on the wing in Rugby League, although he has recently been playing centre for London Welsh in Rugby Union. He says: "I have always aimed to be a good team player, stick by my team mates and do my fair share of the work." Broncos fans remember Scott for his combination of speed and strength, in which ever position he was playing, the two key qualities for a centre or winger in Rugby League. He also showed he could perform against the best in Rugby League with his try scoring in the World Club Championship games.

In 1997, unable to agree a new contract with the Broncos after being offered reduced terms by the club, Scott left to play Rugby Union with London Welsh. Many supporters were surprised he was allowed to leave the club and believe that the qualities he bought to the back line have still not been replaced.

Clive Griffiths, now the London Welsh coach, but with years of experience in Rugby League, clearly recognised his potential for Rugby Union despite his lack of experience in the 15-a-side code. "I found the London Welsh team to be well coached and drilled. Rowland Phillips was one of the best captains I have played with. I missed the club's try-scoring record by two in my first season, after missing the first eight games."

After initially joining London Welsh as a full-time player, a reduction in the number of full-time players at the club means that he now plays part-time and works for an IT consultancy. For the future he says: "I want to stay with London Welsh and keep scoring tries." He does not rule out playing Rugby League again, and is settled in London and being married with a young son. He hopes to stay involved in sport when his playing career is over, but at the age of 30 he still has a lot of try scoring ahead of him in his new code.

Interview in October 1999

136 appearances plus 8 as substitute
86 tries
344 points

Mark Riley

If you asked any London supporter who saw the glorious Tony Gordon season at Copthall in 1993-4 who their favourite player was I would guarantee that 90% would say Mark Riley.

The New Zealand halfback came to London under unclear circumstances. Originally it was stated he was another back-packer who arrived at Crystal Palace in November 1992 from local amateurs Peckham. In truth, he had been brought from New Zealand by the club sponsors Playmaker. He really started to flourish under fellow Kiwi Tony Gordon. Mark was a talismanic figure and indeed his debut was against in the great giant-killing feat, when the then Second Division Crusaders crushed (and this was no exaggeration) First Division Wakefield Trinity 30-0 at the Palace. Mark recalled that he touched down at Gatwick on the Thursday, trained on the Friday and played on the Sunday!

He started his Rugby League career in Auckland with Otahuhu with whom he won a Grand Final in 1990 and Mangere Easts, going onto play in Perth, Western Australia, for the Belmont Steelers, appearing in three Grand finals and winning two. He had tried to come to England for Rochdale in 1987 but could not get work permit clearance, the discovery of a Yorkshire born grandfather allowing him to join London.

It was the move to Copthall that brought out the best in Flicker (nick-named after the tattoo of a horse on his arm). Such was the style of play that Riley scored 37 tries in the 1993-4 season but still finished behind Mark Johnson who was on 43, this in a team that had scored a remarkable 212 tries in a glorious open-rugby playing style.

Mark also held the club record for tries in a game with the four he scored against Highfield on 17 October 1993, a record only overtaken in 1999 by Martin Offiah's five. So much did Tony Gordon think of him, he suggested to the New Zealand selectors that they pick him. However, Mark's only selection honour from that season was being picked for the *Open Rugby* Second Division player of the month and player of the year teams.

During that season Gordon had a cunning plan for scrums in an opponents half. He would stretch the back line from the scrum wide and back towards their own line. This forced the defence to stretch accordingly, Riley would then receive the ball from the scrum and race away under the posts. You had to feel for the opposition as the attacking line-up included John Gallagher, Abi Ekoku, Leo Dynevor, Andre Stoop and Mark Johnson! Although London fans will always fondly remember that season there were disappointments.

The club narrowly lost the promotion race by one point in controversial circumstances. During the game at Copthall against league leaders Workington with London winning 18-4, Riley raced towards the posts and was fouled in the process of rounding the visitors full back, the referee only awarded a penalty when everyone knew Riley would have scored the winning try. Workington then made a sensational comeback and the game was drawn 20-20, a Gallagher drop-goal attempt hitting the post and bouncing out in the final minutes. The club also got to the final of the Divisional Premiership at Old Trafford again versus champions Workington. Alas, disaster struck in first few minutes when Riley was carried off with a serious injury. He claimed his losers medal after a battling side went down 22-30.

The following season saw a change in the style of play under new Australian coach Gary Greinke and we only saw glimpses of the real Riley. One was at First Division Salford in the Regal Trophy, where Mark scored a special, despite this the side (now the London Broncos) went down narrowly 14-16. Soon after Mark broke his kneecap at Huddersfield that put him out for the rest of the season. With the Broncos now put into the top division for the 1995-6 season, and coach Greinke having a very set pattern of play, it was clear that Mark's face didn't fit and with competition for half-back with the likes of Kevin Langer, Leo Dynevor and Ben Walker, Riley was forced into the alliance team.

Even this could not get him down, inspiring them to a Second Division championship title. Mark did get to play in the centenary season, usually coming on as sub with occasional matches on the wing, and scored a try at Castleford in his distinctive jinking way. For the 1996 season, Mark moved on to Second Division Swinton, scoring a club record six tries in a 90-0 win over Highfield. Swinton's club history recalls him as "outstanding". In two seasons there he scored 30 tries. He still is in the London top-ten try scorers list, having scored 62 in four years at the club. He left Swinton at the end of the 1997 season to return to New Zealand.

89 appearances plus 5 as sub
62 tries
1 drop goal
249 points

Mark Johnson

Mark Johnson is the most prominent South African Rugby League star of the Super League era. He has a tremendous rugby pedigree with his older brother Gavin playing for the all conquering Rugby Union Springboks and Saracens RUFC and two younger brothers who also play Union.

Mark, a South African English-speaker, was brought up in the Afrikaans-speaking town of Louis Trichardt in the Northern Transvaal province. There were no English-speaking schools near there, so he went to school as a boarder in Pietersburg. He started playing Rugby Union at the age of seven, and at school played centre. After leaving school, he eventually gravitated to Pretoria where he played Rugby Union for the Harlequins and then on to Johannesburg to play for the Pirates, by now playing on the wing.

He started playing Rugby League "in the Union off season. We played touch rugby after work, but with Rugby League rules. I met Dave Southern and Barry Haslam who were trying to get Rugby League clubs started. There were five or six teams and I joined Dave's team, the Johannesburg Nomads. It was all Union guys who were playing."

Mark had not made the regional Transvaal side in Union and saw that League offered new openings for him. He was soon picked for two tests against the touring Commonwealth of Independent States (later to become Russia) team in November 1992, scoring a try in the second match. The South Africa side won both games and included Jamie Bloem, who was also to make a big impact in British Rugby League.

This led to the international Sydney Sevens in January 1993 which was the turning point in Mark's rugby career. *Open Rugby* reported that the South Africans had "played well" on their overseas debut.

In Sydney he was contacted by Glen Johnson of the Playmaker group which was involved with the tournament. They had links with London Crusaders and had helped recruit Mark Riley to the London club. Mark recalls: "he arranged for me to have trials with Australian Rugby League club Cronulla. I stayed for an extra two weeks after the Sevens tournament, but I was very raw at the time, having just come to the game from Rugby Union. I made three sets of trials, but then the coach said I was too old at 24, so it was back on the plane to South Africa."

But Glen Johnson was soon back in touch and arranged with Mark to be offered a trial with London Crusaders. This coincided with the change of ownership at the club and the appointment of Tony Gordon as coach. Mark played a handful of games at the end of the 1992-3 season at Crystal Palace. "Glen said it was the last six weeks of the season. They would pay for my flight and accommodation, and give me some pocket money. It went really well. Two other players, "Doc" Mulkerin and Chris Winstanley were also staying with me at The Swan Hotel [near Crystal Palace] and made me feel at home. But London was a great shock - I had grown up on a farm in South Africa and was very different to home."

Following that successful trial he was offered a full contract with the Crusaders who had just moved to Barnet Copthall in north London. Playing alongside such gifted backs as John Gallagher, Justin Walker, Scott Roskell and Logan Campbell (who followed him to Hull and Workington), Mark soon adjusted to the League game and smashed the club try-scoring record for a season at the first attempt with 43. His tremendous pace and ability to take tries fitted in very well with the team's attacking style.

Mark remembers: "I must have impressed Tony Gordon. I got offered a contract for just £3,500 plus accommodation and match fees. My mother had recently died suddenly and I felt it was the right time to make a change. It was so exciting to become a Rugby League professional - something almost unheard of in recent times in South Africa."

Some credit must go to the attacking style of play of the coach Tony Gordon who seemed happy as long as the Crusaders scored more points than their opponents - never mind how many. Mark recalls: "That season was great. It was a good life - we celebrated our victories! Sam Stewart played a big part in helping my game develop - I owe him a lot. And Dave Rotheram was very hospitable and very knowledgeable. He always encouraged us at training. But I was still learning the game. In Rugby Union it does not matter if you are tackled over the side line, but giving the ball away like that in League is serious. In one game it happened to me twice in the first half. At half-time Tony Gordon threatened to put me on a plane back to South Africa if it happened again. I made up for it by scoring two tries."

Mark shared a house with three other Crusaders players "all single guys. It was a good life and a great season. I remember playing at York in the snow - a new experience. The Premiership Final at Old Trafford was the climax to the whole season. We had a well balanced team." Although the injury-hit Crusaders lost the Premiership final to a strong Workington team, Mark scored a hat-trick in the match

Not only was Mark the top Crusaders' try scorer but also top in British Rugby League that year. He followed in the tradition of great South African players such as Tom van Vollenhoven, Trevor Lake, Fred Griffiths, Wilf Rosenberg, Jan Prinsloo and others.

You can always tell the popularity of a player - if he has a nickname he's usually popular, Mark Johnson had three: 'Johnno', 'Magic' and bizarrely the 'Cape Crusader', given that he was born nowhere near South Africa's Cape, still it was a good moniker.

Mark stayed with the club in 1994-5 after the Brisbane Broncos' takeover, but never seemed to quite fit in with new Australian coach Gary Greinke's plans. He remembers: "I don't feel I had a fair chance from him. At times I was playing in the A team but felt I deserved a first team place." As Greinke broke up the 1993-4 team, Mark left in July 1995 to join Workington. "The club made me a free agent rather than pay me my outstanding contract money. Workington had been interested in me after the match against them at Old Trafford. Peter Walsh was the coach there and he was the main reason I went there. But as I arrived he left and Kurt Sorensen took over." Workington struggled in Super League. "But for me it was a step up. I got a better contract than at London. And another highlight was playing with Rowland Phillips. He is one of the best friends I have made in Rugby League."

After Mark's contract finished with Workington, he returned to South Africa for four months. Disillusioned after a season of struggle in Super League which had ended in relegation, he tried to get back into Rugby Union. He played sevens in the Transvaal team, but decided that League did offer him a future after all. He was then approached to play for Hull. Two seasons there were followed by move for the 1999 season to Salford. "For the first 10 games, with Andy Gregory as coach, I was in the A team. But then he left and I got a first team spot and ended up scoring 15 tries." Mark was the club's top try scorer. He has signed for Salford for another year and has been joined by Martin Offiah from the London Broncos, who he says in training is fractionally faster over 40 yards.

Another great memory for Mark is playing for South Africa in the 1995 Rugby League World Cup. "I had gone from playing touch rugby in 1992 to representing my country in a World Cup. We played Australia, the World Champions, England and Fiji. They were all a different class from us, but we gave Fiji a good game." Mark was the most experienced player in the team. "For the third game against England I played at stand-off and shouted at our players for 80 minutes telling them what to do. I hope to play in the World Cup in 2000. At least I can say I've played against the best teams in a World Cup competition."

Mark believes that his main strength as a player is his finishing. "I can read the game quite well and see where the breaks will be. Timing is very important. I can't explain it - it happens so quickly. I try to look for work and not just stay on my wing. I'm not the fastest winger in the world but I am a good finisher. I'm trying to improve my weaknesses and I take it personally if opposing teams score on my wing."

For the future, Mark hopes to play for as long as he can. He is now 31 and aims to play for three more years in England before going back to South Africa with his family. He hopes to be able to contribute to developing Rugby League in South Africa and is very committed to playing for the national side again.

Mark has scored 114 tries in 156 games (to the end of 1999) in his British Rugby League career. But he has often been playing in struggling sides, limiting his scoring opportunities. Had one of the top clubs recognised his talent he could have regularly topped the try scoring charts. London fans will remember his contribution to the marvellous 1993-4 team and he remains the only London player ever to top the national try scoring list.

Interview in January 2000

73 appearances
66 tries
264 points

Abi Ekoku

There can't be many people who can claim to have been at Abi Ekoku's first and last game as a professional, but I'm one of them.

Although having spent most of his early years in the north of England, Abi didn't take up Rugby League until he was 27 coming from Athletics where he had represented Great Britain in the discus and had been the

British discus champion. He comes from a sporting family, with his brother having played professional football for Wimbledon and his older brother was a junior Great Britain athlete.

He started playing for St Mary's College. He was recovering from injury and a work colleague suggested he have a game with her husband's rugby team. Her husband was former Fulham player Dominic Cooper who was running the St Mary's team. It was suggested he have a trial for the Crusaders' Alliance team who were playing there at the time. His talent was quickly spotted as Tony Gordon started to put his team together.

He made his debut for the Crusaders against Batley in the first ever game at Copthall in August 1993 and quickly became a crowd favourite with his surging runs from deep in defence. His enthusiasm and commitment fitted in well with Tony Gordon's coaching style (it didn't seem to matter if we conceded 30 points so long as we scored 40). In fact his performance in the Regal Trophy victory against Featherstone persuaded me to join the Supporters Club!

Abi played in the defeat at Old Trafford in the Divisional Premiership - our first ever final, but once Gary Greinke took over, Abi's risky but exciting style of play didn't seem to fit in with the no-risk defensive approach that the team adopted. With a few injury problems Abi's appearances became infrequent and he moved on to Halifax. He then moved to Bradford where he was a part of the team that won Super League II and lost at Wembley. He had intended to retire in 1998 anyway, but ended up being carried off injured in his last game against Saints in the play-offs. It's good that he wasn't lost to the game - he continued as Chairman of the players' union, the second former London player to hold that position. He then joined Keighley Cougars as their chief executive. And in January 2000, after only three months at Keighley, he suddenly was recruited by Bradford Bulls as their new Chief Executive. He is also taking up the discus again with a view to competing in the Sydney Olympics.

27 appearances, 15 tries, 60 points

By Andrew Jackson - Treasurer, London Broncos Supporters' Club
(Based on an article in *Whatever happened to Fulham*)

John Gallagher

Before the Super League era, and the recruitment of Martin Offiah and Shaun Edwards, international stars were fairly rare on the London Rugby League scene.

Hussain M'Barki was a Rugby Union international for Morocco when he signed for Fulham in 1981. In the same Craven Cottage era, hooker John Dalgreen played one test for Great Britain and both Adrian Cambriani and Martin Herdman won League caps for Wales. But while these players were heroes to Fulham supporters, none could really be seen as international sports stars.

In 1990, John Gallagher won the International Rugby Union player of the year award. This was the culmination of a successful career in New Zealand Rugby Union, playing mainly at full-back, which included a World Cup winners' medal in 1987 and superstar status in New Zealand. He was never on the losing side for the All Blacks in 41 appearances, 18 of them internationals. In Rugby Union and sport generally, he could truly be called an international star.

Many London Rugby League fans were unaware that when John joined the London Crusaders in 1993, the club was in fact signing a Londoner. Born and raised in Lewisham, he played his early club Rugby Union for London Irish and Askeans.

An important development in his rugby career came when a Rugby Union scholarship took him to New Zealand in 1984. After a brief return to London and short spell in the Metropolitan Police, he then returned to New Zealand in 1985. In 1986, he won his first All Black honours and success followed success in union.

Not surprisingly, his development in union attracted the attention of leading Rugby League clubs. After winning the international award in 1990, he switched codes, much to the surprise of his friends in New Zealand and signed for Leeds for a fee reported to be £300,000. League magazine *Open Rugby* reported that the signing "sent shock waves through the old school tie world of Rugby Union and has already set the city of Leeds buzzing."

Big money signings from Rugby Union have always attracted attention in Rugby League. There is a long history of such players being the target for opposition forwards, and John was no exception.

John was thrust straight into the first team at Leeds, with little chance to adjust to the different demands of League. A spear tackle in an early game, which went unpunished by the referee, seemed to reduce his confidence further and, by his own admission, although he played 30 games for Leeds in his first season, he did not set the world on fire in his new code.

A further setback came with a change of coach at Leeds. At the end of his first season, David Ward, who had signed John, left the club and was replaced by Doug Laughton.

On the surface, this should have been a positive move for John, as Laughton had a fine record of developing former Rugby Union players in League, including Martin Offiah, Jonathan Davies and Alan Tait at Widnes. But he clearly didn't rate John, who was often consigned to Leeds's A team, playing only a handful of first team games over the next two seasons. An injury in his third season did not help. Interviewed later, John said: "Doug hadn't signed me, didn't rate me and made it clear he didn't want me. I never really got a chance..." Fellow All-Black Frano Botica, who made a successful transition to Rugby League with Wigan, felt that John would have developed better at another club. "I couldn't believe they let him rot [at Leeds]", he said. "I'm sure he would have made it at Wigan."

So when the opportunity came to return to the capital and relaunch his League career with London Crusaders in 1993, John grabbed the chance. Crusaders coach New Zealander Tony Gordon had confidence in him and he fitted into the Kiwi feel the club had at that time, as Gordon built a multi-national team that would play some of the most exciting Rugby League ever seen in London. John's signing also attracted a great deal of press interest, with some welcome and positive publicity for the club. Here was someone playing for the Crusaders who people outside Rugby League had actually heard of, which gave the club some much-needed credibility. As well as adding to the Crusaders' playing strength, John helped with the club's promotion and development work.

John Gallagher receiving a trophy from Liam Bushell
(Photo: Barry & Gwen Warren)

John started the season at full-back and took the goal-kicking responsibilities. When Abi Ekoku was injured he moved to the wing and also played a couple of games at centre.

Maybe he wasn't the best defensive player in Rugby League. But he was an astonishingly consistent goal-kicker and scored tries regularly, both from full-back and on the wing. His experience of the big occasion was also beneficial for a team which included a number of young, inexperienced players.

Tony Gordon's team just missed out on promotion to the First Division in John's first season. Ironically, one of John's kicks most memorable that season was a rare miss - a drop goal attempt against promotion-seeking rivals Workington in the thrilling 20-all draw at Copthall. The kick grazed the outside of the post and could have won the game for the Crusaders. That result was the difference between winning promotion and finishing third, just outside the two promotion places.

Tony Gordon left the club in May 1994, replaced by Gary Greinke. John continued playing the next season in Greinke's more cautious, stereotyped team, but found it difficult to combine attending training with his new job as a school teacher. He retired, but then in January 1995 made a temporary return as injuries saw the Broncos short of a goal-kicker. He retired finally from Rugby League at the end of that season.

In the summer of 1995, Rugby Union went open, allowing players who had switched to Rugby League to return to union. John joined Blackheath where he resumed his familiar full-back role. He later retired from playing to become Director of Rugby at Harlequins, linking with his former All Black colleague Zinzan Brooke who became the club's player-coach.

John only played two seasons of Rugby League in London. However, he still holds two club records, both set in the momentous 1993-4 season: most goals with 159 and the most points, 384. He was an integral part of the club's success in that wonderful year. It is interesting to speculate on how he would have fared in Super League working with Tony Currie. But by the spring of 1996, when Tony Currie joined the Broncos, John had returned to the code where he made his name. But he is still remembered as London Rugby League's first internationally known star.

51 appearances
19 tries
196 goals
2 drop goals
470 points

Sam Stewart

The acquisition of Sam Stewart in 1993, an ex-Kiwi international and a player with Australian Winfield Cup experience, was a real sign to Crusaders' supporters that London were once again on the right track and this proved to be the case, at least on the pitch. In a pack that was sometimes overlooked due to the try-scoring exploits of the back division, club captain Sam ensured that the basics were done in a quiet unassuming manner. More than this, it was Sam's creative handling and kicking that broke done many a stubborn defence. His leadership qualities helped keep the team together during an often turbulent season, when the club ownership and future were often under question.

Sam was born in Wellington, New Zealand and played for Randwick in Wellington before moving across the Tasman Sea to join Newcastle Knights for whom he played from 1987 to 1993. Sam also appeared for the Wellington representative side and for New Zealand Universities

Sam Stewart (Photo: Barry & Gwen Warren)

before going to play in Australia. He made his test debut in 1985 and played in 17 tests, including two tours of Great Britain.

Sam was signed for London by fellow Kiwi, Tony 'Tank' Gordon, who had coached him for New Zealand, but Sam had heard of the Fulham club during the New Zealand Great Britain tour in 1985, and had discussed the possibility of moving here with fellow Kiwi Mark Elia who played for Southend Invicta.

In Australia, at Newcastle Knights, Sam was the first player to play 100 games for the club and was also the first player to be made a life member of one of Australia's newest clubs, playing in front of 26,000 on a regular basis. It must have been some shock to the system to play in front of a few hundred at the small scale Copthall stadium. In a London side replete with strange nicknames (Flicker, Kipper, Pig Dog, Tiger, Sir Alf) Sam's nickname was just as strange, Wheka, apparently some flightless bird from New Zealand.

In Sam's first season the club finished third in the Second Division, just missing out on promotion and made the Divisional Premiership Final. This game was showed the limitations of the club's small squad, because Sam, along with star half-back Mark Riley and Scott Carter, was injured. He had to play the whole game with a problem rib. Despite these problems, the Crusaders rallied in the second half and only lost to

64

Workington by eight points. Sam had also played a key role in the giant-killing act against First Division Featherstone Rovers in the Regal Trophy. Very rarely did anyone get the better of him that season.

After staying with the club for the 1994-5 season, and continuing as captain, Sam moved on to Hull Kingston Rovers. The players that he had joined the club with had largely moved on following the takeover by the Brisbane Broncos and coach Tony Gordon's departure at the end of the 1993-4 season.

His disillusion with the London set-up later caused him to remark that Rugby League success in London was as likely as it was in the middle of the North Sea. You could understand his frustration after efforts he had made and that he was discarded by the Broncos management just before the step up to the top level in the Centenary season. However, whether he would have had the pace for the higher level at that stage of his career is debatable. He played another two seasons for Hull Kingston Rovers before returning to New Zealand.

70 appearances plus 2 as substitute
8 tries
32 points

Leo Dynevor

Leo Dynevor had a stark introduction to British Rugby League, moving from sub-tropical Queensland to play for the Crusaders at a sub-zero Mount Pleasant, Batley on his birthday. Welcome to Britain! It was rumoured that he played in tights and gloves because of the cold. Leo had joined the Crusaders in February 1994 along with prop Victor "Turbo" Timms as part of an aid package from big brother and new owner the Brisbane Broncos.

Both players were big hits with the fans, but the cold weather and heavy winter grounds did not suit Dynevor's running style. It was suggested that season that Leo looked like Bambi, all big eyes and spindly legs that kept slipping on the muddy ground. He also did not like playing in the rain.

Leo returned again for the 1995-6 Centenary season and played in Super League I in 1996, but struggled to hold down a permanent place at

Leo Dynevor (Photo: David Stevens)

scrum-half where Kevin Langer often played. Thus Leo played in several places in the back division and made more appearances from the bench than starting appearances. However, one highlight was a hat-trick in a 37-8 win at Castleford in November 1995 as the Broncos took the Yorkshire side apart.

Leo was born in the outback Queensland town of Moogan, which is three hours from Brisbane. He started playing for a local team in the second row, but then as he got older, found his true role in the backs. He played for Cherbourg juniors before being snapped up by the Brisbane scouting system. Leo is an Aboriginal footballer and was inspired to seek the heights of the game by fellow Aboriginal Steve Renouf.

Despite his great attacking style and his good kicking game Leo found it difficult to break into ARL big time as the Brisbane half-backs were internationals Allan Langer and Kevin Walters, and was just glad to be part of the London Broncos Super League set-up despite competition from Kevin Langer and Tulsen Tollett for the scrum half spot.

Leo was described by the *London Calling!* fanzine as "the great entertainer" and fans soon warmed to his all action style and the cry of "Leo, Leo" would echo round The Valley where he played many of his matches. It was such a pleasure to see the silky skills of Leo teamed up with the class of stand-off Ben Walker, another product of the Brisbane finishing school.

After his time at the Broncos, he returned back to Australia at the time of the split between the ARL and the Super League clubs and signed for Newcastle. This proved to be a good move and he played 19 games for them in 1997. He was their top points scorer that season with 104. His goal kicking assisted the Knights to a Grand Final victory and he became part of a very select club of players who have left London and gone on to play in an Australian Grand Final, the others being Glen Nissen, Tony Martin and Rusty Bawden. Leo then played for Sydney based side Wests in the NRL. For the 2000 season he has joined Kurri Kurri in the Newcastle Rugby League.

37 appearances plus 13 as substitute
21 tries
27 goals
138 points

The Bucking Broncos

Kevin Langer

"There's only one Kevin Langer", sang the Broncos travelling supporters as he scored the first try for London in the First Division for 10 years, at Warrington at the start of the Centenary season in August 1995.

Kevin had come from Brisbane to the new Broncos in December 1994 to try to bolster the club in the Second Division. It was not a happy time as coach Gary Greinke struggled to find a winning side in both the Second Division and the 1995-6 Centenary season. Langer was the nuggety scrum-half type, full of guile and craft. Kevin comes from a famous Rugby League family. His younger brother Allan played for the Kangaroos, the all-conquering Brisbane Broncos and has joined Warrington for the 2000 season. It was symptomatic of Kevin's sense of humour, or possibly his modesty that when London rang him he thought they really wanted his (more famous) brother.

He joined the club from Ipswich Jets and made his debut in the Regal trophy defeat at First Division Salford in December 1994 when the then

Second Division Broncos nearly caused a shock. Langer's bouncy carefree attitude was a real strength as the fledgling Broncos tried to find their feet both on and off the pitch. Numerous players remember Kevin's contribution to the development of the Broncos not only as a player, but as a member of the squad off the pitch, where his sense of humour provided many memorable moments and helped build team spirit.

During his short stay the team played at four different grounds in London, but it was interesting to see Kevin play better as the quality of his colleagues improved with the step up to Super League. He was player-coach of the Alliance side in 1996, but in fact played fairly regularly in Super League at the same time.

Kevin returned back to Brisbane at the end of the 1996 inaugural Super League season to run his brothers' clothing empire and coach in the Brisbane competition.

43 appearances plus 14 as substitute
13 tries
52 points

Peter Gill

Of all the Australians who have played for the club over the years, one of the most popular - and best - players was Peter Gill.

Peter first played Rugby League as a four-year-old. He remembers "My father was captain-coach of a local team in Toowoomba. He introduced me to the game. In my first game I scored - but over our own line." After that inauspicious start, Peter played League at school and then graduated to the Queensland State League. He played for the Queensland Country team for two years, including a tour of New Zealand.

He had an offer to join Penrith, but felt that going to Sydney was too big a move. So he joined the Brisbane Brothers in 1986, where Ross Strudwick was coach. Future London Broncos Tony Rea and Dan Stains were fellow players. He recalls "Ross Strudwick was one of the best coaches. He took me under his wing and I learnt a lot from him."

In 1987, Brothers won the Brisbane Grand Final and for Peter a move to Sydney to join ARL side St George soon followed. There, he won the Panasonic Player of the Year - an award for a first grade mid-week competition. He played 77 first grade games for St George in four years before moving to Gold Coast.

"Financially, it was a good move for me, but football-wise I should have stayed at St George. Gold Coast couldn't compete with their local rivals Brisbane Broncos. I worked on the marketing side there as well. And in 1995 I signed a Super League contract and the opportunity to play in England came. Had Ross Strudwick stayed at Halifax I could have joined him there." Halifax's loss in 1988 was the Broncos' gain in 1995.

Peter found the game here different from Australia. "It was far more attacking, whereas the game in Australia was more defensive. Club director Barry Maranta said come for a month and if you like it stay. We were based at Copthall, it was cold and travelling to training was a nightmare. I was going to join Canterbury at home but that fell through. Now I wish I had come here earlier - I've enjoyed my time here."

He recalls the victory against Leeds at Brentford FC in 1995 as one of the highlights of his time in London. "The victory against Canberra was fantastic and we competed well against Brisbane Broncos in the World Club Challenge. The Castleford Challenge Cup semi-final was so exciting. I can't remember what I said in the interviews after the game, but it was a game I will never forget. Walking out at Wembley in front of the huge crowd is another great memory, but in the end the score line wasn't in our favour. But playing at Wembley was everything I expected and more, even if the end was disappointing."

Peter Gill
(Photo: Peter Lush)

Of the other Broncos players he has played with, Peter outlines that "Steve Rosolen was great in defence. He would always keep going. Scott Roskell was great - big and strong for a winger and he would also come in and help the forwards. Terry Matterson had great ball skills and was a good leader. I worked well with Rusty Bawden - we had a good combination. Tony Martin would always listen and learn. Kevin Langer was an inspiration - and great fun off the pitch. It's been great to play with Shaun Edwards, he's done everything in the game. And Martin Offiah is still one of the best finishers in the game."

Peter prefers playing at loose-forward, because he says it gives him more freedom. In his younger days he played at full-back or stand-off before moving to loose-forward. He says "At least I will retire before I get so slow I have to play in the front row." He was reluctant to talk about his strengths as a player, but when (gently) pushed said "Handling the ball, off loading out of tackles and keeping the ball alive. Defence is important - my dad always taught me that, and tackling practice." Broncos fans have learnt to appreciate his eye for a gap and creating tries for others, or scoring himself as in the Castleford semi-final.

Peter sees his future in coaching or development. "It is important to do an apprenticeship working with juniors. I have the level one coaching qualification and did some development work at Gold Coast. I definitely want to stay in Rugby League." He considered retiring at the end of the 1998 season, but says: "I'm glad I gave it one more year." Despite a long-running lower back injury, his form in 1999 was still consistent in a team that at times struggled. Another honour was to pass the 100 appearances for the club. He was also selected for the "Stones Dream Team" in 1996 and 1997, 13 players chosen by the Super League club coaches as having been outstanding during the season. He succeeded Terry Matterson as club captain in 1998, but was replaced by Shaun Edwards in 1999.

He recognises the key role played by the club's staff and fans. "I would like to thank Dr De Jennings and her son Simon, Trevor Howard, Steve Magee and kitman Clive Townsley. Director David Hughes is always cheerful, despite supporting us and Charlton. And the supporters are the best of any club I've been at. I'll miss them when I return to Australia."

Peter was one of the key players in establishing the Broncos as a force in Super League. His efforts on behalf of the club are recognised by all Broncos supporters and he will be hard to replace.

Interview in August 1999

108 appearances plus 7 as substitute
25 tries
100 points

Terry Matterson

When Terry Matterson joined the London Broncos during the Centenary season in 1995, the Broncos were being transformed from a side often out of their depth against top flight opposition to one with serious Super League aspirations. Along with fellow Australian Peter Gill, he added that element of class and experience that had been missing. He was signed as a loose- forward and was a key play maker from that position, although later in his Broncos career he also played at hooker. His side step and passing ability to create openings for others were an important part of the Broncos attacks.

In terms of experience few could match Terry's record with the Brisbane Broncos. He started his career with Eastern Suburbs for whom he played just two games before moving to the Broncos. He played in the Broncos' first game in the Winfield Cup in 1988, scoring a club record twenty four points in a 44-10 win over one of Australia's giants, the Sydney side Manly. This was to be the start of a glittering career, with Terry making his State of Origin debut with New South Wales as a substitute in a 16-36 defeat against Queensland. Not that he finished on the losing side very often. Terry won two Premierships with the Broncos plus a World Club Challenge victory against Wigan at Central Park in 1992 in which he kicked three goals. He also kicked four goals in Brisbane's 22-8 Grand Final win over St George in 1992. Terry also held the Brisbane points scoring record of 156 in 1992, which lasted until 1995, beating his own record of 150 in the inaugural 1988 season. He is the record points scorer for the Brisbane Broncos with 744.

Echoing his role in Brisbane's inaugural season, he then signed for the London Broncos in 1995. He stayed for three-and-a-half seasons to boost London's return to the top flight. Terry started as club captain at London. However, the club suffered a loss in form at the end of the last winter season after which coach Gary Greinke was sacked. Terry was one of a triumvirate of players who took a temporary coaching role for a Challenge Cup game at Dewsbury in February 1996, only to see the side slide to a shock defeat on a snow covered pitch.

The new coach Tony Currie was far more to Terry's liking as the Broncos finished fourth in the inaugural Super League season, with Terry kicking a record 11 goals and scored a try against hapless Workington in a 58-0 win at the Valley, which was also a Super League record until 1999.

Terry's straight-on kicking style was sometimes erratic and could be frustrating. But Broncos fans remember with relish his deciding last-minute goal from the touchline to secure an 18-all draw at Wigan in 1996 after the Broncos who had been 18-4 down at half-time. That dropped point effectively deprived Wigan of the Championship title as they finished the season one point behind St Helens.

One real triumph for Terry was the role he played in the World Club Championship match against Canberra at the Stoop in 1997. The Broncos had been pasted 66-20 away in Australia and despite a full house at the Stoop nobody expected a different result against a side that had won the Australian Premiership and was brimming with stars. The home side soon went behind 14-0 and Broncos fans feared the worst, but it was Terry's decisive opening try that that gave the Broncos hope and he scored again to send the home crowd into raptures as Mal Meninga's Canberra side were humiliated 38-18. In his final season in Super League III Terry again took the reigns as coach temporarily when Tony Currie had to go home on personal business. His final season was one of anti-climax as London slipped in the table and Peter Gill took over the captaincy. However, on his retirement he had captained the launch of two clubs into the big time.

74 appearances
23 tries
116 goals
6 drop goals
330 points

Darren Shaw playing for Scotland (Photo: Barry & Gwen Warren)

Kevin Langer collects an award
(Photo: Barry & Gwen Warren)

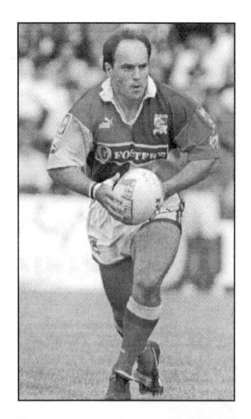

Terry Matterson (Photo: David Stevens)

Tulsen Tollett
(Photo: Peter Lush)

Tulsen Tollett

With the departure of Peter Gill back to Australia at the start of the 2000 season, Tulsen Tollett became the club's longest serving player. He is also the only London Broncos player to be selected for a Great Britain squad while with the club.

Tulsen was born in Sussex, but his family emigrated to Australia when he was six. Consequently he was the first player raised in Australia to be selected for a Great Britain touring squad.

Tulsen started playing Rugby League at the age of 10, "against my mother's better judgement." He was soon being selected for junior representative sides and joined Penrith, playing as a 17-year-old in their under-21 side, including an under-21 semi-final against Parramatta at the Sydney Football Stadium.

"That semi-final was a good experience. In 1991 I progressed to the reserve grade when I was 18 and, in 1992, played nine or 10 games at first grade. But I played scrum-half or stand-off and ahead of me were Greg Alexander and Brad Fittler. So in 1993 I moved to Parramatta where I could play regular first grade football. I had two good seasons in 1993 and 1994, but then was injured in 1995 and had a shoulder reconstruction."

The ARL-Super League war saw Tulsen sign for the Broncos. "I signed for Super League but Parramatta stayed with the ARL. I spoke to Barry Maranta and he recruited me for London. I found it a big change coming here, a real culture shock. I was only 22 and on the other side of the world. But it was a good bunch of guys and they made me feel at home. In my first game I scored two tries against Paris - it was certainly very exciting."

Apart from the 1999 Challenge Cup Final, Tulsen's best memories of his time with the Broncos in club football were the World Club Challenge games at the Stoop. "Beating Canberra and coming back from 14-0 down to win 38-18. And the game against Brisbane. The ground was full to the brim. It was very exciting." He also has vivid memories of the Challenge Cup semi-final against Castleford. "Steele Retchless got the ball, threw a dummy and was straight through to score the winning try. It was a really special day."

The 1996 Great Britain tour was a major highlight for him. "We flew to Singapore and trained there in 80 per cent humidity and on such a hard ground that Bernard Dwyer got blisters. Then it was Papua New Guinea. That was a new experience for me. The grounds were rock hard and we did well to win the games there. Then on to Fiji - we went scuba diving there. New Zealand was totally different - rain and mud." It was a tough time for the Lions and they suffered from a controversial directive from back home at the RFL. "Before the second test 12 players were sent home to save money. I went back to Sydney and then tour manager Phil Lowe phoned me to come back to provide cover because Andy Farrell was injured for the final test. But it turned out he was fit so I returned to Sydney. It was great to be with players I did not usually meet. I developed some good friendships on tour."

Tulsen played five matches on tour, including two as a substitute, scoring one try, but did not play in any of the test matches. He believes the 3-0 series defeat against the Kiwis was not a fair reflection of the play. "Kiwi John Timu scored twice in the last 10 minutes of the first test after we had been 12-2 up." And Great Britain were winning the second test 15-12 before narrowly losing by three points.

At the end of the 1997 season, Broncos fans were shocked when Tulsen signed for Harlequins Rugby Union club. "I had played Rugby Union at school and wanted to have a go. But I had an understanding that I could return to Rugby League if I wasn't happy. I played centre in union and played with some good players. I enjoyed my time there but I missed the atmosphere at the Broncos." Tulsen had established himself in the Harlequins first team, but rejoined the Broncos, initially on loan to play in the Challenge Cup semi-final against Wigan in March 1998. He soon returned on a permanent basis. He played union again for a couple of months at London Welsh in the autumn of 1999. "I have a lot of respect for Clive Griffiths (the London Welsh coach). Union is tactically different from League. The training is more physical with more contact work."

In League, Tulsen prefers to play at centre or stand-off. He has played all the back positions for the Broncos as well as occasionally filling in at hooker. He recalls: "In one game I went from the wing to scrum-half to centre. It can be difficult to adjust - the angles are different in each position. I would prefer to play just one position but it is good for the team if I cover a number of roles." Tulsen also enjoys goal kicking. "Often the most difficult kicks are the ones nearer the posts - you are expected to kick those, not like the ones out wide."

Looking to the future, Tulsen hopes to work in the media. "I did a column for the *Surrey Comet* and was recently on a sports chat show on BBC Digital. I would also like to get involved on the administrative side of the game, but not the coaching side." Before coming to London, Tulsen did a degree, qualified as a teacher and taught for a year. He also has a Level One Rugby League coaching qualification and has been involved in the Broncos' community work and schools coaching clinics. But for the next few years he wants to concentrate on his playing career, continuing to entertain and excite the Broncos fans.

Interview in October 1999

91 appearances plus 4 as substitute
29 tries
37 goals
1 drop goal
191 points
(to end 1999 season)

Martin Offiah

Mention it quietly in the north of England, the highest English try scorer in Rugby League and highest profile Rugby League player of the last decade is a Londoner! Martin Offiah has been the most successful Londoner ever in Rugby League and his presence on and off the pitch helped raise the Broncos' profile in the capital.

In the 1980s, then club owners Roy and Barbara Close watched Martin play Rugby Union at Rosslyn Park, having been given a press report of his third game, in which he was described as "O'Flyer" - a nickname that surprisingly did not catch on. However, Martin had no contact with the Fulham club. "I was barely aware of their existence and would not have considered Rugby League then. I was approached by someone from Hull when I played a sevens tournament in Wales, but the first serious approach was from Widnes in 1987."

Success followed success for Martin in League, first at Widnes, then at Wigan. In 1992, the publicity for the Great Britain versus Australia World Cup Final at Wembley was based around a photo of Martin - "Can the Aussies catch Offiah at Wembley?" But, by 1996, Wigan had reached their peak and were under financial pressure. Also, the decision by Rugby Union in 1995 to go "open" and allow professionalism cleared the way for Rugby League players to play union. Martin had already had a taste of union with Wigan - the game against Bath at Twickenham and Wigan's triumph, enjoyed by all League fans, in the Middlesex Sevens. These events combined to open the way for Martin's move south.

Martin recalls how the deal with the Broncos arose: "Originally I wanted to play a short season in Rugby Union and to be in London. Then it became apparent that London Broncos were interested in signing me. It all tied in together. I had played against the Broncos for Wigan at Brentford in 1995 and scored my 400th try. I said then that I could see myself playing for London at some stage in my career. The move happened quite suddenly. But if it feels right, do it." So Martin did it and alongside his move to the Broncos he also signed to play Rugby Union for Bedford in the winter.

Martin had only lived in London for two years since his primary school days. "It was a big change. I thought London was a good place to have fun, but that the quality of life was not that great." He made his debut for the Broncos against Warrington on 2 August 1996 at The Valley.

It is often forgotten that Martin was an up and coming player when he left Rugby Union, on the verge of international honours. "I am seen as a League player, but before signing for Widnes I had played for the Barbarians, England Students, London Division and in the Middlesex and Hong Kong Sevens tournaments."

However, things did not work out at Bedford, with his move back into Rugby Union only lasted one season. "I found I was a professional in a non-professional environment. Less than half the squad were full-time, so we trained in the day and then again at night. It was very different from Wigan which was run very professionally. Also, it was a 70-mile trip from home to Bedford and I was stuck there during the day after training. I would get home at 11pm and then have to go out early the next day. But I did score a few tries, including one against Blackheath who had John

Martin Offiah (Photo: Peter Lush)

Gallagher at full-back. I went round him to score. Another memorable try was the winner against Newcastle at Bedford. I played against League and union international John Bentley - we continued the ruckuses we had had in League! I found there were less opportunities in union for a winger. But union has improved as a game - the Super 12 tournament in the southern hemisphere has had an impact."

Playing both codes resulted in the unique experience of playing a match for each club over the same weekend. If this was not complicated enough, Martin was also going to Buckingham Palace on the previous Friday morning to be awarded the MBE. The ceremony over, he got a helicopter to Manchester airport to play for the Broncos at Warrington that evening, followed by playing for Bedford at Rotherham the next afternoon. This was covered by a number of national newspapers.

The Challenge Cup Final was one of the highlights of Martin's time with the Broncos. "Losing to Wigan in the 1998 semi-final was a low point. It was good to be involved at Wembley in 1999 and score the first try in a Challenge Cup final for the third time." He also recalled the 1997 season as being very successful. "The World Club Challenge games in Sydney helped us bond as a team. Beating Canberra Raiders at The Stoop was a big night. Beating Bradford and Wigan here to finish second in Super League was also very good. Everyone thought the club would take off. But some players were released and big names who were bought in didn't work. I was so excited at that time, that we could compete with the other clubs. But that team broke up and there has been a high turnover of players. Tony Mestrov, Rusty Bawden and Tony Martin have all done well since leaving the Broncos."

Martin recognises the problems the club faces establishing itself in London. "I am not sure if having one team called 'London' works. Sometimes people think I play American football when I say I play for the London Broncos. Where should the club play? A stadium in central London would be easier for access, but expensive. The club has been nomadic - at the moment they're still not sure where they are playing next season (2000). And small crowds means a lack of atmosphere. Maybe the club needs a wider vision about where it's going. I respect Maurice Lindsay and Gary Hetherington - they have the vision to take clubs forward. It's not just about hard work. The players do more promotion than any other club. Two days before the Wembley final I was up at 6am to appear on breakfast television. We have a loyal hard core of support, it just needs to be bigger. But I am sure that Tony Rea can sell the club to the London public."

Martin enjoyed working with former coach Tony Currie. "It was very similar to playing at Wigan." He also encouraged other northern-based players to come to London. "I helped bring Shaun Edwards to the club, as well as Wes Cotton and Robbie Smyth."

Martin was not offered a new contract at the end of the 1999 season, with the club making measures to economise and developing younger players. But it could be that this is proved to be short-sighted. Martin is one of the few Rugby League players known to the London public and his presence on and off the pitch has helped give the club credibility.

Despite a series of niggling injuries and, at times, not fitting into Dan Stains' plans for the team, he still scored 36 tries in 50 appearances and now holds the club record of tries scored in one game, with five against Whitehaven in the Challenge Cup. He has also contributed to the team's defensive play, contributing memorable try-saving tackles as well as scoring tries at the other end for the Broncos. Inevitably, he played his part in Salford's victory over the Broncos in the Challenge Cup at the start of the 2000 season.

Looking to his future, Martin hopes to continue playing for a couple of years with new club Salford, then develop his work in the media. "I would not go into coaching. Shaun [Edwards] would be good at that, not me. I have enjoyed my time in Rugby League and it has given me a good living. The tours were especially good and without Rugby League I would not have been to Papua New Guinea. I learnt from Ellery [Hanley] that the sun won't always shine and to make the most of your time in the game. But I am glad to have played a part in putting Rugby League on the map in London."

Interview in October 1999

45 appearances plus 3 as substitute
36 tries
144 points

Shaun Edwards

There are few Rugby League players to whom the word "legend" can justifiably be applied. Shaun Edwards is one of them.

Shaun was recruited to Wigan by another Rugby League legend - Alex Murphy, their coach at the time. He received a then record signing on fee for a schoolboy of £35,000 and the signing ceremony was live on breakfast television on his 17th birthday in October 1983. Shaun had played both League and Union at international level as a schoolboy and followed in a family tradition as his father Jackie had played Rugby League for Warrington and Lancashire, Shaun went on to win more medals than any other player in Rugby League and was central to Wigan's domination of the game in the second half of the 1980s and the first half of the 1990s. In 1994 League television commentator and journalist Ray French wrote of Shaun that: "His relentless, single-minded drive for success still continues to shatter all records…" Ray included Shaun in his book *100 Great Rugby League Players*, published in 1989, when Shaun was only 22 years old. In that book, he wrote that: "Within four years of his signing for the Lancashire club Shaun Edwards had achieved all there is to achieve in Rugby League". Amongst many honours, Shaun was the youngest ever Great Britain test player, the youngest ever Challenge Cup finalist to appear at Wembley and, in 1988, the youngest ever Challenge Cup Final captain. He has also scored over 300 tries in his career in the professional game.

Neil Hanson, in his book *Blood, Mud and Glory* on Wigan's 1990-1991 season, wrote of Shaun: "Edwards has blistering pace off the mark, great vision and constant alertness for the half-chance. He has a fine passing and kicking game, demands perfection from himself and expects it from colleagues."

Shaun shocked the Rugby League world when he signed for the London Broncos in March 1997. He wanted to move to London for family reasons and was surprised at being unable to reach agreement with Wigan to live in London for part of the week. He now believes that the coach at Wigan at that time saw the chance to move him on.

London Broncos supporters felt that the Broncos' coach Tony Currie was taken aback to suddenly find a Great Britain scrum-half in his squad. The signing had happened very suddenly when Shaun's hopes of staying with Wigan were dashed. Currie had signed a new scrum-half, Josh White, and it took a little time for Shaun to become established in the Broncos team. But, looking back, his experience and determination added an extra ingredient to the Broncos side.

At first Shaun found it difficult to settle in London. He recalls: "My personal profile was smaller in London. I had joined a smaller club, but one with big potential. I found the training very different. But that first season was one of my happiest years in Rugby League. We finished higher than Wigan. Even five years ago, the idea of that happening would have been laughable."

But at the end of that first season in London, again mainly for family reasons, Shaun headed back up north, signing for the Bradford Bulls. That move did not work out. There was also a well-publicised feud with Bulls' player Graeme Bradley, which Shaun attributes to him having replaced Bradley's friend Glen Tomlinson in the Bradford team. However, Shaun did find the Bulls a very professional club: "Bradford were the best run club I have been to - the staff there were fantastic. They have become the standard bearer for Super League."

Two legends at scrum-half. Shaun Edwards and Allan Langer at
Warrington March 2000 (Photo: Peter Lush)

In Shaun's absence, the Broncos made a disastrous start to the 1998
season, with many of the 1997 team having left and the new players
failing to gel as a unit. Shaun's return to the club at the beginning of July
was a huge boost and saw the team reach mid-table respectability.

One of Shaun's best memories of his times with the Broncos was
beating Bradford at Edinburgh in a Super League "on the road" game
soon after his return to London. Bradford scored near the end of the game,
but could not catch the Broncos. With the final hooter about to sound, as
the Bradford kicker prepared for the conversion, Shaun went round the
whole Broncos team, shaking hands with each player, congratulating them
on a memorable victory that clearly meant much to him. "It was nice to
stick that one down their throats," he remembers.

Another highlight for Shaun was the 1997 World Club Championship
games. "We did well - for the rest of the British clubs it was embarrassing
at times. I didn't play in the match when we got stuffed by Canberra. We
were winning in Brisbane until near the end and just lost to Canterbury.
We should have won that game."

Getting to Wembley in the Challenge Cup in 1999 was a further
highlight of his time with the Broncos and his delight at the end of the
victorious semi-final against Castleford was obvious to everyone. Despite
all his previous Wembley appearances, he had done it once more, this time

83

for the Broncos. His determination again came to the fore as he played for the Broncos at Wembley with a broken thumb, a legacy from the semi-final victory. That he played should not have been a surprise - for Wigan he had played most of one Challenge Cup Final with a fractured eye socket sustained early in the match.

Shaun is very positive about the future for the Broncos. "I am pleased to see the club develop and attract players from the north, especially fellow Wiganers. In John Monie we have got one of the greatest coaches in Rugby League, his record is the best of all time. I think there is more potential for the club in south-east London. I never thought south west London would work - we need to be in a working class area."

Peter Gill and Terry Matterson stand out for Shaun of the Broncos' players Shaun has played with. "I have a lot of respect for both of them". He also enjoyed playing with Martin Offiah and is angry as he feels that former coach Dan Stains effectively ended Martin's career with the Broncos by not picking him for the team.

Away from Rugby League, Shaun's son James is a very important part of his life. James is now nearly three and enjoys playing football. According to Shaun "he has a lot of determination, taking after both his parents" [his mother is singer Heather Small]. Shaun is also pleased with his younger brother Billie-Joe's progress in Rugby League. He played for the England Schools under-16 team on their successful 1999 tour of Australia and has recently signed for the Wigan academy team.

Shaun announced his retirement as a player in April 2000 because of injury problems. He received a spontaneous standing ovation before the Broncos match at Wigan the day after announcing his retirement, the crowd recognising his magnificent service to Wigan and Rugby League. For the future, when interviewed, he said that he is looking to move into coaching, although at the time of writing is taking a break from Rugby League. He completed his coaching qualifications by the age of 24, and clearly has much more to offer the game.

Interview in February 2000. Updated in April 2000.

42 appearances plus 10 as substitute
23 tries, 1 goal, 94 points (To retirement in April 2000)

2. The Coaches

John Monie (Photo: Peter Lush)

During the past 20 years, the club has been fortunate to often have coaches of a high quality. The first, player-coach Reg Bowden, was both an excellent player at the peak of his game and an inspired choice by managing director Harold Genders. After the club's departure from Craven Cottage, Roy Lester did a remarkable job of coaching and man-management to rebuild the team after the departure of so many of the club's established players. Had his team in 1984-5 been together for the whole of the season, promotion back to the First Division would have been a realistic target, because they showed promotion form for the last three-quarters of the season.

The third coach, Bill Goodwin, was a key figure at the club for five years, both as first team coach and in other roles, the culmination of years of service to southern Rugby League. At the start of the 1987-8 season, Bev Risman became team manager, with Bill Goodwin continuing in a coaching role. Bev said when he took the post that it would take three years to rebuild the club's fortunes, but as with so many managers in sport he was not given that time. He returned to the club in 1996 as director of development, where he played a key role in building the Broncos' youth structures.

Phil Sullivan was a successful short-term appointment in 1989, with the club committee split on whether or not to retain him. He was released after only four matches in charge.

Ross Strudwick was a remarkable capture by a struggling Second Division club, having a very high reputation in the game, undermined by lack of success when taking over an ageing Halifax side. Ross developed the club's structure, playing strength and coaching, but ultimately was given too much work with matters off the pitch, being chief executive as well as running the coaching side, putting a great deal of responsibility on one person.

Tony Gordon was only coach for just over a season, but produced the marvellous 1993-4 side, denied promotion by the width of a goal post when John Gallagher's drop-goal attempt against Workington at Copthall just missed the target.

The new regime under the Broncos brought in their own coach - Gary Greinke. Although dedicated to the sport, his lack of experience of the British game and stereotyped coaching style never worked and he left the club just before Super League started. He had also let many of Tony Gordon's players go, some of whom went on to success elsewhere in Super League.

The Broncos' next choice was far more successful. Tony Currie's experience of the game in Britain and internationally, combined with a determination to succeed paid dividends. His three seasons in charge represent the most successful period in the club's history. Had the club retained the 1997 team, further challenges for the Super League crown could have materialised. As it was, key players were allowed to leave and Tony only lasted one more season.

His successor, Dan Stains, faced similar problems to Gary Greinke. He had not coached at the top level before and, despite taking the team to the Challenge Cup Final, clearly had problems with team morale and in handling the more experienced players. The club's worst defeat for years, at Bradford in June 1999 saw him depart. Assistant Les Kiss took over along with chief executive Tony Rea, working as joint coaches and rebuilt team morale and confidence, but by then a top-five challenge was impossible. At the end of the 1999 season Les left for personal reasons and returned to Australia.

The recruitment of his successor John Monie is undoubtedly a huge signing and he is the most successful coach ever to come to London. His profile and experience should help establish the club in a position to challenge for the Super League crown.

Reg Bowden

Reg Bowden was probably the most important signing made by Harold Genders when building the first Fulham team. Not only was he a top quality scrum half, still at the height of his game at the age of 30, but an inspired choice as player-coach. Fulham paid Widnes £25,000 for him - at a time when the record Rugby League transfer fee stood at £40,000.

Reg had been a key player in the great Widnes teams of the 1970s, which won every honour in the game. Born in Widnes, he was bought up on Rugby League, playing for the town team as a schoolboy. He then played for Diton Youth Club. Together with Keith Elwell, who was to become another Widnes stalwart, he went for trials at Hull KR. Reg recalls: "Colin Hutton, the manager, missed us at the station - he thought we were too small to be Rugby League players. You should have seen the look on his face. We played in the A team, and I was offered terms, but I preferred to stay in Widnes and it was an excellent move". Soon Reg joined the Chemics and in 1969 made his first team debut. "I was man-of-the-match - we won at Blackpool. But the next week I was back in the A team. Regular first team star Jimmy Boyd was the scrum-half then."

By 1970, Reg had won a first team place. But then injuries saw him in and out of the team. When Vince Karalius became coach, he introduced weight training and Reg grew to 12 and a half stone and subsequently tended to avoid injuries.

Reg learnt a lot from working with Karalius. "We were fitter than the other teams. We trained right through the summer. We were still strong in the last 20 minutes and had less injuries. Frank Myler continued this when he became Widnes coach".

Reg was still working as a diesel mechanic, despite being a household name in Rugby League. But he recalls: "It was marvellous to play for our town and to be at the top of the sport."

But, by 1980, Reg had been doing the same off-field job for 15 years when Harold Genders offered him the chance to be Fulham's full-time player coach. When initially approached by Harold about Fulham, his first comment was "I know bugger all about soccer." But he was won over by Harold's vision for the club, convinced his wife Brenda it would be crazy to turn the opportunity down and signed a four year contract. He was also aware of the young up-and-coming Andy Gregory at scrum-half in the Widnes A team and realised his first team place could be challenged.

Reg says that "I had been captain for five years, but had never done any coaching. I aimed to build the same camaraderie and fitness we had at Widnes and bought players who could fit in to that vision. It was a daunting task. We had six weeks to get 13 players on the pitch to face Wigan in our very fist match. Harold Genders dealt with the management side and I learnt a lot from him. I persuaded Tony Karalius to come out of retirement to play for us - he lived round the corner from me. He had a will to win and a professional attitude. Slowly the team grew - from three players to five to seven. We trained at the Golborne Sports Club in Leigh.

The week before the Wigan game we only had 13 players, the day before we had 18."

The first game was crucial. "If we won, it would be a masterstroke. If Wigan only just won, that would still be OK. But we had to avoid a massacre. However, most of our team were experienced professionals although I was worried about Adrian Cambriani - it was his first game of League, but he came through with flying colours. That game against Wigan was as good as any of my Wembley appearances."

Reg has fond memories of his four years at Fulham. "It was a tremendous time for me. The supporters were second to none - they didn't always understand the game, but they were so enthusiastic. We beat Bradford Northern in the now legendary pre-Wembley challenge match and gave the 1982 Australian tourists a good game. But we didn't have enough money to spend on the team. By 1983-4 we were struggling. Harold Genders left and we never had the strength in depth to stop being a "yo-yo" team. If we had suspensions or injuries sometimes we had to use amateurs. To establish the game in London we had to be successful in the top flight."

In June 1984, with regret, Reg left Fulham and joined Warrington as coach. He recalls that: "I wanted to finish playing at the top. Warrington

Reg Bowden (Photo: Peter Lush)

offered me a job. But it hurt me to leave Fulham. The people there were fabulous. But I felt I could not turn down Warrington."

Reg was coach at Warrington for two years. Some of the club's established players had retired and he was faced with rebuilding the team. Despite winning the end-of-season Premiership in his second season and reaching a Lancashire Cup Final, his contract was not renewed. He has not coached at a professional club since - surely a loss for the game.

For 10 years he was a director at Widnes, with responsibility for running the club's lottery. He now owns a social club on the outskirts of the town. He has started an amateur Rugby League team linked to the club, which he will coach. He is building dressing rooms for sports teams attached to the club.

He says that: "Fulham was the best time of my life. If the Board had put in the same effort as the players and more resources the club would have thrived."

Playing record:
116 appearances plus 4 as substitute
14 tries
42 points

Interview in June 1999

Roy Lester

Harold Genders made a number of great signings when he was assembling the first Fulham squad, but none better than the first signing of the lot, Roy Lester.

In 1980 Roy, then 33, was firmly identified with his home-town club Warrington. But over the next six years he became the epitome of the renewed London League crusade - first as a player and then for two hugely eventful seasons as club manager.

Twenty years on he is a successful businessman who has the trappings of that position - elegantly cut suits and an impressive car. But he remains the unpretentious, decent, dedicated man who was such an inspiration to Fulham fans through one of the club's toughest periods precisely because of those qualities.

Roy still lives in the same house in Leigh as in his Fulham days. Sitting in his front room he recalls memories which remain vivid in spite of the passage of time. He still remembers getting the call: "I was told Harold wanted to talk to me about playing for a new team in London. At first I thought it was a joke. After we'd talked about it I said I'd have to think about it but in my mind I'd already said 'yes'."

The decision gave an underachieving career a new lease of life. Roy played for Lancashire and was once named in a shadow Great Britain squad: "There was talk of tours, but it didn't happen," he remembers. He believes he had the ability to play at the very highest level, but blames himself for not doing so: "I don't think I was as committed as I might have been - I was always given to looking for excuses for things going wrong. I'd have a brilliant game followed by mediocre ones - consistency was the problem - and I wasn't the greatest trainer in the world. Other people had more confidence in me than I had in myself."

Harold Genders's vote of confidence in his ability to do a job for the new club sparked off one of the best spells of his career: "The first year at Fulham is my best memory as a player. It was privilege to play with such an array of talent - even though they were getting on, they were still superb players. I'd always loved playing for Warrington, because it was my home town and they were the team I'd always wanted to play for. But London provided a different angle - it was exciting, challenging and gave me the chance to play with players I'd always admired like Mal Aspey, Harry Beverley and David Eckersley. The support was terrific. Fans used to say how much they enjoyed the fact that they could watch us on the pitch and have a drink with us afterwards - they couldn't do that with the Fulham footballers.

"There was a showbiz element as well - people like Colin Welland [who was a club director] and Brian Glover. Michael Parkinson sometimes came to games, and Bernard Cribbins."

Roy was a regular that season, playing 20 times including the debut match against Wigan, and scoring three tries: "We had a fantastic season, winning promotion. In the end of year challenge game against Bradford we hammered the First Division champions, then the club took us off on holiday for a fortnight. It was very hard to better that."

He believes the first false steps were taken in preparation for the second season: "We always knew it was going to be much tougher and the squad needed strengthening. I don't think the players who were brought in were good enough to make the difference. Steve Diamond and John Crossley were good players but, in my opinion, they were a disruptive influence and ended up doing a lot of damage to the club."

The second season also saw the beginning of the end of his own playing career through injury: "I tore the ligament off the side of my knee. Initially they thought it was just a strain, so I went back into training pretty quickly. We had a game at Whitehaven and I was named in the team for it, but I just collapsed in agony in training. I had an operation, then cartilage problems which led to another operation within a year."

After starting the first eight games of 1981-2, he was to make only 15 more appearances, all but four as a substitute - the last in the final 17 minutes of the 'Battle of Stamford Bridge' against Cardiff Blue Dragons, when three players were sent off, at the end of 1982-3. An injury suffered in his other job as a welder then put a firm stop to his playing career.

But his most significant contribution to Fulham was only just starting. Roy trained as a physiotherapist, turning up to classes even when his leg was in a splint following operations, and was appointed to the club's coaching staff, looking after the forwards. When David Eckersley left the club, Roy became assistant to player-coach Reg Bowden.

Roy Lester playing against Doncaster 20 April 1981
(Photo: Barry Taylor)

In the summer of 1984 Bowden left for Warrington and the Board, now only interested in the football team at Craven Cottage, closed the Rugby League club. Fortunately, supporter and businessman Roy Close, who had already paid the transfer fees for some players, rescued it and asked his namesake to continue as coach: "We were on holiday in Devon and I spent a lot of it nipping off to the phone box to call Roy Close."

His first task was to reconstruct a club torn apart when several players went to court in pursuit of free agent status: "Not all the players were fully committed. I began to dread training sessions - there'd be people off in corners having meetings and others just not turning up. In the end I said to the players 'you are either with us or against us. If you aren't with us don't bother turning up'."

The 1984-5 season was an extraordinary struggle, with a hastily assembled squad doing very well to finish eighth in the Second Division: "It was a battle week-to-week, a real struggle just to get 13 men plus a couple of substitutes on to the field. Looking back I don't know how we managed it. If the players weren't as good as those we'd had before, the spirit was better. There were a lot of good characters in the side and it was a pleasure to go training, coach them and watch them play."

An important early signing was the veteran half-back Ken Green: "Ken was a godsend. You need someone who other players respect to take what you think on to the field for you. Other players would die for him because they knew he would always look out for them, and take on any opponent for them - however big. He did get sent off occasionally - Kenny used to count to 10 but he didn't always get there before he reacted - however, he made an immense positive contribution."

Another significant signing was the Cumbrian veteran Harold Henney, always tagged "larger than life" - and that life was pretty substantial. Roy remembers: "John Wilkinson at Salford, who was a good friend, had warned me off him. I got hold of Harold, told him what John had said and told him 'I've been told not to sign you. I know you're a good player, and I'm going against the judgment of someone I respect to sign you, so you'd better not let me down.' And he didn't either."

Henney's Fulham career ended after a set-to with Roy on the team bus: "Harold was having a go at Don Duffy, who was a nice lad to talk to and a completely professional player but never the most popular with the others - he was a bit of an oddball. Harold wouldn't leave it alone. I told him to let it go and he carried on. I then said 'if you want to have a go at anybody have a go at me'. He hit me and I hit him back and took one of his teeth out."

By 1985-6 Fulham had moved to the primitive but homely Polytechnic Ground at Chiswick: "There was a terrific atmosphere about the place. In the bar afterwards you felt as though everyone had been out on the field with you. People had worked incredibly hard to get the ground ready." Roy himself had drawn on his old skills with a welding torch to restore broken down turnstiles and the public address system.

There were higher expectations following the remarkable efforts of the season before: "The spirit was always there and there were some excellent performances - even after having Chris Wilkinson sent off we nearly beat Leigh, who were that year's champions. There were two minutes of injury time and they won in the last second. But it was a bit up and down."

And all the time the threat of closure loomed as Roy Close discovered that running a Rugby League club was a very costly and unprofitable business: "Roy used to say 'we can't go on like this'. The last straw was when they went to Whitehaven and Barbara wasn't allowed in the board room in spite of being the club chairman. They went home and that was that. I remember Roy phoning me and hearing Barbara behind him saying 'close it, close it'."

His final game in charge, at Huddersfield, remains one of the most vivid memories. The players offered to play for nothing, with Frank Feighan saying he would walk up the M1 if necessary to play. The pre-match moment when Roy walked into the bar at Fartown is remembered as if it were yesterday, by Roy and everyone else who was there: "We had a makeshift side out, but it seemed as though everybody was there in the bar. They cheered and clapped and kept on going. I couldn't believe it and I had tears in my eyes."

New club proprietor Paul Faires asked him to stay on, but he refused: "I could never have worked for him."

But it wasn't long before he was back in the game - Carlisle, impressed by his work in London, hoped that he could do a similar job for them. He became their coach in June 1986.

Quite how similar the Carlisle job was soon dawned on Roy: "I would never have thought things could be as difficult again as they had been at Fulham, but they were." Memories of Crossley, Diamond and the free agency dispute were revived by a squad of largely Yorkshire-based players: "Every one of them was an Arthur Scargill in his own right." A clear-out followed the 112-0 defeat by St Helens in a cup tie, his third match in charge: "We had a couple of small lads in the centre and [their coach] Alex Murphy was shouting 'run at the midgets'."

It was once again a matter of scratching around for players, living hand-to-mouth and using old contacts to put a team together - Ken Green joined him again, while off-field Fulham's super-fan Bob Evans travelled up to help with the club. Roy even found himself in the ground construction business again, as Carlisle constructed their own stadium close to a railway line after the football club kicked them out of their Brunton Park ground.

Roy spent three and a half years travelling vast distances to training up and down the M6 before a near-disaster on the road convinced him that he'd done enough: "I feel asleep on the road and ran up a bank. I rang the chairman and said 'that's enough'. I was also getting frustrated - we had some decent players there, but I didn't think I was getting the ones I needed for us to be successful."

His time at Carlisle helped launch his business career, in partnership with a club director in a company called Cumbrian Leisure. When his partner ran into financial troubles, Roy moved on to a company called Pentacan, where he has been a director for 14 years: "We run pubs and night clubs in Lancashire and Cumbria. At the moment we've four clubs, three restaurants and six pubs. I look after the club and four pubs in Lancashire. The idea is to develop big places as quality venues. I've learnt a lot doing the job, and I've effectively been clerk of the works for the building refurbishments."

He also credits his Fulham experience for his success: "I learnt a lot from talking to Roy Close - about things like business organisation. I also had to deal with a lot of paperwork and administration at Fulham because in effect I was in chief executive, although I never had the title."

After Carlisle he went to Warrington as assistant coach. He'd be there still, if it were not for the introduction of full-time professionalism with the advent of Super League: "It would have meant giving up my business career and I wasn't prepared to do that at my stage of life. I'm still involved with the club in an unpaid capacity - for instance I'll often talk to players they are looking to sign."

He retains a deep affection for the game and immensely warm memories of his time in London: "I've managed to keep in touch with people and it was marvellous to see the club go to Wembley".

The warmth of those memories was evident soon after Wembley when he travelled down from Lancashire to attend Bob Evans's funeral, joining a large group of mourners which swamped Mortlake crematorium's capacity limit.

Looking back to his Fulham days, Roy says: "The supporters were unbeatable. There weren't very many of them, but they were so committed they more than made up for their numbers. They kept everybody going. It is because of them that a club has been kept alive in London for 20 years - if you look at what has happened in Rugby League history that is an immense achievement by itself."

That regard is mutual. Ask supporters who remember Fulham's earliest days, and they'll tell you that a fair bit of that achievement belongs to Roy Lester.

Playing career:
28 appearances plus 19 as substitute
4 tries
12 points

Interview by Huw Richards in January 2000

Bill Goodwin

Bill Goodwin was a key figure at Fulham from 1986 to 1990. Before his arrival there he was involved for many years with the Peckham amateur Rugby League club in south London, both as a player and then a coach. In 1978-9, Peckham won the double of cup and league in Southern Amateur Rugby League. Mark Newbrook wrote in his history of the Southern Amateur Rugby League that this "owed much to coach Bill Goodwin, formerly of Doncaster, who had encouraged a style based on solid teamwork and forward dominance."

His entry into the professional game in the south came at the unlikely venue of Maidstone, where in 1983 Paul Faires started the Kent Invicta club. Bill's background in southern amateur Rugby League and his coaching experience made him the ideal person to take this post. He also developed links between the Peckham club and Kent Invicta.

Sadly the Kent venture only lasted one season, with the club moving for 1984-5 to Southend. That club attracted even less support and only lasted one season. Paul Faires had left the Kent Invicta club during their only season, but re-emerged in April 1986 to take over Fulham from Roy and Barbara Close.

His plan was to have a southern based team and he brought in Bill Goodwin as coach, with the aim of including London based amateur Rugby League players as the mainstay of the playing squad, rather than the northern based players who had been the backbone of the club's playing strength until then. Bill also recruited some players who had played with him at Kent Invicta and Southend.

Paul Faires's ownership of the club only lasted a few months and club sponsor Richard Lawton and match manager Tim Lamb became directors for the 1986-7 season. But Bill Goodwin stayed as coach and, according to Huw Richards in the *Rugby Leaguer*: "constructed a competitive team in an incredibly short time with some astute talent-spotting in the London Amateur League and some useful Australian acquisitions."

However, the new set up had limitations with little capacity to cover for injuries and suspensions, despite a new area of recruitment being southern based Rugby Union players. By February, Bill was saying: "I've got 15 players of certain Second Division quality and I'm having to ask

Sandra Goodwin, Richard Lawton and Bill Goodwin
(Photo: Barry & Gwen Warren)

Ross Strudwick and Hussain M'Barki at The Stoop April 1999
(Photo: Peter Lush)

them to go out and take all the pressures and blows week in, week out." Fulham finished that season in 12th place, a creditable result for a club that had come very, very close to not starting the season at all, and then conceded 140 points in the first two matches. By November, things had improved enough to hold First Division Castleford to a 10-point margin at Chiswick. Bill said in his programme notes for the last home match: "This season has shown that we were right to refuse to let the club die."

In that summer, 1987, former international Bev Risman was appointed as team manager, with the club hoping his high profile and experience in the game would help attract new talent. Bill remained as coach.

Bev's period as manager lasted until October 1988, when the committee decided that a new direction was needed and he left the club, with Bill again taking over temporary full control of team affairs.

This lasted until January 1989, when Phil Sullivan came on trial from Australia, but his appointment only lasted a month, with the committee split on whether he should continue and finally deciding to terminate his work at the club.

Once again, Bill took over, although business commitments meant that he did not want the job on a long-term basis. Club director Tim Lamb, recognising Bill's role at the club, said that: "there will always be a role for Bill Goodwin at Fulham in whatever capacity he chooses."

In July 1989, Australian Ross Strudwick was appointed as team manager, with Bill Goodwin again reverting to the role of coach. He stayed in that capacity until October 1990, when he left the club saying he wanted to do "the things that I have not been able to do during that time [22 years involvement in Rugby League] and to experience now rather than to regret later."

The club programme recognised that with his departure "a considerable amount of experience and knowledge is being lost to the game." Bill's attitude to the game was summed up when he said: "All I've ever wanted, is to see southern kids playing Rugby League and being given the opportunity to do so."

Bill now lives in Spain. However, he did return to London to see his old club in the 1999 Challenge Cup Final, a very different scenario from the struggle to keep the club alive at Chiswick, when winning a cup tie, let alone reaching a final, was a rare event.

Ross Strudwick

Ross Strudwick played a key role in the development of the club's set-up of the late 1980s and early 1990s. He established higher playing standards, introduced many innovations in coaching and recruited better quality players. He left the by-now renamed London Crusaders in February 1993.

Ross first played Rugby League as a youngster on the family farm deep in the New South Wales countryside. His father was a "bush" League player. The family moved to Sydney when he was nine, and from junior football he joined the famous Sydney club St George. He played four seasons at first grade there, playing with famous Australian stars Johnny Raper, Graeme Langlands and Billy Smith, while future Kangaroo boss Jack Gibson was one of the coaches. In 1973, he moved to the Brisbane Valleys club in Queensland. At that time (before the Brisbane Broncos started in 1988 and became the first Queensland club to play in the Sydney competition), the top Brisbane clubs would have held their own against the Sydney clubs.

Ross played at scrum-half, twice represented Queensland against New South Wales and was capped once by Australia, against New Zealand at Lang Park in the World Championship in June 1975, the Kangaroos winning 36-8. After five successful years at Valleys as a player, in 1978 he became captain-coach and won the Brisbane Premiership. In 1979, Valleys, including future international star Wally Lewis, beat Souths 26-0 in the Brisbane Grand Final. The Souths' side included a young Mal Meninga, later captain of Australia, who remembers the match, saying that: "Captain-coach, the former Australian halfback Ross Strudwick, was an inspiration".

In 1982, Ross retired from playing, but stayed at Valleys for a further two seasons as coach. Three years at Brisbane Brothers as coach followed, where his team included future London Broncos Dan Stains, Peter Gill and Tony Rea, and culminated in a Premiership win in 1987

By 1987, with the Brisbane Broncos on the horizon, which he feared would inevitably undermine the remaining Brisbane competition, he decided to come to coach in England, taking over from Chris Anderson at

Halifax in July 1988. One of the players he signed for Halifax was future Broncos' coach Dan Stains.

He says he inherited "a side on the slide" and thought he could turn them round. His unfamiliarity with the English transfer system did not help matters, and his tenure at Halifax finished in February 1989 with the team facing relegation.

He was planning to go back to Australia when Fulham contacted him. Several meetings followed and by mid-April he had agreed to join the London club. Huw Richards said in the *Rugby Leaguer* that he was "generally recognised outside Halifax as one of the world's leading coaches" and was a "major capture" for struggling second division Fulham. He was also credited with inventing the "sliding" form of defence, now widely used by many teams.

Using his Brisbane connections, he was able to sign up-and-coming Australians such as Russell Browning and Wayne Sanchez. Mick Taylor was recruited from Halifax, the first established northern player to join the club since 1985. A few other northerners followed, including Nick Halafihi and Colin Atkinson. But the basis of Ross's teams was always Australian players.

He still remembers with delight his first game in charge as "the York chairman said he would eat his hat if we won" which Fulham did 10-9.

From only 10 players at his first training session, he concentrated on developing the club's structure. "We started junior development and tried to get into the schools. We got conditioners, use of a gym and weight machines for the players".

The Polytechnic Stadium in Chiswick could not offer a long-term future for the club as it could not secure a long term lease that would have allowed some development of the ground and, in 1990, Crystal Palace became the team's home again. However, a layer of fans was lost to the club through this move, as it was a difficult journey from west London and the seats did not offer a good view of Rugby League.

By now Ross had taken on the role of chief executive as well as coach. The club were now able to attract players from Sydney, such as Steve Rosolen and Scott Roskell, both of whom served the club well. Ross also managed to attract better sponsors, some with Australian connections, and the national daily *Today* newspaper.

The team improved considerably in this period, playing in a highly intensive eight team Second Division. In each of Ross's full seasons in charge, the club reached the end-of-season Premiership competition. But the crowds failed to come to the wide open spaces of Crystal Palace, the usual gate being less than 1,000. The lack of atmosphere even at big cup matches made it difficult to keep new fans that the club did attract.

Although Ross developed a coaching staff to support him, looking back he now feels that towards the end of his tenure his coaching suffered because of his wide workload. "I spent an enormous amount of time finding sponsors, producing the programmes and newsletters and running the club. This made me less tolerant with the players. In one match the tension was so strong I was screaming at the players and nearly walked out. Then they scored and I calmed down."

The club had been looking for new owners for at least two years when, in February 1993, Richard and Samantha Bartram took over and Ross left the club. He returned with his family to Australia. Looking back, he believes that even at that time the plans for Super League were being made and, had he known this, he would have hung on in London with the prospect of a Super League club in the capital.

Back at home, he coached the Queensland under-19 team for three years and was a selector for Australia.

He now runs a successful chain of sports shops and spends more time with his wife Lisa and their five children. He enjoyed his time in London and was responsible for major improvements in the club's playing and coaching standards.

Some of the players he recruited and helped develop were important for the club in the period leading up to Super League starting. He tried to build a structure for a successful professionally run club. But he was always held back by a lack of resources, a problem only remedied by the arrival of the Broncos in 1994.

Interview in May 1999 when Ross and Lisa visited London to attend the Challenge Cup Final

Tony Gordon

Of all the coaches who have taken on the onerous task of directing the recent fortunes of London's Rugby League club, Tony Gordon perhaps needs the least introduction to readers of this book. Yet the man who is still held in affection by London's supporters was only in charge for little more than a year. But what a few heady months it was. During the 1993-4 season, he took the London Crusaders to within a goalpost's width of promotion and to a Premiership Final at Old Trafford. And all this on a shoestring budget.

To supporters brought up on Super League and a Wembley Challenge Cup Final this may sound like small beer. But with a team of mainly little-known players, Tony Gordon turned his club into potential First Division material. It was a remarkable achievement which only ended with the arrival of new club owners Brisbane Broncos. Yet there is little doubt that, had London Crusaders failed in 1993-4, there would have been no club for the Broncos to purchase. Finances were parlous and only the results on the field showed that the club was worth buying. That was Tony's Gordon's great legacy.

Supporters who followed the club then will need no introduction to the story of that season but many may not know about the man who made it happen. Just who was this talismanic guru who changed the face of Rugby League in London?

Surprisingly, Gordon was not an out-and-out League man. Growing up in New Zealand he dreamt of becoming a union All Black. Born in Waimiha in 1948 on the North Island, he was one of six children of a union-playing father. Not surprisingly he shone at that game as a schoolboy, gaining representative honours.

Three years as a physical education instructor in the army changed his physique from a slightly built, elusive player into a dynamic, muscley back. But the best years of his Rugby Union career came after he left the forces. In 1972 he was playing alongside legendary All Black Colin Meads for King Country, and Gordon's strong running and devastating attack saw the first appearance in the newspapers of his now famous nickname "Tank".

Across the Tasman Sea, Australian Rugby League clubs began to take notice, yet when he did switch codes it wasn't for one of the big Sydney League teams but the Auckland Maritime club. By the end of his first season in League he was selected to tour Europe with the Kiwis.

Back home he switched clubs to Mangere East, forming a stunning partnership with Olsen Filipaina, before heading to Australia to become player-coach of the Surfers' Paradise club which won three consecutive Gold Coast titles. Over the next few years he progressed through the Australian coaching scheme and when he returned to New Zealand on holiday in 1982 he was one of his nation's most highly qualified coaches.

That holiday proved to be the turning point that set him on the road to the London Crusaders, although via a roundabout route. In Rotorua he met Joe Donaldson of the Central club. It was a chance meeting which culminated in Gordon being offered the club's coaching position. He took it and, when Central were successful his style attracted the attention of the perennially dismal Bay representative side. Never one to turn down a challenge, Gordon left Central for Bay in 1984 to join a team that he said needed three years to turn around. On cue, three years later, in 1986, Bay won the national Division One championship.

By now his stock was high in New Zealand coaching circles, so much so that when Kiwi national coach Graham Lowe split with the NZRL administration, Gordon emerged from the selection process in pole position and in 1987 became the national coach. And there were some fine memories from his era. Gordon reckons the highlight was the famous 13-6 victory over Australia at Brisbane in 1987 only nine months after taking charge. "With only three professionals in the team we defeated the Invincibles who hadn't lost a game in Europe," he says. That match is still talked about today.

But, of course, with the highs came the lows. "Losing to Australia in the 1988 World Cup Final at Eden Park was disappointing," he admits. "The game was lost by half-time." Series defeats to Australia and Great Britain were to follow in 1989 and Gordon decided not to apply for an extension to his contract. "Three years was enough for me," says Tank, yet he left with his reputation intact as he stepped down to coach the New Zealand colts.

Which is where London Crusaders came in. The club, stricken with financial problems, was being coached by Ross Strudwick. The Australian had been in charge since 1989 but new direction was required. At administrative level that was provided in the spring of 1993 with the purchase of the London Crusaders by the Bartrams' Britannic Touchdown Promotions (BTP) company. The takeover had the backing of Rugby Football League chief executive Maurice Lindsay and he helped strike the deal that brought Tony Gordon to London.

Lindsay had, in practice, been keeping professional League in London alive during the financially difficult years of the early nineties. When BTP came along he pointed them in the direction of one of New Zealand's finest. "I got a call from Maurice," recalls Gordon, "he wanted to know if I'd be interested in the London job. He was persuasive. His support convinced me it was a good move. I thought long and hard before deciding to move but if I hadn't believed I could succeed, I wouldn't have dragged my family halfway round the world," he adds.

Gordon's arrival was a huge coup for the club and shortly after he landed this author had the opportunity to meet him at the Queens Hotel in Crystal Palace, near where the Crusaders played their home games in 1992-3. His was a gruff and affable nature. I took enough tapes to cover a two-hour interview - I used about 15 minutes. A multitude of questions were reduced to monosyllabic answers but his style that day characterised the man. He had just arrived to take up a new post. He knew little of his new team and merely answered honestly. Some coaches would have elaborated about how their regime would revolutionise the club, but Tony told it straight, honestly and with a self-confidence that soon found its way through to his players.

His team went on that day to defeat Huddersfield and start a remarkable run that many London Rugby League supporters remember today. Tank's team moved quickly away from the defensive approach employed by his predecessor. "I needed to make changes," he says. "The club was a home for holidaying Aussies, that wasn't right. I needed players prepared to take up longer contracts. Either attitudes changed or the team sheet did. My teams always competed."

His Crusaders certainly did and as *Touch and Go*, the history of professional Rugby League in London, tells us: "No one could have predicted the drama to follow." A mere list of achievements does not do justice to the transformation of the team into a swashbuckling and adventurous unit.

A switch from Crystal Palace to Barnet Copthall stadium was coupled with three major summer signings. Former union All-Black John Gallagher was followed by the powerful presence of Sam Stewart the ex-Kiwi Rugby League forward and Abi Ekoku, the strong-running former international discus thrower.

Add in Neville Ramsey, the man Gordon described as his "organiser", South African winger Mark Johnson who was to top the Rugby League season's try charts with 43, nippy scrum-half Mark Riley, attacking fullback Andre Stoop and hard-working Steve Rosolen, and it was clear Gordon had a fine nucleus.

Victory after victory, amid ongoing financial problems, took the Crusaders to the verge of promotion in 1993-4, only a goalpost denying John Gallagher a drop goal in a draw against Workington Town and with it a promotion spot. Perhaps the highlights of the season were victory over First Division Featherstone Rovers 26-12 in the Regal Trophy and a subsequent quarter-final against mighty Bradford Northern only narrowly lost. And there was also the end-of-season Premiership run that culminated in a Final appearance at Old Trafford against Workington. The match was lost 30-22 but a season such as this cannot be told in statistics alone. It is better described by the man responsible. "I really enjoyed it," he says, "despite the club being in the middle of financial problems. The supporters were excellent and the team like a family.

"In my opinion we were there to play exciting League. Players were allowed to express themselves and this is my philosophy. Under this system the players that stood out for me were Sam Stewart, Neville Ramsey, Mark Riley, John Gallagher - especially for his kicking, Abi Ekoku, Steve Rosolen, Scott Roskell and Dave Rotheram. But it wasn't just the guys on the field. Neil Robinson was a great manager of our resources and Steve Magee our kit man travelled everywhere with us for the love of the game.

"Yes, John Gallagher's drop kick against Workington would have put us in the top division but promotion would have brought problems. The squad lacked depth and perhaps we would have needed more players, but they did deserve promotion that's for sure. It was a shame to lose at Old Trafford but injuries to key players put us behind the eight-ball that day."

It was a truly remarkable season and one following which any coach might feel his position was secure. But for professional Rugby League in London, 1993-4 was remarkable off the field too. This was the year the Brisbane Broncos began to take an interest in British Rugby League. The Broncos shocked the League world in February 1994 when they announced their takeover of the Crusaders, soon to be known as the London Broncos.

There is no doubt that without the financial input of the Broncos, the Crusaders could have gone to the wall, but there is also no doubt that their arrival spelled the end for Tony Gordon. Over from Queensland came conditioning staff, marketing men, accountants and players. The achievements of the hardy bunch who had pushed Rugby League in London to unexpected peaks were largely forgotten. Just before the end-of-season Premiership competition started, Tony found he was on his way out of the club.

Perhaps he was a victim of his own success. Had his Crusaders performed badly maybe the club would not have been such an attractive target for Brisbane. They may have looked elsewhere for their English operation. Whatever, Tony had seen problems looming from the day Brisbane first made contact. "I did not know if their arrival would be for the best," he relates. "At first, when they told me how much they had to spend, I thought it could only be good for the club. And they also told me they would like to renew my contract. I worked hard to make that happen, working on reports, player contracts and finances, and I was invited to visit Brisbane.

"However, I began to realise that the club was to be used as a feeder for the Brisbane Broncos, as a way of defeating the Australian salary cap. Australian players were going to come and go with no sense of team-building. I wasn't happy with this, nor the coaching methods being forced upon me. I tried to explain the situation but my opinion did not go down well with John Ribot, Brisbane's chief executive." (Interestingly, Ribot told me earlier that he was impressed by Tank's approach, but he obviously changed his mind somewhere down the line.)

107

Neil Robinson and Tony Gordon at Hendon FC - an occasional home in the mid 1990s (Photo Barry & Gwen Warren)

Tony Currie (Photo: David Stevens)

Tony Gordon finally heard the bad news. "A week after making my views known I heard via a reporter that I wouldn't be coaching the team the following season."

The Broncos appointed Gary Greinke, a successful coach from the Brisbane local competition, as Gordon's successor and the Tank was out of a job. I recall meeting him at the London Amateur Final at Wasps RUFC just a few days before the announcement was made public. "I won't be here next season," he confided. He was right. And things were never to be quite the same again at London's professional club.

Tony is very frank about the whole affair. "To be honest I was pissed off," he says. "And because little was said about my departure, it looked like I walked away. But that wasn't the case, I was just never offered a position in the new set-up. It wasn't long before my players were gone too - Neville Ramsey, Mark Riley, Sam Stewart... what a shame. I loved the club, made a lot of friends and often think about that time. I'd be back there tomorrow if I was offered the job I never wanted to leave."

My own report on Tony Gordon's departure, written in *The Greatest Game!*, sounded more like an obituary, yet on the positive side I wrote "Tony Gordon and his team created an upbeat mood at the club that will take something catastrophic to destroy overnight."

But gone he was and it seemed that Hull was the club most likely to benefit. Gordon's work had not gone unnoticed and the First Division club quickly brought him on board. Yet success did not follow.

"It was a bad experience," he admits. "The players were not up to scratch and I shocked the Hull board when I said only five or six could have made my Crusaders side! There was no money to buy players, yet the board was looking to play Crusaders-style rugby... I told them with the players they had it couldn't happen overnight."

However Hull couldn't or wouldn't wait that long and, after poor results, Tony Gordon's career there was over. "In the end I was glad to leave," he says. "I'd still say it was the worst administration I've been involved with. The payments on my car and home were not kept up to date and I lost both. I was glad to return to New Zealand."

Sadly, on return to his native land, things did not get better. A failed business venture led to gambling debts, a charge of extortion and, ultimately, a brief spell at Her Majesty's New Zealand Government's pleasure. "To be honest because of who I was the judge felt he had to make an example of me. A prison sentence was a stupid outcome," says Gordon, while still admitting his mistake. And, while inside, things got worse with a foot infection leading to him having a toe amputated.

Fortunately, the more recent past has been kinder. Gordon is now in charge of sales and marketing for Tuffsports, a company making tackle aids for rugby clubs. The Tony Gordon-designed Tuffman looks like a huge polyurethane Subbuteo player and "Tank" tacklebags also sell well. And he is back coaching too, helping to take a club from the Rotorua area to the regional semi-finals.

Supporters in London will be glad to hear that the first result he checks for on a Monday is theirs and that he considers he's really just marking time until he gets the call to return to the Broncos. "I'd be back tomorrow," he repeats. Many people would see that as the return of a golden age. For in that article I wrote for *The Greatest Game!* I added: "Tony Gordon wasn't the most successful coach Britain has ever seen but given the chance at London maybe he could have been. Winning the respect of those around him and on the terraces is never an easy task. Tank made it seem like a doddle..."

By Michael O'Hare

Tony Currie

Tony Currie, or TC as he was affectionately known by the supporters, transformed the fortunes of the London Broncos from a side that struggled to a side that at times were as good as any other. Before Tony's appearance the club had finished second bottom during the 1995-6 Centenary season, and had just suffered the indignity of being knocked out of the Challenge Cup by lowly Dewsbury. Gary Greinke's teams had played what the fans felt was a stereotyped pattern of play. Only a few weeks before the start of Super League in March 1996, he was replaced by Tony Currie.

Tony had been on the Brisbane Broncos coaching staff as the first team defence coach. He was also a successful player at the highest level. He played at centre for Brisbane Wests, Redcliffe, Canterbury-Bankstown and the Broncos, and won seven caps for Australia in 1988 and 1989, scoring two tries. He played seven times (with a further eight substitute appearances) for Queensland in the annual State of Origin battles against New South Wales between 1982 and 1989, scoring three tries. But the London Broncos marked his debut as a first team coach at the age of 33.

He is fondly remembered by Leeds fans for having played two seasons there in the mid 1980s, scoring 35 tries in 65 matches. According to British Rugby League journalist Dave Hadfield, he was "a player of unquestionable class." The list of coaches that Currie had played under is impressive: Bobby Fulton, Arthur Beetson, Wayne Bennett, Phil Gould plus British coaches such as Peter Fox and Maurice Bamford.

TC brought in some young players and blended in the skills of experienced stars such as Terry Matterson and Peter Gill. He feared no one and was always upbeat and positive before a game. In some ways he was fortunate to take over a club new to Super League and also had the backing of a progressive owner in Barry Maranta.

In his first season he brought on such talent as academy player Tony Martin who became a first-team star, and piloted the club to a very respectable fourth place, claiming the scalps of Leeds both home and away and a memorable draw at Wigan that virtually settled the inaugural Super League title in favour of St Helens, taking it away from Central Park, but more importantly, also signalled London's own aspirations. TC saw the jump from defensive coach at the Brisbane Broncos to the top job in London as a great challenge as he said " If we catch on down here, just the sheer size of the population will carry the club on to success". In an amazing piece of crystal ball gazing just a few weeks after arriving in London, Currie mused about the idea of signing Shaun Edwards in an interview with *London Calling!*

He said: "...if we get a high profile player, for example, Shaun Edwards, would the London population really know who Shaun Edwards is?" Sports fans in London do now.

In some ways it was the brash confidence of Tony Currie that raised the Broncos' aspirations and enabled the club to sign such stars as Edwards and Martin Offiah. These two signings really put the club on the Rugby League map and showed that it had now more on its mind then merely survival in Super League.

In 1997, even though Tony Currie was now longer a newcomer to coaching in Britain, he still managed to surprise the other Super League coaches. His success in both Super League and the World Club Championship really made people look up. Despite three defeats in the Australian leg of the World Club Championship, the Londoners were leading at World Champions to be Brisbane at three-quarter time.

However, nobody gave London a chance in the British matches and it was probably novelty that drew a near capacity crowd to the Stoop to see the match against Canberra Raiders, former Broncos coach Gary Greinke and all, especially as the Broncos had lost 66-20 to the Raiders' "Green Machine" down under. Things started badly, with the Broncos going 14-0 down with Scott Roskell in the sin bin. But London were level at half-time with two Terry Matterson tries and the second half will go down in British Rugby League history as the reigning Australian champions were swept aside by a final score of 38-18. Currie could not repeat the trick before large crowds against Brisbane or Canterbury but had done enough to make sure the Broncos were one of the European qualifiers for the quarter-finals. However, opponents Cronulla were on their guard and emerged victorious but London had proved their point and were now serious contenders on the Super League scene.

In the league campaign there was a tremendous thumping of Wigan at the Stoop by 38-12, a real landmark result. Nonetheless, clouds were gathering which ultimately led to the side being dismantled at the end of the season. Rumours abounded of agents, contractual and work-permit problems and by the end of the season the likes of Roskell, White, Mestrov, Krause, Bawden, Martin, Barwick, Tollett and the talismanic Edwards departed the Stoop. The last great victory was a wonderful last league match of the season when the Broncos, who had finished second pulled off a magnificent win over champions Bradford Bulls at the Stoop.

In his final Super League season, 1998, Tony was dealt a difficult hand with the above players leaving even though they were replaced by big name signings Mark Carroll, then a current Australian international prop and John Timu ex-All Black and Kiwi international.

Bizarrely, although the new side struggled they did manage to get the club to the Challenge Cup semi-final, for the first time in its history, only to be obliterated by Wigan at Huddersfield. Fortunes improved with the

112

return of the prodigals Tollett (from Harlequins RFC) and Edwards (from Bradford Bulls), but it was too big a challenge to make the top five. There was a memorable win over Bradford Bulls at Edinburgh in an "on-the-road" game, but it could not make up for a disappointing season. The final straw was a tempestuous home defeat by bogey side St Helens, which was to be one of the last incidents in Tony Currie's Bronco career. He was released by the club at the end of the season, much to the disappointment of the supporters. His replacement, Dan Stains, while credited with taking the club to Wembley, only lasted six months, leaving after a record defeat at Bradford Bulls in June 1999.

Tony reflected on his time at the club to journalist Julian Easterbrook in July 1999: "I still consider it an achievement - I had a 60% success rate which is pretty high for a newly-founded club. We had some great victories and I feel that London were a force to be reckoned with. It all tapered off in my last season but I don't believe it was caused by the coaching. There were a   lot of internal problems that needed to be rectified.... We climbed mountains when I took over in 1996. These mountains have been eroded, and London has gone back at the rate of knots. The 1997 squad should have been largely retained at least, but players went elsewhere. Tony Mestrov, Scott Roskell and Shaun Edwards were all allowed to leave while Tulsen Tollett was allowed to have a go at union - more effort should have been made to keep those guys. By the end of it they paid just as much for replacements, if not more."

Tony Currie still follows the fortunes of his old club, he evens keeps the fixtures stuck on his fridge! For the future, he is investigating various business possibilities and is keen to return to coaching in some capacity, but probably not in England, as family commitments and his children's education will probably keep him in Australia. He remains one of the most successful coaches the club has had, especially as all his results were achieved at the highest level.

With thanks to Julian Easterbrook

John Monie

When Shaun Edwards says that a coach is: "one of the greatest in Rugby League", you pay attention. He was talking about John Monie, arguably the most important recruit for London Rugby League since Harold Genders persuaded Reg Bowden that he didn't want him to change sports and play football for Fulham, but to be the player-coach and focal point of his new Rugby League venture at Craven Cottage in 1980.

The club has had some fine coaches since then - Roy Lester, Bill Goodwin, Bev Risman, Ross Strudwick, Tony Gordon and Tony Currie all made significant contributions to the development of the playing side of the club in different ways. But John Monie's record in club Rugby League, both here and in Australia, is unequalled in the modern era. According to Tony Adams, who includes John in his elite selection of 15 coaches for his book *Masters of the game - Coaches who shaped Rugby League*, he was: "the first coach to win major titles in both hemispheres." Neil Hanson, in his account of Wigan's 1990-1 season, *Blood, Mud and Glory* says that John was: "a cool, thoughtful, methodical and brilliantly effective coach."

John first played Rugby League at primary school. "I started in the under-5 and under-6 teams, like most kids in Australia. My family moved to Ocean Beach, near Woy Woy and I rose through the grades there, under-12 and under-13. Country Rugby League has four grades and I started in D grade, which is under-17. In my last year in country football I played for the first team. I played at stand-off and also played for the Southern New South Wales Division representative side."

John then signed for Cronulla in the Australian Rugby League and played three seasons at first grade level. It was his love for surfing that saw him return to Woy Woy where he became captain-coach. This was a big responsibility for a relatively young player in his early 20s. But John says that "I had always understood the game and played under good coaches. Also, I've always got on with players. I played in the Newcastle Rugby League for a season under Dennis Ward and I felt that he had problems handling players."

When he was 32, John broke his arm and decided to concentrate on coaching. The legendary Australian coach Jack Gibson had just been

114

appointed as coach at Parramatta and, as John recalls: "sacked all the coaching staff. He took me on as skills and second grade coach. He was great. Everyone was scared of him, but I got on really well with him. I was not afraid to talk to him on coaching issues. It was a super three years." John's reserve grade side reached their Grand Final in 1981, while the first grade team won three consecutive Grand Finals. Then Jack Gibson decided to move on. "Jack had had enough", John remembers, "and recommended to the Board that I take over as he believed that I could do the job. In 1984 we had a very good season but lost the Grand Final 6-4. In 1985 we were eliminated in the play-offs, but in 1986 we won everything including the Grand Final."

By the end of the 1989 season John had been involved at the top level for nine years and was looking forward to a break from the game and some surfing. Then Maurice Lindsay, at that time Wigan's chairman, phoned him. John vividly recalls being recruited by Lindsay: "I got a phone call from Maurice Lindsay who said he was talking to the new Wigan coach. I said I was not interested. He rang me every day for the next two weeks and in the end convinced me to come. I had never been to England before, never even thought of it."

Paul Wilson's account of Wigan's domination of British Rugby League in the 1980s and 1990s, *The Best Years of our Lives*, quotes Lindsay saying that: "...I knew there was something special about Monie. I had seen him operate and wondered at the calmness of the man... He had a presence that instantly commanded respect." To follow one highly successful coach in Jack Gibson had been a major challenge, but John was now taking over at Central Park from Graham Lowe, who had built Wigan's domination of British Rugby League. A hard act to follow. When asked about his first spell at Wigan, John simply said: "I was there for four seasons. We won the Challenge Cup and the League four years in a row. Maurice Lindsay left after three years, but asked me to stay for one more season. I was not convinced that Jack Robinson was the right man to take over as chairman, but we won everything anyway. The pressure was not as bad as in Sydney, but there was pressure within the club in my fourth season and the pressure to keep on winning built up. But I think I am good at not putting too much pressure on myself." Apart from Challenge Cups and League Championships, Wigan won the World Club

Challenge, Regal Trophy, Premiership and Lancashire Cup in this period. Not surprisingly, John was coach of the year for British Rugby League every year from 1990 to 1993.

It is easy to say that both at Parramatta and Wigan that John inherited successful sides. But there are many examples of coaches who have been in that position and failed. Wigan captain at that time, Dean Bell, recalls in his autobiography *The Ultimate Warrior*, how when he came to Wigan, John: "...simply observed the team to see who did what and how we played before he slowly started putting things into place". Bell also says that John tightened up on defence and that he was: "obviously a very professional coach." It could also be argued that Wigan spent enormous resources at this time and bought success. But again, other clubs have spent large sums on players but failed to knit them into a successful team. John just saw his job: "to get the best out of the players. For example, I didn't want to sign Frano Botica. I'd lined up [Australian] Phil Blake for Wigan, but Jack Robinson wanted to sign Frano instead. I had a first class Rugby League player ready to join, but instead got someone who'd never played Rugby League. But my job then was to turn Frano Botica into a Rugby League player. I started him in the lower grades, then playing on the wing, introducing him slowly. He became a good friend of mine. He joined me in Auckland, but then broke his leg."

At the end of four highly successful years at Wigan, John moved to the Auckland Warriors, to prepare the club to enter the Australian Rugby League, a huge step forward for the sport in New Zealand. The Warriors were one of four new clubs that entered the ARL in 1995. John recalls: "It was an exciting concept. I was recruiting the players, physically setting up the club, getting a gym and training locations. I had a season a and a half to do that before we started playing. But in the middle of my third season [1997], I was sacked. I wanted to build the club on good New Zealand players. But the board dropped that philosophy. However, the main problem was the ARL-Super League War. The players decided to go with Super League and the club was split down the middle. Also, the press and media were very hard on Rugby League because of the [Rugby Union] All Blacks who were the superior side at that time."

There is an old saying: "never go back". But after four years in Auckland that had seen the new club become established, John was offered the chance to return to Wigan, who by their standards had not been successful for a couple of years. He explains: "I wanted to go back and straighten the club out. I bought in three players from Australia with good work habits - Danny Moore [who has followed John to the London Broncos], Robbie McCormack and Mark Bell. I turned the playing side around in one season, but the problems were deeper than that. There were financial problems, the salary cap and in the club's management structure. There were changes in the Board. I had disagreements with the new chairman, Peter Norbury and in 1999 he sacked me." In 1998, under John's direction, Wigan had won Super League, including a triumph at Old Trafford in the first Grand Final. They had also reached the Challenge Cup Final, before losing to Sheffield Eagles in one of the biggest Cup Final surprises for many years.

It was the potential that he believes the club has that bought John to the Broncos in October 1999, not any particular desire to move to London. "I was seeing what jobs were around and had been working for Sky television. I believe this club should be a top five side and potentially could make the semi-finals. I talked to Tony Rea about the plans he has for the club. I believe I have a good squad of players here. The junior development in the club has been impressive and I hope I can give some of the younger players the chance to play at first grade. But it is also important to attract players from the north to London. If we have a competitive team and good organisation then we can do that."

John sees the development of the playing side as a whole, not just the first team as his overall responsibility. "I am responsible for the whole organisation, but I have never had a problem with letting other people do their jobs. If someone is good at their job, let them get on with it. We have a collection of people - the coaching staff, conditioners, the football manager. The way the players think and train is our responsibility. My philosophy and priorities should go through all the coaches. But I also rely on other people's opinions. I'm not always right or wrong. I don't want flexibility in defence, but I want some in attack and players to express themselves, to play with flair in the right place at the right time. We have got players at the club with special skills and we should use them. I want players thinking about the game the way I do."

At the time of writing, it is too early to assess John's contribution to London Rugby League at this time. But he faces a challenge similar in many ways to the one he faced with the Auckland Warriors in 1995. The move back to The Valley for the 2000 season is a vitally important one for the club. The achievement in reaching the 1999 Challenge Cup Final in some ways disguised the decline on the playing side since the glory days of 1996 and 1997. The return to south-east London must see a growth in the club's support.

However good the promotion activities and work in the community the club does, unless this is matched by a competitive side on the field, new support at the turnstiles will not happen. Since the club became the Broncos in 1994, apart from three months in 1999 when Les Kiss and Tony Rea were joint coaches, three relatively untried coaches have had the helm. One, Tony Currie, was successful. The other two were not. The change in direction to recruiting an established coach was an important move. The club have managed to capture one of the most illustrious coaches the sport has ever known. If anyone has the pedigree to build a successful team to put the London Broncos on the sporting map in London, it is John Monie.

Interview in March 2000

3. Club Officials

Harold Genders at Fulham (Photo: Courtesy Harold Genders)

1999 Challenge Cup Final Parade. Roy Close is the second in line.
(Photo: Peter Lush)

Choosing the people to be included in this chapter was very difficult. It would be possible to write a whole book about those who have worked for more than 20 years to keep Rugby League alive in London, both professionally and in a voluntary capacity.

Starting at director level, apart from the people featured, Colin Welland was an important presence in the Craven Cottage period and continued to work for the club at Chiswick. Tim Lamb and Richard Lawton gave the club much needed stability and direction from 1986 to 1990, supported by many people doing voluntary behind-the-scenes work for the club. Tim is still involved today providing the players' match statistics. Sir Richard Branson has financially supported the club to give it a more stable existence than at any previous time and his involvement has helped to raise its profile.

As club officials, Chris Blanchard (who was also a director for a time) gave much needed support with others to Ross Strudwick at Crystal Palace. Neil Robinson, as club secretary played a crucial role in keeping the club alive at Copthall before the Broncos arrived. Robbie Moore was central to establishing the Broncos presence in London. More recently, Tony Rea has been at the centre of developing the club's structure for Super League. In the background, timekeeper Dennis Samuels has served the club for many years, as has Nicki Welding in a number of roles.

The experiences of the people featured in this chapter offer an insight into the different activities of the club at various times in its history. From marking out the pitch to - at times - avoiding the bailiffs, they have all helped Rugby League develop in London.

Harold Genders

In 1980, Rugby League in Britain was in a healthier state than for many years. The introduction of the "six-tackle" rule, floodlit matches and playing on Sundays had all helped the game's revival. The 1982 Australian tour, when the playing deficiencies of the British game would be exposed, was still on the horizon.

The major weakness, as for so long, was the failure to break out of the game's traditional heartlands. It was nearly 30 years since Cardiff's one season in the professional game. Student Rugby League was just starting to build a base in new areas and the London Amateur Rugby League was keeping the flag flying - just about - in the capital.

As so often in its history, the game seemed to lack any development strategy. Had it not been for the vision of Harold Genders and his key role in establishing Rugby League at Fulham, 20 years' activity outside the north might never have happened.

Harold had played Rugby League professionally, signing for Rochdale Hornets as a 19-year-old. " At the same time as I turned professional I was studying and doing exams for my City and Guilds and Higher National Certificate," says Harold. "At 21 I was conscripted into the RAF to do my national service. I played Rugby Union for the RAF and was captain-coach of the RAF Stoke Heath team. We played in a sevens tournament at Waterloo's ground and were knocked out in the semi-final. Before the final I played for a combined select team picked from the teams who had been knocked out, against Waterloo. It was an exhibition match. They were captained by Gordon Rimmer - the England Rugby Union scrum half - and were going to show us how to play. I gave him the run around and we beat them 35-5."

From Rochdale Hornets, Harold joined Widnes and then finished his playing career at Blackpool, deciding to concentrate on his work in the construction industry. "I was concerned about my long-term future - it was poor money playing professionally in those days. But I enjoyed my time playing Rugby League."

Harold's next involvement with the game came at Warrington, when he became a director in the late 1970s. "I was asked by the late Sir Oswald Davies, the chairman of major construction company AMEC Ltd, who had become the chairman of Warrington to come onto the Board. My main role was in finding and signing new players. I had also founded the Primrose Club to raise funds for the club."

It was at the 1979 Rugby League Cup Final that he had the idea of establishing a Rugby League team in the south. "I could not find anything about the cup final in the southern papers. I thought that something must be done to spread the gospel. The only possibility would be the creation of a Rugby League club in the south."

In 1980, Harold approached club chairman Ernie Clay at Fulham Football Club and convinced him that using the ground for two sports -

then unheard of except for a couple of football grounds that also staged county cricket - would be a worthwhile enterprise. Fulham FC had just been relegated and needed the extra income. "At my initial meeting with two of their directors, Gregory Clay and Brian Dalton, I suggested that Fulham should sell their soccer team and take up Rugby League full-time. The other alternative was to play Rugby League at Craven Cottage every other week, which they accepted."

Harold's activities initially were rather clandestine, as he was still a director at Warrington. But once Fulham were accepted into the League, he resigned from his position there, to become managing director at the newly formed Fulham RLFC.

Player recruitment was now an urgent necessity. Using his extensive knowledge of the game and contacts in the north: "I bought a team in eight weeks that played Wigan, never having played together before, and beat them 24-5."

The impact of that game was enormous. National newspaper coverage, BBC's *Match of the Day* cameras and nearly 10,000 people saw the new club burst into action. "That first match was something special. It was not the best Wigan team ever, but they were still a big club to beat. No one gave us a chance of doing it."

Harold had promised Ernie Clay promotion and achieved it. "The first year was exciting. We were out to achieve something and we did it."

Fulham never quite repeated the impact and excitement of that first season. The next year, despite new signings such as Steve Diamond, John Crossley and John Dalgreen, as well as Moroccan Rugby Union star Hussain M'Barki, an injury hit squad struggled and were narrowly relegated. Four stalwarts of the first season had gone and soon after the season started three other players went into dispute with the club, leaving the team desperately short of players. Harold says that he had been promised more money to develop the team if promotion was won, which was not forthcoming. "Players wanted to come to Fulham. We needed to get top class players and we could then have become a leading club. I tried to persuade Ernie Clay to pay for better players so we could become established at the highest level. It also took time for the new players to fit into the team."

Promotion as Second Division champions in the club's third season followed, despite very little money being put into the club. Arguably, this team played the best rugby of the time Harold was involved, dominating the Second Division. Harold says that was the best season in his time with the club. "That year was tremendous. We did extraordinarily well with the squad we had." But by the start of the fourth season, it was clear to Harold that the Rugby League team was not going to be given the resources it needed to be a consistent success.

"I resigned because promises of money to buy players had not been kept. That was what prevented us staying in the First Division. If we had been given the funding to strengthen the team, the gates would have improved. We needed to speculate to accumulate." Harold left the club after six matches of the 1983-4 season.

In 1988, Harold joined Swinton as managing director, with a brief to rebuild the club's playing strength. Chairman John Way outlined: "We feel that we need a new man with drive and energy and a thorough knowledge of Rugby League." Although the new players were successful in reaching the Divisional Premiership final, losing to Sheffield Eagles, they had finished fifth in the Second Division and missed out on much-needed promotion. Frustrated by financial problems at the club, which was trying to deal with debts and the upkeep of its huge Station Road ground, Harold left the club.

Harold retired from AMEC in 1997, having been managing director of Fairclough Civil Engineering Ltd and finishing his career as special advisor to the AMEC Chairman, Sir Alan Cockshaw. He still follows Rugby League and takes a party to the Challenge Cup Final every year for AMEC.

His other sporting interest is cricket and he is a member of Lancashire CCC. He still has an interest in Rugby League in London and hopes that the game will develop there successfully in the future.

Interview in December 1999

Roy and Barbara Close

In July 1984, Fulham fans were shocked by the announcement that their Rugby League club was to close down. In retrospect, the signs of a serious crisis were clear. Managing Director Harold Genders had left in the previous October, coach Reg Bowden had just joined Warrington and the team had just been relegated again to the Second Division. Not surprisingly, the club's crowds had been declining.

The club's future was saved by Roy and Barbara Close. The papers had already carried reports of "a Maidenhead businessman" taking over the club. In fact, that businessman Roy and his wife Barbara, had supported the Rugby League club from the beginning. They became majority shareholders from 1984 to the end of the 1992-3 season, except for a short period in 1986, and were directors from 1984 to 1986 and again from 1989 to 1990. Barbara was the first female chairman of a Rugby League club and Roy represented the club on the Rugby League Council for many years.

Roy and Barbara were Fulham Football Club season ticket holders when Rugby League started at Craven Cottage. All season ticket holders were given complimentary tickets for the first game. They recall: "We thought we'd go along to give our support and see what it was all about." They were impressed, so much so that they sponsored kit for the Rugby League team and then funded the transfer fee for Steve Bayliss from St Helens. They also paid half the transfer fees for Steve Mills and Charlie Jones from Widnes.

Roy recalls: "I had the ambition of owning Fulham FC and the Bayliss transfer started our moves to buy the Rugby League club." Roy saw that as a move in the right direction. "We were negotiating to buy the Rugby League club for two years. I saw this as a first step towards buying the football club. Ernie Clay used to talk of our two families working together, but we couldn't agree on anything."

Roy and Barbara later realised that the purchase by Ernie Clay of the freehold of Craven Cottage prevented them from buying the Rugby League club at that time. "Ernie Clay had managed to have a covenant restricting use of the ground removed, making it potentially very valuable for development." This meant that they did not want to give the Rugby

League club a lease as it was a further obstacle to possible property development. The football club was subsequently sold by the Clays to a property company.

The Rugby League club was put into liquidation. Roy and Barbara then started negotiations to buy the assets, including, so they believed, the players registrations. They were immediately plunged into a crisis. They had an agreement with Fulham FC to continue playing at Craven Cottage, but two days before the end of a 28 day "cooling off" period for the agreement to buy the club assets, they were told that Craven Cottage was not available for the Rugby League club. They recall: "We held a board meeting - the two of us - and decided to go ahead with buying the club. We thought if we held the registrations of the players we already had, strengthened the team and got the Supporters Club involved, we could get the club into the top half of the First Division. So we let the cooling off period lapse and bought the club."

They appointed Roy Lester as team manager - an inspired choice. "Roy taught us a lot about Rugby League. We taught him about management and business." Desperate to find a new home ground, with the season about to start, the club moved to the Crystal Palace National Sports Centre. But towards the end of that season "it was obvious that we couldn't continue there. It had a good pitch and good floodlights - onto the track around the pitch - and 16,000 seats. But it was difficult to get to, was desolate in winter and it was clear that we had to move." The club had played one game that season at the Polytechnic Stadium at Chiswick and with help from the Supporters Club in rebuilding the ground, Fulham moved there permanently for the 1985-6 season.

Another crisis arose almost immediately after they took control concerning the players they thought they had taken on when buying the club. Most of the players claimed - on legal advice - to be free agents and took the club and the Rugby League to court. The club lost the case and most of the original players, which "was a huge setback".

Elsewhere, the club was breaking new ground. Barbara was the first female chairman of a Rugby League club, at a time when most boardrooms were still male only preserves. She recalls: "We agreed that I would become chairman. I was not trying to prove anything, although it did gain us some publicity. My intention was to run the club, as with other things Roy and I had run together. We could run a business, a family, etc. Roy would run the administrative side as managing director and so I became chairman." There was uncertainty amongst the home officials at the first away game at Swinton but then their chairman, Ian Clift invited Barbara into the boardroom and generally they had no problems after that. Specifically, they remember the hospitality at perennial strugglers Highfield - a club that was always short of resources but willing to share what they had.

The club recruited young Australians to strengthen the team. To save costs, they often stayed with the Closes. Barbara recalls: "I used to creep into the laundrette with all their muddy kit." They have a lot of good memories of the Australians who stayed. "On one occasion Glen Haggath organised a do for the players at a pasta place in London, to try to promote togetherness in the team. They borrowed our car. We were woken up at 2am, hearing Neil Diamond singing very loudly. I found Greg Pratt in the lounge fast asleep and Glen asleep in the front of the car, with the tape deck blasting out for the whole of Maidenhead to hear. Another time, they came back from training and at about 1.00 a.m. and there was a strong smell of cooking. Glen and Greg had put a pizza in the oven, then fallen asleep. The pizza was very well done."

A British winter provided new experiences for their Australian guests as well. "Christmas was very cold and there was ice on the swimming

Barbara Close presenting Michelle Snares with a Player of the Match award
(Photo courtesy of the Snares family)

126

pool. Pat O'Doherty put shorts and a vest on and had photos of Christmas Day at zero degrees. In the New Year there was snow, so they bought a toboggan and went tobogganing in the park. The local kids couldn't believe it - great big men tobogganing. Some of the Australians had never seen snow before."

On the playing side Roy and Barbara have fond memories of Lancashire Cup matches against Wigan. "We went to Central Park and had Wigan on the rack. They were still losing 10 minutes from the end. We lost, but Maurice Lindsay had been getting very upset and Shaun Edwards was worried." Of the club's players, apart from the Australians, Alan Platt, a high profile signing from Oldham, stands out from the players they signed.

Following the Rugby League team in the north gave Roy some new experiences. Barbara's mother is from Liverpool and she had spent some time there in her youth. Roy remembers one visit to Huyton. "I had a Jaguar XJS sports car. I parked in the car park by the ground. We came out after the game and there were four young boys - aged eight or nine - around the car. I went over to it with trepidation, but they were just looking at it. I let them sit in the car - they all squeezed in. I said 'I bet you've never been in a car like this before'. They replied 'Mister, we've never been in a car before'. I was very shocked by this and asked them where they lived. They were from the estate by the ground, so I drove them home. We would have liked to have taken them out again, but it wasn't possible."

Roy and Barbara clearly wanted to do things properly at the club. Barbara remembers going to Chiswick to clear up litter after the games. Roy recalls one occasion when there was racial abuse towards the players. "Barbara told the people involved to shut up or leave. They did shut up - and apologised later." Barbara remembers that at Chiswick someone spat at the referee at the end of the game. "I wrote in the programme the next week that if that behaviour didn't stop, we would close the club down. It makes me cross when people say 'what can you do'. There is always something you can do. I don't get angry very often, but I do at behaviour like that."

Roy and Barbara's involvement with the business side of the club finished in 1992-3, when the husband and wife team of the Bartrams took over. After that period the Broncos took control and since then the Closes have been given boardroom facilities in recognition of their work for the club. Roy still attends matches regularly. "It's ideal - I just go and enjoy the games. No worries abut the gate or the results." But with the club moving back to Charlton - a 140 mile round trip for them - Roy says that unfortunately they will attend fewer matches in future.

One area of the club's work in which they are still actively involved is sponsoring awards for the Academy players. This started as a sponsored meal for the 16-year-old players at The Stoop. Now it has developed into a dinner with annual awards for the player at each age level of the traineeship scheme who has shown the best all round development, both academically and at Rugby League. The award is split into a first prize of £700, second prize of £200 and third prize of £100. Roy and Barbara said that: "We want to help the young players. They are the future of the club - there are hundreds of potential Martin Offiahs out there for the club to find."

The important role they have played at London's professional Rugby League club was recognised when Roy was invited to be one of the club's representatives in the pre-match parade at the 1999 Challenge Cup Final. Had the couple not rescued the club in the summer of 1984, professional Rugby League in London would have collapsed, which would have been perhaps the ultimate setback to the development of the game in London and indeed anywhere outside its traditional areas.

Interview in December 1999.

Barry Maranta

The transformation from the under-funded London Crusaders of the early 1990s to the Super League London Broncos was not easy. The man who can take much of the credit for successfully guiding the club through those times was Barry Maranta.

Barry played Rugby League in the Brisbane competition in his youth and worked as a college lecturer. His business ventures then developed into real estate, producing text books and forming Queensland's largest private funds management company. He also was involved in sports management with Greg Chappell, the former Australian cricket captain. His business interests gave him the financial base to become one of the four founding directors of the Brisbane Broncos Rugby League side when they joined the Australian Rugby League in 1988.

The Australian Rugby League/Super League "war" in Australia which ran from 1995 to 1997 for control of the game there has made Barry Maranta a controversial figure in some quarters. Mike Colman in *Super League - the Inside Story* wrote that the Broncos: "... proved by far the most successful new club in the competition, although they set record crowds, attracted new fans and played attractive football, they bought a new rogue element into Rugby League. No more was it just about football and trophies and tradition at club level. It was about profits and percentage points and market share." What is beyond dispute is that the Brisbane Broncos were a success, although Barry pointed out that their crowds were "3,000 when we first won our licence for the Brisbane club, we've gone to 44,000. The game is the top sport in our community."

At the beginning of 1994, the Rugby Football League, with the support of chief executive Maurice Lindsay was guaranteeing the London Crusaders' existence while the club looked for new owners. The Brisbane Broncos were the successful bidders, beating a consortium that included Andrew Robson, former England football manager Bobby Robson's son.

The Brisbane Broncos loaned their new sister club a couple of young players and saw their new operation narrowly miss out on promotion to the First Division at the end of the 1993-4 season.

Barry now accepts that the new owners made mistakes at that time. Interviewed by Michael O'Hare in *Open Rugby* in 1996, he said: "When we first took control of the club we had what we thought was the correct coaching and playing staff to take us into the First Division at the first attempt. We sat back in Brisbane and foolishly expected it to happen. When it didn't we lost a lot of money and reports of our impending withdrawal weren't far from the mark."

Apart from employing a coach, Gary Greinke with a very stereotyped style, which was a huge contrast from the open, flowing game of New Zealander Tony Gordon's 1993-4 team, some of the players the club signed from the local teams in Brisbane were clearly not experienced enough, or in some cases good enough, to achieve promotion from the Second Division.

The club's prospects were saved by the arrival of Super League in 1995, which "promoted" the Broncos to the top flight, because the new League wanted a London club, despite having only finished fourth in the Second Division in 1994-5.

There can be little doubt that the concept of Super League, with the British and Australian leagues playing at the same time, culminating in a World Club Championship Grand Final was being discussed in 1994, or even before and was a factor in the Brisbane Broncos' directors deciding to establish a London base. A vicious court fight in Australia meant that Super League only started there in 1997, in direct competition to the Australian Rugby League and lasted one season before merging into a unified format as the National Rugby League in 1998.

Barry Maranta at the book launch of *Touch and Go* in August 1995
(Photo David Stevens)

Despite the often negative experience of the 1994-5 season, Barry still believed that a Super League club could be established in London. In 1995, he sold his 25 percent share of the Brisbane Broncos and bought out the other Brisbane based shareholders of the London Broncos, to take control of 75% of the club. He became chairman and chief executive.

He saw the future for the game as being in Super League: "Big city matches between big city teams in modern stadiums in fine summer weather." However, he was critical of how Super League was set up in Britain, recalling that he pleaded with the sport's bosses not to try to impose mergers on long-standing clubs who were often bitter local rivals.

Barry realised that coach Gary Greinke was struggling and just before the start of Super League in March 1996 sacked him and as his replacement appointed former Australian international Tony Currie. Barry "guaranteed" that the Broncos would finish in the top six in the first Super League season and, reinforced by new players, the team made good his promise, finishing fourth in the table, a stunning improvement on their 10th place in the Centenary season.

Barry was also responsible for appointing Bev Risman as director of development to build the club's Academy structures for young players. This is now bearing fruit as more young, British, London-based players are coming into contention for first team squad places.

Barry's guidance of the club in 1997 was even more successful, with second place in Super League and near capacity crowds at The Stoop for the World Club Championship games, including the remarkable victory over the Canberra Raiders. Also, he could watch his London Broncos in two closely fought matches with the Brisbane Broncos, the team he had helped found just 10 years before.

But at the end of that season, he decided it was time to return to Australia and he sold his majority shareholding in the club to Sir Richard Branson, famous as head of the multinational Virgin group.

Much of the credit for establishing the club in Super League must go to Barry Maranta. In 1995, the Brisbane-based owners were very close to pulling the plug on their expensive London operation. Yet, Barry's confidence in the possibility of the sport becoming established in London at the top level has been borne out.

As former club staff member, Nigel Waters recalls, Barry Maranta was an inspiring figure to work for when he ran the club. Barry was also popular with the fans. At the Valley, Broncos fans remember him buying drinks for Charlton football supporters at the Rugby League games, enthusing to them about the sport. At The Stoop he would often walk around the ground before the game, checking everything was in place and greeting supporters he knew. It was his ability to give the club a high profile, combined with his ability to relate to the club's supporters, which helped give the club a solid foundation and its highest profile in London since the early days at Fulham.

Bev Risman

One of the most encouraging developments for Rugby League in London since 1996 has been the Broncos' youth academy set up. The leading force behind this was the club's director of development, Bev Risman.

Bev joined the club from Student Rugby League, after a lifetime's involvement in the game. "I was due to retire as co-ordinator of the Student Rugby League because all Rugby League employees have to retire at 60. So when Barry Maranta approached me to come and work for the Broncos to run the development programme I was happy to join. There was some money available and the *Framing the Future* document produced by the Rugby Football League when they were planning the future of the sport said that Super League clubs had to have a development programme, hence my appointment. But we had very little time to put things in place - from November 1995 when I was appointed I was given until March 1996 to have an Academy team in place. So we bought over seven young Australians on scholarships and then looked to Rugby Union for other recruits. I went to representative games and approached lads who I thought had potential. We also advertised for players. There was resistance in some Rugby Union schools but, in others, former League players who were teachers helped. We also got some first year university students, some of whom had League experience. We ended up with between 30 and 40 players at training. They were very keen but some of their Union coaches were still telling them they could not play Rugby League. Some were afraid of being banned from playing Union."

The academy team finished sixth in their first season. "We decided to compete at the highest level. We had some famous victories, and the players learnt on the hoof. Some who had never played before suddenly found themselves playing Wigan! Two players came through from that group - Dominic Peters and Wayne Sykes. Wayne was a basketball international but had always been interested in League. He had trials with Hull and Wigan. Dominic Peters came from Gunnersbury School, where Jason Wing, a former London Crusaders player, was a teacher. It was a Rugby Union school and we had to negotiate about when the players could play for us in the winter when our under-16 schools team clashed with their fixtures. We lost a few who did not want to let their school down, which is understandable."

It took time to build the squad. "Dozens of players came - many found it too hard compared to Union. The professionalism was far ahead of anything they were used to in Union. We insisted on training twice a week, preparation on Saturday mornings and playing on Sunday. In Union they trained if they felt like it and turned up on match days. Only the keenest and most enthusiastic survived in League. But even then we had more players than we could cope with and had to tell some they wouldn't make it. There were tears…"

Once the Academy team was established then came the under-16 team. "My philosophy was that we needed an Academy team immediately. We built from the top downwards. In 1997 we cut back to four Australians

Bev Risman speaking at the dinner after the Fulham versus Papua New Guinea match in 1987 (Photo: Stephen Froggatt)

133

and in 1998 the team was totally London based. Then we set about building a team below the Academy. We got a phenomenal response to starting the under-16 team. We had over 60 lads at the first training session at Crystal Palace. It paid dividends. Players such as Yusuf Sozi and Chris Weathers started coming through into the Academy team. Today we have players coming into the Academy having gained experience in the under-16 team. Dave Evans as Development Officer did a lot of the work establishing the game in the schools. He became coach for the under-16s."

Another very important development was the traineeship scheme. "We had to find an academic as well as a playing structure for players coming out of the under-16 team. So Richmond Adult College, where my wife Ann is the principal, organised a programme for them. They do NVQ levels two and three over two years. This is the equivalent to 'A' levels. The first group has just graduated. It was an amazing experience for them - some, such as Leon John, had no GCSEs. He should now get his level three NVQ. I think that as well as finding the stars of the future we have given some of them a chance in life. For example, trainee Wayne Parillon has just been offered a professional contract. We aim for two or three Super League players from each year. Four players from the first group to go through the scheme have just been offered part-time contracts to play in the Alliance (mainly under-21) team."

But this success has also brought problems. "In the south apart from the Broncos there is the London Skolars club and the summer conference teams. We must give the young players who have come through the Academy the chance to stay in Rugby League or we will lose them to Union. We need them for our under-21 side and must keep them involved in the game."

The club is now recruiting young players from outside London to the traineeship scheme. "Peter Lupton comes from Barrow. He was our top Academy player last year and is just 17. I hope he will be blooded in the first team soon."

The London development scheme now at last has the resources that it once lacked. "We have three Development Officers funded by the Rugby League and three funded by the Broncos working in schools. Forty secondary schools and 20 primary schools are now playing Rugby League with more to come. We have an infrastructure there and that is helping the under-13 team to develop. The best is yet to come. The highlight of my time with the club has been giving young lads the opportunity to play Rugby League, especially the young black lads and ones from under privileged backgrounds. Seeing Dominic Peters play for the senior team was great - he was the first one to come through the ranks. I am thrilled that all this is happening."

Bev brought a lifetime's experience in sport and sports development to the development role. "I was born into Rugby League. I have a photo of me at 12 months old sucking an orange watching my dad play for Salford. I've been passing a ball ever since." After the war, the family moved to Cumbria, where Bev's father Gus became player-coach for the new Workington club. Bev's younger brother John also followed in their father's footsteps, his Rugby League career including playing full-back for Fulham in the first season at Craven Cottage. He had also previously been capped for Wales.

Bev's early experience covered both codes. "I played Union at school and then Rugby League on Sundays. But when I went to university it was all Union - there was no student Rugby League then."

In 1959, Bev was selected for the Union British Lions tour of New Zealand. "I missed my finals to go on the tour, which lasted four months. So I went back to Manchester University the next year to take my exams and then went to Loughborough College."

In 1961, Bev turned professional with Leigh. "I mainly played at stand-off. I learnt a lot about the game there and had a great time. But we had an ageing pack and the club did not replace them. I found myself covering different positions and in the end became a bit disillusioned. At that time I think you lost out on international ambitions if you were not just playing in a single position. I was on the bench for Great Britain a couple of times."

However, in February 1966, Bev moved to Leeds and experienced a period of great success, winning the Challenge Cup and the Championship. "I was 27 and it was time to move on. People say that was the best ever Leeds team. The four-tackle rule had just started and we threw the ball around from the first tackle." Roy Francis was the coach and played Bev at full-back and also gave him the goal-kicking role.

However, many followers of London are unaware of his illustrious history. Some Broncos supporters were surprised to see Bev in the Leeds group of past players in the parade that took place before the 1999 Challenge Cup Final.

For three years running, from 1967 to 1969 he was the leading goal-scorer in British Rugby League. "I got close to Lewis Jones' record, which was recently beaten by Iestyn Harris. But we did score a lot of tries too." Another highlight was Leeds's Challenge Cup triumph in 1968, in the notorious "watersplash" final. "The conditions were farcical. Normally it would not have been played." However, the referee, John Hebblethwaite, did not want to be the first to postpone a Wembley Final despite the monsoon conditions and gave the go-ahead.

Further international honours also came Bev's way, with five Great Britain caps, including being captain of the side in the 1968 World Cup played in Australia.

In 1970, Bev retired from playing. "I was 32 and was completing a masters degree at Leeds University. I wanted to go into higher education and wanted to finish playing while still at the highest level. It was a positive decision." Bev and his family moved south and he took a job at Bulmershe College, lecturing in PE and sport. There was no Rugby League at the college, so he coached student Rugby Union. Later he became involved in League again. "I couldn't keep away. Student Rugby League was now established and I joined the committee. I was involved in both codes and tried to build bridges at the student level." Typically, Bev came up against some resistance. "I was almost put on the national Rugby Union Executive representing the English Students Rugby Union, but then someone at Twickenham said it was 'not appropriate'."

On the playing side, not wishing to return to Rugby Union, because former League professionals were banned from returning to Union, Bev played soccer in the Reading and District League until he was 43.

A move to West London Institute for Higher Education followed. "I formed the Rugby League team there. Dave Rotheram and Russ Bridge (among others) played and later joined Fulham. I became more involved in Student Rugby League. Also I started getting involved with the London Amateur League, working with its administrators Gordon Anderton and Cliff Buckton. From the late 1970s I was the Regional Coach for London, trying to get people involved in coaching and promoting the game in the schools with help from people like Dave Part and Reg Pearce. But there was no infrastructure to build on."

At one time, Bev almost returned full-time to Rugby League when some other football clubs were considering launching League teams. "I had talks with Michael Glikstein at Charlton about starting a Rugby League club. But he was outvoted by the other directors."

In 1985, Bev took early retirement from West London Institute of Higher Education and went into sports consultancy. "I had been working for the Lawn Tennis Association, coaching young players and as a fitness consultant for the Davies Cup squad. "I worked with Mark Cox, Buster Mottram and the Lloyd brothers. In those days I had to convince them that fitness was important. Now everyone recognises this."

The LTA wanted Bev to work for them full-time, but he did not want to give up his Rugby League activities. In June 1987, he became team manager at Fulham RLFC. "I said to Roy Close we had to recruit players from London. We looked at Rugby Union and the London amateur Rugby League players and invited some along. There was a lot of enthusiasm - we had 40 to 50 players at training. We also reinforced the team with three or four young Australians. I did not have a contract and from the beginning said it would take three years to develop the team. In my first season the objective was survival. We finished fourth from bottom. But we competed and London-based players such as Steve Guyett and Mick Hutchinson came into the first team. Glen Haggath and Pat O'Doherty were the Australians we brought over and Glen was outstanding."

But at that time the club was struggling for resources. "We did not have the money to sign players from Rugby Union. And the second season we wanted Glen and Pat back but they wanted more money and we could not afford them. We did not start the season well and then the committee decided to try someone else in charge of the team. It was very disappointing - I had said it would take three years, but people expected success in the second season. So I went the way of many coaches and managers..."

At the time Bev left Fulham, the first London Rugby League development officer post was being appointed. Bev applied for the job, but then withdrew to become co-ordinator for the Student Rugby League, a post he held until he joined the Broncos in 1996. His time at the Student Rugby League was very successful. "There was a massive explosion of interest, following on from the 1989 Student World Cup. From 28 universities it quickly grew to 50 or 60. We started the four home nations' championship and I was involved in a further two Student World Cups. The SRL now has a strong committee including David Oxley, the former Chief Executive of the RFL." Bev also had a family interest in Student Rugby League - his son John was the first Union and League double blue at Oxford University.

Bev is still involved with the Broncos and enthuses about the young players coming through the Academy set-up. With his wife soon to retire, they are planning to spend part of each year in Cumbria, near his brother John. "People are already asking me what I will be doing in Rugby League up there. And I am sure I will be coming south regularly for the Broncos matches," he concludes. It's obviously going to be difficult to keep Bev Risman away from Rugby League in London.

Interview in November 1999

Steve Magee

Only one member of the club's staff has been involved all the way through the club's history from its beginnings in 1980 at Craven Cottage - kitman Steve Magee. Steve was on the Fulham groundstaff when Rugby League first started there.

"I was born in Parsons Green and supported the Fulham football team from an early age. I met Mr Clay in 1976, when he was a Director at the club. When I left school I went to work for him at his factory in Reigate, making insulation products. Then I worked at his home - an enormous house and grounds on the side of Boxhill - doing maintenance and gardening work. He felt that was good enough training to be a groundsman," the job he had in mind for Steve at Fulham FC, "which he saw as just cutting grass. Of course it's far more than that".

Initially, Steve worked with the outgoing groundsman. When he retired, Steve became head groundsman. "I was the only one," he recalls. "There was a small staff throughout the club, because the football team was not doing that well." Steve remembers former football international Malcolm Macdonald, then the club's commercial manager, and Mr Clay telling Steve they wanted to stage Rugby League at the stadium. "It didn't carry much weight with me. I had been brought up on football. I had watched League on *Grandstand* with Eddie Waring. It was an alien sport to everyone involved, except Mr Clay because he was Yorkshire born and bred. However, all the staff took on dual roles to make it work. I believe this was unique." Steve's job at the time had many responsibilities. "I dealt with the field, the grounds, security, maintenance work, everything. We also had to overcome problems. Sometimes there would be football on Saturday, Rugby League on Sunday and then football again on Tuesday or Wednesday. We had to change the pitch markings, the posts, the adverts. Often I worked through the Saturday night to get things ready. But it was worth all the trouble - Mr Clay had introduced Rugby League to a new audience."

And even though the London Rugby League Club has long-since left Craven Cottage, Steve has stayed with them. This means that with all the grounds the club has used, Steve has put up posts and dug pitches all over London. "In 1983 we played one game at Stamford Bridge. We took the posts there from Fulham and I remember one of Mr Clay's sons helped me dig the holes". Three home games were taken away from Craven Cottage, with two being staged at Widnes. This made some supporters doubt the club's commitment to the Rugby League team. Steve recalls: "It was Malcolm Macdonald, by then the football team's manager, who wanted the games moved. He felt if the football team was promoted that would bring in huge rewards for the club." Macdonald wanted the pitch to be in perfect condition for the football team and believed that because of the Rugby it was suffering. "The real problem was the pitch was knackered. A lot of games were staged on it and it was hired out for private use at the end of the season. That meant there was less time to do annual renovation work. Then one summer it was relayed and the roots never took. We had to weigh down the turfs with sand and it did not create a good surface. It took years of graft to try to get it right."

Steve saw little of the Fulham Rugby League players at Craven Cottage. "They were like an away side. They would arrive, get changed, play, have a meal and a pint afterwards and be back on the bus by seven to head north. Occasionally I would see player-coach Reg Bowden in the week if he was down for a meeting." But by this time Steve had taken an interest in Rugby League and began to follow the club. "At away games, as a supporter, I would see more of them."

When the club moved to Chiswick in 1985, after a season at Crystal Palace, Steve's talents were called on again. "Roy Lester, the team coach, and Mr Close, the managing director, asked me to do the pitch. The groundsman there was already working six days a week and refused to do any more. I had an army of helpers to lose the football markings, move the football posts, put the Rugby posts up and do the pitch markings."

The move back to Crystal Palace in 1990 saw Steve take on a new role, at the request of coach Ross Strudwick. "He asked me to help with the kit. I got on great with him - his manner and direct approach was like working for Mr Clay. He told you to do something and you did it. Dr De Jennings was recruited in the same style by Ross Strudwick at this time. I also liked working with Strudwick's successor Tony Gordon - getting us to the Divisional Premiership Final in 1994 was a great achievement with such a small squad of players. That final was the biggest game I had been involved in at the time. As there was only one set of dressing rooms at Old Trafford, we had to change at the [nearby Lancashire CCC] cricket ground and warm up on the cricket outfield. Then we got a police escort to Old Trafford. We could use the main dressing rooms only for a team talk and at half time. We had a brilliant second half. I have great memories of that day, even though we lost to Workington."

Steve Magee (Photo: Peter Lush)

Apart from these matches, the tour of the Soviet Union in 1991 and the 1999 Challenge Cup run are other highlights of Steve's time with the club.

In 1997 Steve came to work full-time for the Broncos. "Barry Maranta had taken over and I spoke with him and Tony Rea. My role now is to try and ensure that the players have nothing to worry about with equipment and clothing, so they can focus on playing and training. I make sure equipment is available for training and that everything is right on game day. I suppose my job is like a 'roadie' with a band. Get everything right, like equipment, kit, food and drinks." Steve used to be seen running on with the water bottle and messages for the team from the coach. "I do that less now - I am more in the dressing room checking everything there. This means that at away games I see any tries I have missed on the video on the coach going home."

Steve also tries to deal with all the requests coaches make. "With Ross Strudwick it was bananas for the players as a high energy food. He even liquidised them to make a banana drink". Another idea by Dan Stains was only tried once: "He wanted live tackling practice when the players got off the coach on an away trip. My colleague Trevor Howard and I were on the end of this. Trevor copped a knock so I took over. The lads tried to be gentle, but…" However, Steve does remember playing on the wing on a tour game in Holland and was proud to be able to wear the club colours.

Rugby League has clearly come to have first place in Steve's sporting outlook. "I went to more than 1,000 consecutive Fulham football matches. But then at the start of one season the Rugby League Alliance team were playing at Staines on a Saturday. I went to do kit duties for them instead of going to the football. Now I don't go. In football, with the exception of the Clay family, I was never made to feel as welcome or as involved as I do with the Broncos. There have been so many highlights over the years, but really it has been my overall involvement with the club that I have enjoyed. This sport has grown on me, from the one I had regarded as alien when Mr Clay had the vision to bring it to Fulham." And the club is fortunate to have one of the most loyal and hard-working backroom staff in the sport.

Interview in November 1999

Dr De Jennings

One of the key back room staff at the club since 1990 has been club doctor, De Jennings. She was first recruited to the club by Ross Strudwick when the team moved to Crystal Palace. She recalls: "I was conned by Ross - I was minding my own business working in the Sports Injury Clinic at Crystal Palace Stadium one Wednesday when Ross turned up to say that he needed a doctor for the first game of the season at their new venue. He had some sob story about having no doctor. 'No doctor, no game,' he said, so with considerable anxiety and foreboding I agreed to be there. Then came the rest of the season. I thought that I had arranged for a suitable young sports doctor to help . He lasted one game then withdrew."

Dr. De has always been interested in sport. "At medical school I played lacrosse and tennis and watched a lot of rugby union." Her first date with husband Mel, who is an urological surgeon, was at a mixed doubles tennis tournament. Mel was involved with the Barts Hospital Rugby Union Club and is a member and ex-player of Harlequins. All their three sons have played Rugby Union for their school and hospitals and are now surgeons. The family connection now extends into Rugby League. De's middle son, Simon, an orthopaedic surgeon with a Sports Medicine Diploma, is now heavily involved with the Broncos, treating players at matches both at home and away.

Doctor De Jennings (Photo: Barry & Gwen Warren)

Away from the Broncos, her main work is in General Practice in Reigate. Her interest in Sports Medicine developed after her sons left school, and she was no longer able to watch them play on Wednesday afternoons - her half day - and be available if medical attention was required. In order to keep involved in sport she took the Diploma in Sports Medicine and this led to her work at Crystal Palace Sports Injury Clinic.

Apart from her work with the Broncos, she is a governing body doctor for the British Judo Association, having met them at the Atlanta Olympics where she was headquarters doctor and she is looking forward to attending the Sydney 2000 Olympic Games with the judo squad. Another responsibility is as medical officer to the Middlesex Rugby Union, mainly looking after the under-19 team. She has been on Rugby Union tours to South Africa, Singapore and Hong Kong, and to Australia for the Rugby League World Club Championship. Back in 1991 she went to the Soviet Union with the Fulham and Ryedale-York clubs on a tour to promote Rugby League. The players' language and antics do not worry her. "For a long time I was involved with medical school and Rugby Union antics. Both are worse than Rugby League and together are far worse still."

As club doctor she plays an important supporting role for the players. Asked if she gets attached to them, she replied: "I seem to be Mum to them all and thoroughly enjoy getting to know them and their families who are always welcome at our home. I consider them our extended family." When the game was played in the winter, some of the Australian players would spend Christmas Day with her family, "which was special." She keeps in touch with a lot of the club's former players and has watched Scott Roskell play Rugby Union.

She describes herself as a "League addict, and very keen follower of the game". She sees the players as gladiators. "Summer Rugby League is fast and a great spectacle to watch, requiring great skill but there is an high price to pay on the players' bodies." For the past few years she has looked after the Little Leaguers who play immediately before each Cup Final at Wembley, but in 1999, when the Broncos reached their first Cup Final, "had the privilege of looking after my own Big Leaguers! This obviously was an amazing experience I will never forget".

Based on interviews in *London Calling!* and by Sue Webber on the Broncos' club website.

Nigel Waters

Nigel Waters was one of the people who played a key role in the development of the club's administration in the mid-1990s.

Nigel became involved with London Crusaders in 1993, stewarding the match day buses the club provided. He was persuaded to do this by his old friend from his days on the beat in the Metropolitan Police, club secretary Neil Robinson.

He had no previous involvement in Rugby League. "Union was my first sport" he says. "I played for Brixham in Devon, then for the Met Police team, occasionally in the same side as John Gallagher who at the time was a young recruit at Hendon Training School. I never had the opportunity to play Rugby League except for a handful of games for the Crusaders/Broncos Alliance which was always a case of being in the wrong place at the wrong time. For one game I was dragged out of the club shop to play Aylesbury before going back in and then doing the PA announcements."

After club owners, the Bartrams left the club in the autumn of 1993, Nigel became involved working with club secretary Neil Robinson and coach Tony Gordon to keep the club functioning. "I started doing a couple of hours a day but in order to keep the money coming in, this had to grow." Match day, along with a lot of other people, meant wearing a variety of hats. Programmes needed putting together, sandwiches needed making (if I'd sold "The Corporate Box" - the club only had one box at Copthall stadium!), bars needed controlling and, on a couple of occasions, toilets needed cleaning. The club's financial situation was dire and during the week bailiffs became regular visitors. "Although armed with bits of paper, they never seem to leave with anything - certainly not money. Fortunately, the Rugby League guaranteed our debts but did little else than take the gate money. That was until the Brisbane Broncos rode in on their white charger. There was certainly a sense of relief but I was sorry they let Tony Gordon go - I thought he did a marvellous job but probably had the wrong passport."

Nigel's role changed when the Broncos took over. "Robbie Moore arrived and I gave him the keys to the stadium. Nigel was given the title of Commercial Manager because "we didn't have one." Shannon Robinson and Trevor Howard also joined the administration at that time. "The Broncos clearly knew a lot about the game but didn't understand London. I think they found my expertise in this area vital and among other things, I did keep away some of the vultures that the club attracted. The club was taking up more and more of my time so I finished up doing a deal with Robbie for the merchandising rights in exchange for my labour."

Nigel's work continued to develop in the Centenary season when the club had a nomadic existence. Indeed, the club shop lived in the back of his van being transferred from ground to ground. The first game at the Stoop saw it located under an umbrella on two trestle tables. That season also saw Nigel take on the roll of PA announcer, much to the consternation of rival fans.

By now Barry Maranta had bought out his fellow Brisbane based directors and became chairman. "Barry was great for getting things done or at least inspiring those around him. You would leave a meeting with him thinking that nothing was impossible and everyone worked phenomenally long hours". Nigel's official role now included PR and media manager and soon after, he became an employee of the club in a deal which included the return of the merchandising rights to the Broncos. He still ran the shop.

Nigel left the club at the start of the 1998 season after a bust up with one of the club's directors - since resolved. "Although I knew it was the right time to leave I still regret that I left in those circumstances. The club meant everything to me and to a certain extent still does. Ironically, the club had just recruited new staff and I actually had four different people to hand over to". Nigel now works for Brand Asset Management, a sports marketing agency which has a contract with among others, Super League.

Another important role Nigel played was liaison with the Supporters' Club and the supporters generally, as well as running the telephone service "Broncoline". "I saw this as a vital role and I am glad to see that Tony Rea is continuing with it. There is not the same culture between a club and supporters in Australia and as a result the Broncos often appeared aloof and uncaring which wasn't always the case." Nigel also had his 15 minutes of fame on BBC television's consumer programme *Watchdog* defending the club's reputation following a dispute over the club's goal kicking competition. "In the end, we received 10 minutes BBC prime time coverage and left with our name intact - not a bad deal."

On the pitch, Nigel has vague (he was very drunk) but good memories of the opening World Club Challenge match in Australia against Brisbane. "With an hour gone, we were leading the best team in the world on their own pitch and I was one of the few Englishmen in the stadium. Additionally the Castleford Challenge Cup and Doncaster Premiership semi-finals stand out but, for sheer excitement, you can't beat Justin Bryant's try in the last seconds against Whitehaven to keep the 1994-5 season alive."

Of the people he knew at the club Nigel says "Robbie Moore remains a great friend and I will always be grateful to Neil Robinson for getting me involved. I also remain great pals with Dominic Fenton, Steve Magee and Trevor Howard."

Nigel played an important part in helping the club through the transition from the penniless Crusaders to the evolving Broncos. His popularity with the club's supporters was recognised with a well-received presentation when he left. He laid the foundations of much of the club's commercial activity today.

Interview in October 1999

Trevor Howard

Since 1996, Trevor Howard has been the club's football manager. Unlike football, where such a title would mean having responsibility for the team on the pitch, in Rugby League this job entails dealing with everything connected with the players off the pitch. Trevor explained "This title came when Super League arrived and it is an Australian concept. It does confuse people - sometimes they ask if it is hard to sack a player. But fortunately I am not the coach."

Trevor joined the club in July 1994, helping to create an administrative structure for the club's new owners. He was born and bred in St Helens and was brought up on Rugby League. By trade he is a bricklayer and work in building management first bought him to London. "I used to watch Fulham at Chiswick and I regret that I never saw them play at Craven Cottage. But I was not involved - I just used to go to games."

Nigel Waters - on the phone (Photo: courtesy Nigel Waters)

Trevor Howard (Photo: Peter Lush)

Since 1988, Trevor's parents have lived in Australia. In 1993 he went there for a year. He worked at the World Masters Games, a veterans' athletics tournament, as a volunteer and met Barry Maranta, soon to be a London Broncos director, who gave him tickets for a Brisbane Broncos game. The Brisbane Broncos were in the middle of buying the London Crusaders. "I said to Barry "gis' a job". He asked for my CV and what role I could play. I think my passion for Rugby League came over and I was given a three-month trial. Five-and-a-half years later I am still here. I wanted the job because I love this sport and this club. That has never changed in all the time I've worked here."

"At Copthall I was the programme editor and investigated running a lottery for the club. But it was three months before the National Lottery was launched, so we abandoned that idea. So my role expanded into administration - any job that came up really. We only had four full-time staff. I got on well with the players so I organised the away trips."

Trevor's responsibilities now cover a multitude of administrative roles. "This can be anything to do with the team - liaising on fixtures with the League and Super League, work permits, medical issues, training facilities, where we stay on away trips, even the food the players eat when we are away. I try to ensure they have good nutritional food for breakfast and pre-match meals. Most of our guys are educated about food and make the right choices. We try to stay loyal to hotels and use the same one and the same coach company for trips to the north."

Another key responsibility is arranging work permits for overseas players. "As long as you follow the rules it is not a problem. There is a special department that deal with sport and entertainment at the Department of Employment. I was asked to join a committee to help redesign their application form, with people from the BBC and entertainment promoters. But Immigration procedures can be slower and more complicated."

With so many players from outside the city, another vital role for Trevor is helping players settle in London. "I arrange housing for the players, but we are trying to get them to be more self-sufficient. We find them somewhere when they arrive, then they can choose where to live. The Australians don't realise how small houses are in London compared to Australia. Our players from the north are also shocked - Karle Hammond

148

moved from a four bedroom house in Widnes to a two bedroom place in Isleworth. But then they do have the excitement of being in London."

Trevor also organises the club's training facilities, working closely with Steve Magee "one of the best right-hand men in any sport. I liaise with the coach and the conditioners. But I have to try to stay within budgets." One of the more unusual equipment requests was from Dan Stains. "He wanted tractor tyre inner tubes to use for tackling practice, to roll them along and for the players to tackle them as they moved."

The club did not have any facilities at The Stoop for training. "We train at Meadhurst, the BP sports centre and do weight training at St Mary's College. I want to try to bring all the training to one base in the future and combine it with physiotherapy facilities." For the 2000 season, with the move across London to the Valley, the club have found new training facilities at Charlton Park RFC, with all the facilities on one site.

Trevor also has some responsibility for the Alliance team and the Academy. "Most of the Academy work is done by Dave Evans. Really its about putting systems in place for each team. I try to make things go smoothly so that the players only have to worry about the game."

Working for the club can sometimes involve very long hours. Returning from an away trip, Trevor was in the office at 2.45am having just unloaded the coach. The phone went. "It was someone from Australia wanting information about the club. When I pointed out the time, he said 'well you're there' and wanted answers to his questions. Another time I came in at 7am to phone Australia, to find the man I wanted to speak to had taken the afternoon off and gone home."

Another of Trevor's roles is as a water carrier during matches. "I started doing this for Tony Currie and have been doing it ever since. I wanted to stop for the 1999 season as it means working every weekend. But there was a new coach, Dan Stains, so I agreed to continue. I am glad I did because it meant I was involved at Wembley, which was a wonderful experience. Coming out in front of the crowd, the walk down the tunnel, the noise, the fireworks. Money could not buy an experience like that. I think that Richard Branson was the most nervous. It was great to have him there."

Apart from Wembley, another highlight for Trevor was beating Canberra Raiders in the World Club Challenge. "I didn't go to Australia

149

for the games as I stayed here to keep the club running. I watched them stuff us, and saw Tulsen Tollett being interviewed. Behind him was Gary Greinke, our former coach, with a big smile. It surprised everyone when we beat them here and I managed to return the smile when Tulsen was interviewed following the win. Beating St Helens this year was great. When we go there my friends chant "Judas" at me from behind the dugout! Last year they hammered us, this year we returned the favour. Barry Maranta used to say to me that when we played St Helens I couldn't lose. He was wrong - there was no team I wanted to beat more. When we beat them, Peter Gill gave me a hug - we had done it at last."

Players that stand out for Trevor are Peter Gill, Tulsen Tollett, Steele Retchless, Darren Shaw and Steve Rosolen. Of the present team he finds Karle Hammond and Greg Fleming "real jokers and good fun". Of the back-room staff, he has enjoyed working with Nigel Waters, Clive Townsley, Steve Magee and Dominic Fenton.

For the future, Trevor hopes to continue working for the Broncos. "I couldn't go and work for another English club - it would be disloyal to the Broncos. I want to help make this club successful in the future."

Interview in October 1999

Director David Hughes receiving the Broncos' 1999 Club Man of the Year award. David is also a director of Charlton Athletic FC. (Photo: Peter Lush)

4. Memories and Reflections

Tee-shirts! From the left: Broncos Super League launch, Fulham on the road, Tony Gordon, and Hot Action with the Broncos (Photo: Peter Lush)

The people in this part of the book all have particular memories of London Rugby League that illustrate what the game in the south of England has meant to people in different ways over the last twenty years.

Twenty years

My Dad and I went to the first game in 1980, and have been unable to break the habit since. There were so many great games in those early years, or at least they have become great in my mind with the passing of time. The forwards in that first season were giants, the mighty van Bellen, the alarming-looking Harry Beverley, who charged into opposing defenders knees raised and wouldn't have lasted five minutes with today's officious whistleblowers, and the pugnacious John Dalgreen. My own hero from that era was John Wood who seemed, to an impressionable 14-year-old, to have superhuman powers, once dragging four or five defenders the best part of 20 yards with him before scoring at the far corner of the Hammersmith End.

The arrival of Hussain M'Barki and his willowy running style brought a touch of glamour to the rough, tough, Rugby League players who made up the early sides. The fact that we managed to score a try against the 1982 Kangaroos was wondrous in itself. That our very own Moroccan superstar had crossed the whitewash made it doubly so.

My star-struck admiration for the Fulham icons of the early days was not diminished by meeting them in later years. The highlight for me of that emotional day at Huddersfield in 1986 came in the bar after witnessing the match that looked like being our last ever. I was standing at the counter trying without success to get served, when a burly moustachioed Yorkshireman leaned forward, asked me what I was having, attracted the barman's attention immediately and got the drink for me. As other Fulham fans near me started to chat with him it dawned on me that I was in the presence of the great Ian van Bellen himself. Sadly I missed my cue and didn't manage any more than a mumbled "Thanks" whilst others around me engaged him in conversation about his Craven Cottage exploits.

I still hadn't learned how to overcome being awe-struck when meeting Hussain M'Barki some years later in the bar after a game at Chiswick. I'd stayed to have a drink with Noel Keating, with whom I worked in a bookies in West Kensington at the time. Noel was a promising young second-rower who had only recently broken into the team. While standing in a group with him and other players we were joined by the unmistakable Moroccan. I spent the next half an hour earnestly nodding at everything he said, in fact I was probably nodding at him even when he wasn't talking. I don't remember actually saying anything to him other than "Hello". I certainly wasn't going to admit to him in front of everyone else that he was my all-time sporting hero, whose autograph I'd collected and still treasured and that I'd been heartbroken when he left us the first time to try his luck playing in the north.

Talking of Fulham icons, My Dad and I made a trip to Southend one Boxing Day to watch Fulham take on Southend Invicta. We had never been to the place before but managed to find a cosy little chippy for lunch. When we finished eating I turned to the locals sitting behind us to ask for directions to Roots Hall. A broad Yorkshire accent, strangely reminiscent of the Tetley Tea adverts, told me that he didn't have a clue but wanted to know himself.

Unfortunately I was too pre-occupied at the time with getting to the game to actually stay and chat with the late Brian Glover and Colin Welland his dining companion. So I just apologised for disturbing them and asked the people on the next table instead. It was probably just as well as I hadn't yet got over my inability to string two sentences together to anyone famous and/or vaguely connected to Fulham Rugby League Club.

The late eighties and early nineties seemed to be a succession of lows, occasionally broken by the odd glimmer of hope, but the onset of the Tank Gordon era and the excitement generated in that 1993-4 season made it all seem worthwhile.

I remember travelling to watch a game with my girlfriend against Runcorn Highfield, played in neither Runcorn nor Highfield but Knowsley. We'd had a long drive, it was a cold day and there was no tea or coffee on sale in the clubhouse. However, by improvising with a scarf up the jumper and some ham acting we managed to persuade the club secretary that my partner was heavily pregnant. This led to royal treatment, a pot of hot tea, seats in the boardroom and sandwiches - and we won - a great day out!

The relative success that we've enjoyed since the arrival of the Broncos and Super League has seemed unreal at times. I'd have to say that one of the happiest days of my life was Monday 21 July 1997. I'd found out that afternoon that I was going to be a Dad for the first time so I was already walking on air by the time I reached the Stoop. The fact that we thrashed Canberra Raiders 38-18 wasn't just icing on the cake, it gave me the chance to jump up and down and shout out to the whole world just how happy I was - without being arrested!

Of course, Headingley '99 can't be left out of any recollection of Broncos memories, and I know I shared the knife-edge excitement and last-minute joy with many others that day. I want to know how many other people suffered bruising to their shins from jumping out of their seats every other minute and banging them on the row in front. Those bruises filled with a warm, satisfied glow for weeks every time I looked at them!

Paul Dunne

The Fulham Maintenance Crew

What does the committed Rugby League supporter do on the morning before a home game? Nice lie–in? Wash the car? Walk the dog? Not if you were a member of the Fulham RLFC Maintenance Crew you didn't. Some people thought we were mad – looking back on it they could well have been right.

It all started in the summer of 1985 when Supporters' Club chairman Ron Snares asked for volunteers to help put the Polytechnic Stadium, Chiswick, Fulham's new permanent home to-be, into some sort of order. Before the first match there against Runcorn in March 1985, it had last been used in anger back in 1968 and even the most optimistic estate agent would have been hard pushed to describe the place as having "potential". However, after several weeks of digging out turnstiles, painting, cleaning, unblocking lavatories and accidentally digging up one of the polytechnic ground staff's vegetable garden, assisted at one point by the chairman and secretary of the Whitehaven Supporters Club while on a week's holiday in London, we arrived at the first game of the 1985-6 season at home to Blackpool Borough exhausted but unbowed.

The Fulham Maintenance Crew in action.
Top: Securing the post
Middle: "Planting the flag at Iwojima" - Fulham style
Bottom: Nearly there - fixing the cross bar
(Photos: Stephen Froggatt)

Things then settled down into a fairly predictable routine (running the bars and catering came later). One of the jobs involved erecting the posts for each match. At this time we had the Craven Cottage posts but not the sockets and sleeves and so we had to use the posts from the Rugby Union pitch at the railway end of the ground, put them up on our pitch and then reverse the process at the end of the match. Getting them out was bad enough, but to put them back in involved pushing them upright - bear in mind that they were about 30 feet tall and narrow, so it was difficult for everyone to get a decent grip - and then shuffling over to the socket, checking the post was completely upright and then dropping it in.

This was bad enough in fine weather, but on a wet morning in cloying mud it was murder, particularly because if the sockets had filled with water suction made it almost impossible to get them out again. After one game we had to finish working in the dark by the light of car headlights! Once this was finished we did some cleaning while Supporters Club officers Mo Snares and Barry and Gwen Warren dealt with the club shop. Then we set up the P.A. and waited for the game to start.

All this changed in March 1986. Following a fairly depressing trip to Whitehaven I arrived at Chiswick on Tuesday evening to find everyone standing around as if someone had died. It wasn't someone, it was something – the club, the money had finally run out – so following a small wake we drifted unhappily into the night, thinking that was that. Oh no it wasn't! On Friday evening I had a phone call from committee member Stuart Barlow, who had just heard from the then club secretary John Rathbone that all was not lost and the next game at Huddersfield was to go ahead. This heralded the start, although we didn't know it at the time, of a strange period that even now has an almost unreal feel to it.

For those of us gathered at Hammersmith Odeon at 9am on Sunday 16 March it seemed like we were going to a funeral (future kit man John Bryant spoke for many of us when he described it as the worst day of his life so far), and you couldn't have a more suitable graveyard than Huddersfield. For probably the vast majority of current London supporters Huddersfield means the ultra-modern credit to the game that is the McAlpine Stadium. This means you never had the dubious privilege of seeing a game at Huddersfield's original ground, Fartown. At one time it had been a modern, well-maintained place but by the mid 1980s it had degenerated into a heap of rotting timber, rusting corrugated iron and crumbling concrete terracing, more suited to an edition of television archaeology programme *Time Team* than Rugby League, and this was the place where for Fulham it was all going to end!

The journey to Huddersfield had some moments of macabre humour – I remember the driver of the coach I was on forgetting that he had to come off the M1 at Junction 6 to pick up some supporters, slamming on the brakes and reversing down the up slip road, long-standing supporter Bob Evans hitching a lift ("could someone please check he's on one of the coaches when we leave – we don't want a repeat of Featherstone in 1983") and Castleford supporters behind us on their way to Wigan speeding past us on the M62, slowing down, dropping into the inside lane and then coming up close to check that we were who they thought we were.

The black comedy continued when we reached the ground. Fartown was and as far as I know still is, a multi-sport site with a cricket pitch and bowling greens and before the game people used the bowling green bar, where we all headed when we arrived. The sight of more than 100 of us proved too much for the elderly barman, who fled into a back room, slammed the door after him and could be heard frantically phoning for reinforcements. Eventually they arrived, and we were able to a certain extent soothe the soul and calm the pain of the day with a brisk internal alcohol rub. The arrival of the team and the story of the game is told elsewhere. In the absence of the regular kitman, supporter Chris Bandey did the honours, a job he continued to do during the following season, and the crowd was augmented by the arrival of Fulham's first season hero Ian van Bellen, also a former Huddersfield player who lived locally.

After the game and yet another mini-wake we had a peculiar journey back, the driver refusing to stop on the way. At Hammersmith Odeon everyone parted, with only a Supporters' Club meeting to look forward to.

However, all was not lost. At the last minute Paul Faires bought the club from owners Roy and Barbara Close. This meant that the Doncaster game on 6 April was the first time we had to put on a game completely on our own and things were understandably a trifle chaotic. The outside caterers had withdrawn, so we had somehow to arrange bars, mark out the pitch (referee Cliff Hodgson agreed to get to the ground early to check that supporters John and Steve Bandey had done it properly) and still do everything else we had already been doing. The bar was the big problem, because it had only been on Tuesday night that anyone knew there was going to be a match! This was solved by running a shuttle service of glasses and bottles in Steve Bandey's taxi between the wine bar supporter Liam Bushell managed in the City and the Polytechnic Stadium. We also were unable to get hold of any beer glasses so everyone ended up drinking from the bottle. Luckily a man then turned up with a burger van and we were off again.

Given the circumstances things didn't go too badly for the rest of the season both on and off the pitch, with the team winning five and drawing one of its last 12 games, finishing only one place lower in the table than they had the previous season. Off the pitch things were made easier by the last four home games (including a weekend double-header) being played in brilliant sunny weather. By the time of the Friday evening match against Hunslet on 16 May things were running smoothly enough for us to start offering a limited catering service in the bars. The club burger van didn't start until the 1987-88 season – so up until then the man who turned up on spec for the Doncaster game provided the rest of the catering.

There was still a feeling of unease about the situation, however, and the end-of-season bash at the Clarendon in Hammersmith on Cup Final night together with the Lancashire Supporters Federation end of season Player of the Year awards at Wigan in late May (where Fulham's Tony Kinsey was runner up) had more the feel of farewell parties than anything else. It was a pleasant surprise therefore to find ourselves back at Chiswick at the beginning of July, mops, buckets and paintbrushes to the fore. It seemed too good to last and of course it was. By the middle of the month the club turned turtle again – this time apparently for ever. Paul Faires announced that he had withdrawn the club from the Rugby League.

On 4 September Ron Snares called a Supporters' Club meeting at Liam Bushell's City wine bar to decide on our future; the general consensus seeming to be that we turn ourselves into the London branch of the Widnes Supporters' Club and run coaches up to their home matches.

By a strange coincidence that I've never entirely accepted, this was also the day when the Sixth Cavalry once again galloped to the rescue, as Richard Lawton and Tim Lamb took over from Paul Faires as directors with the support of the Closes, and we were back on the road, this time going down to a 72-6 thumping at Whitehaven (a result that was overshadowed in the press by Roy Lester's Carlisle leaking 112 at St. Helens). It didn't matter – we were up and at least crawling, if not running, again. This was followed by a 68-14 loss at home to Sheffield, where I had the dubious distinction of operating the scoreboard and then defeat at Mansfield – the game being played at Notts County FC, in front of a coach load of Fulham supporters and seemingly no-one else.

In the meantime the sockets and sleeves for the Craven Cottage posts had at last been recovered. At 8.30 on the morning of the Keighley game Ron Snares and I turned up to help Stuart Barlow, who was responsible for organising the practical work at the ground, insert the sleeves in the pitch. At 9.15 the Bandeys and the Barlows arrived having agreed on Thursday night that we didn't need to turn up so early after all and then forgetting to tell me and Ron. Once that was sorted out we listened to Colin Welland on the radio blowing the whistle on some of the things that went on in the Craven Cottage days. As a result of this we very nearly didn't finish in time, as to set each sleeve into the ground involved boring a hole some two feet deep and around nine inches in diameter using a hand auger. However we made it and after much huffing and puffing the club's original goalposts adorned the pitch – I sometimes wonder what happened to them. Incidentally, has anyone noticed that League and Union secure the crossbar to the uprights differently?

And that was that. Although the club may have wobbled a bit for the rest of the time I was involved, the real crisis had passed. After the first season back at Crystal Palace, like many people I became disillusioned by a long journey, a ground where it wasn't possible to see properly and the way the players' names kept varying - but not the change of club name. There was a lot of largely misplaced emotional baggage surrounding Fulham and we may have been better off if a name had changed earlier.

There are a lot of ifs and buts in the history of Fulham, the biggest for me being what would have happened if Ross Strudwick had stuck to coaching. In my opinion he was the best coach we had in the time I watched the club. Instead he tried to run the whole club, which I think it is now recognised, never fully worked.

Stephen Froggatt

Playing Leeds

This piece highlights for me the way the club has existed over the last twenty years, and what it has come to mean to me. Ironically, the three fixtures I've written about all involve Leeds.

The first of the clashes took place in Fulham RLFC's inaugural season, in the heady early days of life at Craven Cottage. After all the euphoria of the opening home fixture and the now legendary victory against Wigan, results were going well and the promotion push was gathering pace.

Then in November came the John Player Trophy fixture against Leeds. Now even without a great deal of Rugby League background at that time, I knew that Leeds were a big name. They were a First Division side, and really I expected Fulham to be taught a lesson in League from them. However, it was not to be, and from that first season, this more than any other was the fixture that stuck in my mind.

In terms of details, what I remember most about that game are two particular images. The first is of the Putney End, the "away" end for supporters, packed out with what seemed like an army of blue and amber, with heat rising like a steam cloud from the masses on that cold November day. The second is of the defensive effort of the Fulham line in clinging on to their narrow winning margin. Every time Leeds got near the line, you could feel the collective will of the home crowd in the Hammersmith End forcing the ball away, putting up a barrier to the Loiners' efforts.

Of course that game was 20 years ago, and so the mind plays tricks with how we recall moments and in the way we remember certain feelings. However, no expanse of time will change the feeling of elation I and thousands of others felt that day, and the sheer enthusiasm at having knocked one of the great names in League out that day.

In those early days, 1 think there was a lot more acceptance of the side, with northern-based players and their promotion to the First Division earned through finishing in one of the top positions. With the advent of the special dispensation regarding the overseas quota and then latterly the elevation to Super League, I believe a lot of League people, especially fans of other clubs, turned against London.

There will always be banter. It is part of this great sport, but my next experience typified a lot of the prejudice that exists regarding London.

This fixture took place at Headingley in August 1997. Leeds basically had run riot in the second half and given the Broncos a right run around. The game as a contest was very much over but, with a few minutes to go, Shaun Edwards was sent off. Standing at the scoreboard end, I didn't get a good view of the incident which took place in front of the South Stand. The referee had no hesitation, so off he went.

At this game I was standing with members of my wife's family who all live in and support Leeds. I stood out a bit, resplendent as I was in quartered Broncos shirt. As Shaun made his way to the tunnel, I was aware of somebody very close behind me. This person then launched into a tirade of abuse aimed at the departing player, with his final insult something along the lines of it served Edwards right for all the filth he dealt out while at Wigan.

I was annoyed and pointed out this was Leeds versus London, and I couldn't see what his playing record at Wigan had to do with this particular fixture. This was, I thought, a fairly logical point, but it only provoked another volley of abuse. This time I was his target. Excluding the expletives, he said, what did I know about the game...I was only a Southerner...it was just a team of has been Australians...Rugby League didn't want our sort in the game, or the likes of Paris...we had no fans...he'd rather watch local teams. What was also very unfortunate about this incident was that his young son (eight or nine years old) witnessed the whole incident. I hope he proves to have a more enlightened attitude than his father.

Like other London supporters, experiencing such prejudice won't be new. Most of the time incidents like this would be brushed aside, but in this case it was just that it was such a personal attack, and it illustrated to me just how much bad feeling existed and maybe still does exist against the London club.

Even the 1999 appearance at the Challenge Cup Final brought mixed reaction from the League public judging by what appeared in the Rugby League press. Comments ranged from those supporting London in making the breakthrough in getting to Wembley, to those who said the draw had been fixed and they didn't deserve to be there.

For me being at Wembley, watching the side come out the tunnel at

161

Wembley was something I could hardly believe. As the team walked out, so the journey of 20 years came to a defining moment, a milestone that perhaps we never believed would happen.

The game itself of course set all sorts of records, and won't be fondly remembered by Broncos fans. However, with that start to the first half and the score at 10-0, there was in the heart that hope that perhaps the fairy tale could come true. Common sense said otherwise and the floodgates opened in the second half. Unfortunately, that latter period of play will always stay with me. With the final try, I could take no more, my mind and body was in pain, it actually hurt. I had to get out of the stadium.

I realised that day what Fulham/London Broncos means to me. I was like a parent, happy sharing in the growing up of a child, but feeling along the way the painful experiences as well.

Long may the team prosper and develop to take its place proudly in the future of Rugby League.

Paul Hatt

London Calling!

London Calling! is currently the world's longest running Rugby League club fanzine. Perhaps this is a reflection of the determination and tenacity that Rugby League fans have shown in London over the years. After all, not many clubs' fans in a 20-year period have had to contend with the club going bust on five occasions, moving grounds innumerable times and losing half the team through a court case.

Perhaps the lack of Rugby League coverage in the London newspapers, combined with the fact that, for many supporters who do not live near the team's ground the local papers are not available to them, has provided an audience keen to read about their team. And a reasonable number of them also have something to say, so many articles and letters are contributed by supporters to the fanzine, making it a lively forum for debate.

One of *London Calling!*'s strength's over the years has been that it is very much a team effort. The history of fanzines in all sports is full of ones that collapsed after a few issues because they relied on one or two people. However, it would be fair to say that brothers Al and Lol Ferrier have been at the centre of the operation of the fanzine since its birth in September 1993.

Lol first watched live Rugby League at Chiswick in January 1990, when Fulham played Batley. "I had watched Rugby League on *Grandstand* with Eddie Waring in the old black and white television days on Saturday afternoons. I was driving past the Polytechnic Stadium and saw a big board advertising the match. So I decided to go. It was the 21 January 1990 - I remember it well. I had lived in Yorkshire for 18 months five years before this, but never got round to going to a game. Once you go to a game it's addictive. I loved it and wanted to see more."

One of his early converts was his younger brother Al. He remembers: "Lol nagged me to come to a game. I wasn't particularly interested, but went to the cup match against Bradford Northern at Chiswick. We lost 20-2. It seemed a small crowd and generally a poor experience. But I was interested in the action and started going regularly. Lol used to give me a lift. I did not have any other interest in sport at that time."

Despite living near the Chiswick ground, the longer journey to Crystal Palace when the club moved there in the summer of 1990 did not put them off. Lol recalls: "We got season tickets for the next season at Crystal Palace. The more we got to know about the game, the more we enjoyed it. We had an idea of producing posters to help publicise the club, to put them up in shops. Then fellow supporter Steve Woodland suggested a fanzine." Al recalls the idea first being discussed by a few fans on the top deck of a bus back from a game at Crystal Palace. "We thought there was very little for the fans to read. So we produced a questionnaire for the last game of that season [1992-3] against Oldham at Crystal Palace. We checked out the questionnaire with the club and the supporters gave us a very positive response." Lol says that "There had been a fanzine before, but it had only lasted for a few issues. Apart from Al and myself, Steve Woodland and Paul Taylor were involved."

During the close season, the club moved again, this time to Barnet's Copthall Stadium. The first edition of *London Calling!*, including an interview by Steve Woodland with John Gallagher, was sold at the first home game at Copthall. It was an immediate success. Al recalls that "We produced 250 copies - and sold out. We sold at all the home matches," while Lol added that "It all snowballed from there". By the end of the

1999 season, 42 issues had been produced. Around 400 are sold of each issue and the price has never gone up from £1. We operate on a not-for-profit basis and any surplus is donated to the amateur or student Rugby League game in the south.

During that first season, the club was in dire financial trouble. The fanzine was approached by the club owners, the Bartrams, to see if they could help. Al recalls: "We gave the club £1,000, but made sure, on captain Sam Stewart's advice, that it went straight to the players. Some of the money was used to pay for Logan Campbell's airfare to fly from New Zealand to join the club." It still niggles both Al and Lol that apart from Sam Stewart, no one from the club ever said "thank you" for the money.

Despite that, generally the relationship with the club has been good. Al says that: "occasionally they get upset with what we write. We don't expect them to agree with everything we say. But we can usually sell in the ground, although sometimes stewards are difficult." Often, fanzines are banned from selling in their club's ground and some in football have even been sued by club officials, so it is to *London Calling!*'s credit that they have retained a good relationship with the club.

The 1996 fanzine team: (from left) James Sadler, Steve Woodland, Dave Farrar, Lol Ferrier & Al Ferrier. Jade Ferrier in pushchair (Photo: Peter Lush)

One of the fanzine's strengths has been the interviews both with club players and officials and people from the wider world of Rugby League. One of Lol's best memories of his work for the fanzine is interviewing Eddie Hemmings and Mike Stephenson from Sky Sports. "I had written to them but not got a reply. Eventually Eddie wrote back, apologised for the delay and said they would love to do an interview. So I popped over to Sky Sports, which is round the corner from where I live and was there all afternoon. They were great - I couldn't stop them talking." However, Al worries about the "curse of the *Calling!*" as apparently six people they have interviewed all resigned from their posts soon afterwards.

Another of the fanzine's strengths is the diversity of views. Lol says that "We give the ordinary London supporters a platform. We don't always agree with them, but as long as it is not racist or libellous we will publish it. And it's important that we cover general issues in the game, not just London. Sometimes fanzines can be too introspective. General pieces on Rugby League are important," while Al agrees that "strong, incisive copy is very important. People have strong opinions and express them well. We have the best letters page of any Rugby League fanzine."

On the pitch, they both remember the 30-0 Regal Trophy victory against Wakefield Trinity in 1992. Al recalls: "Old Trafford in 1994 as a highlight, and Wembley, with mixed emotions." For Lol, the highlights of his time supporting the club are the victory against Featherstone in 1993 in the Regal Trophy and the victory against Canberra in 1997 at The Stoop in the World Club Championship

Another important part of *London Calling!*'s activities has been backing the amateur game in London and the south. Al says that: "After the Broncos became owners of the club we decided to help fund the amateur game financially, as the Broncos themselves were financially secure.

We have helped several clubs and donated a trophy for a seven-a-side tournament at Reading in 1999. We have also supported wheelchair Rugby League." There is also an international angle to the fanzine's activities, as *London Calling!* has financially supported the Australian fanzine *Loosehead*, as Al says "to maintain an independent voice for the fans there."

Most readers do not realise the amount of work that goes into producing the fanzine. Apart from the layout and photocopying, there is also the stapling and folding, although they claim now to be "streamlined operation", which is shown by its regular publication during the season.

For the future, Al says that: "the main issues are the promotion and advertising of the game in London, and the relationship between the club and the fans." He is confident about picking up new readers now that the club has moved back to The Valley. "Football fans are more used to the idea of fanzines, unlike the Rugby Union types who came to The Stoop." Lol says the fanzine has kept going "because of our passion for the game. We have battled through the hard times. But we give the ordinary London supporter a platform for their views and that is important."

Al and Lol Ferrier were interviewed by Peter Lush in March 2000

Journalist for a day

Ten to five on a quiet Friday afternoon. It was the end of the week and I was tidying the flat and looking forward to Sunday when Broncos were to play in the Challenge Cup against Cumbrian amateurs Wath Brow Hornets, the first home match of the 2000 season. The phone rang. "Peter, it's Tim Butcher from *League Express*. Michael O'Hare [freelance Rugby League journalist] suggested I phone you. Could you cover the Broncos match on Sunday for us?"

I was taken aback. "I suppose so," I said, "but you do realise I've never done a match report on the day before." "Don't worry, you'll be fine," he replied. "It's going to be an easy win for the Broncos. Concentrate on the main details and get quotes from the coaches. The Broncos are usually helpful with access for that. Do the match facts and 500 words should be enough. Phone it through to us between 5.30 and

6pm." I agreed the (not enormous) fee for the work, asked him to send a fax to the Broncos to let them know I would need a press ticket and put the phone down.

Luckily, I was a few weeks behind with collecting my press cuttings from *League Express* and started digging through the pile on the living room floor to find the previous match reports on Wath Brow Hornets, to get some background on them. Slowly, however, the responsibility of what I had taken on started to sink in.

I had written match reports before, mainly for *London Calling!*, the London Rugby League fanzine. But I had never had to do one with such short notice. And if I am doing a report for *London Calling!*, I have the reassurance that I can always check an uncertain fact with the reports in *League Express* or the *Rugby Leaguer*, as there is usually plenty of time to do a report for the fanzine. But for this match I was the "reporter on the spot" for *League Express*.

I did some research - the Broncos' record wins, past scores over 60 points and past matches against amateur opposition. If it was to be a slaughter, this information might fill a couple of paragraphs.

I have supported West Ham United in football for over 30 years and the London Broncos since the club started at Fulham. As a supporter I have been nervous with anticipation before key matches - cup semi-finals in particular. But on this occasion I was more nervous than ever before a match. What if I got the facts wrong, or had "writer's block", or the car broke down on the way, or I got lost finding the match venue, Kingstonian

KINGSTONIAN FOOTBALL CLUB
LONDON BRONCOS
v
WATH BROW
PRESS PASS
DATE 13.2.2000
NAME PETER LUSH
Newspaper LEAGUE EXPRESS

Football Club, which I had never visited before? Even worse, what if Wath Brow won and they suddenly wanted more copy for a "big" story?

Over the past few years I have read and enjoyed Chris Harte's diaries of his years as a sports journalist. They gave me some idea of press box etiquette. I had learnt that you're neutral unless the report is for a local publication (no Broncos scarf), don't applaud and have a telephone handset available. I decided not to take up the offer of the loan of a laptop computer, because it was not a model I was familiar with, and relied on writing out my report longhand.

I arrived at the ground well before 2pm, for the 3pm kick off. I found the window where Dianne from the Broncos was giving out press tickets and there was one ready for me. I was "official"! I found the press box and saw the reassuring figure of Nicki Welding, who runs the press box for the Broncos on match days. She seemed surprised to see me and I explained my emergency call-up off the bench as a late substitute, and my trepidation. "Don't worry", she said, "I'm doing a report as well and we all exchange information on what's going on."

Then my friend sports journalist David Ballheimer arrived. He was covering the match for the *Rugby Leaguer* and a couple of Cumbrian papers. He was also surprised to see me sitting in the press box, but was also very supportive. Part of his work was to give marks out of 10 to each Wath Brow player - at least *League Express* didn't want that.

Nicki gave me a programme with the team changes, so I thought I would phone *League Express* to give them the team lists and assure them I had got to the ground. "No one's here yet, they usually come around 3pm," was the answer from their office. I said I would phone the teams through at half-time.

One piece of valuable practical advice I had been given was to number lined sheets of A4 paper 1 to 80, a number on each line, and then write incidents in the line in the minute they happen. Craig Wilson, editor of the Australian fanzine *Loosehead* told me that this is what the famous football commentator John Motson does. "If it's good enough for him, it's good enough for me," I thought, and it did prove to be very useful.

One problem with the Kingstonian ground is that the stand is quite small and the press box is therefore not very high off the ground. This makes it difficult at times to follow the pattern of play.

I carefully set my stop watch as the match kicked off. And then Wath Brow scored a try in the first minute! Chris Warren, the Broncos' announcer, checked with their bench who the scorer was, made his announcement and I noted it down.

The Broncos' superior class and fitness started to tell, but, to be honest, I can't recall much about the first half. All my concentration was on noting down anything interesting, keeping the penalty count and recording both sides' substitutions.

Half time arrived and I was drained. The Broncos were 30-8 ahead, although the player who had stood out was the Wath Brow number 9, Marc Jackson, who eventually won the Silk Cut Man-of-the-Match award. I phoned through the teams to *League Express* and wrote, in anticipation of a 60 or 70-point win for the Broncos, a couple of opening paragraphs of my report.

Two Broncos' tries in the first seven minutes of the second half seemed to confirm my prediction. But the Cumbrian amateurs kept tackling, scored an excellent try, and with Jackson kicking any kickable penalty, kept the score respectable.

A Mat Toshack try four minutes from time gave the Broncos a 44-18 win, nowhere near the slaughter that had been anticipated. My introduction, written at half-time, was immediately scrapped in favour of a "heroic Cumbrian amateurs fight all the way" approach.

I started working on the report and sorting out the statistics and substitutions while waiting to interview the coaches. John Monie was very affable, paid tribute to the Wath Brow performance, but, understandably, was mainly interested in his own team's performance. I got some "exclusive" quotes from Karle Hammond as well, but *League Express* did not use them in the report. Alfie Griggs, one of Wath Brow's joint coaches was delighted with his team's performance. I jotted down his words and went to finish my report. The hardest task was deciding on a Broncos' man-of-the-match. No one had really stood out, but prop forward Scott Cram seemed to make an impact with his runs, so I chose him.

I phoned the *League Express* office and was put through to the copy-taker. I explained that this was the first time I had done a match report in so short a time. Her reply, "I haven't done this for ages either," did not reassure me.

169

As I was starting to dictate the report, sitting in the cold now deserted press box, the stadium loudspeakers suddenly burst into life. It was Chris Warren, using the PA system in the bar, announcing the man-of-the-match awards. For inexplicable reasons it was now booming out to the empty stadium and drowning out my telephone call. We struggled on and after dictating my just under 500 words, I put the phone down with some relief. I went off to the bar feeling I had earned an orange juice. I left my mobile phone turned on in case Tim Butcher wanted to ring me to check anything.

I am pleased to say he didn't need to phone and *League Express* used around 95 per cent of my report. I resisted the temptation to go to Sportspages to buy a copy on Monday morning and waited patiently until my subscription copy arrived by post on Tuesday.

"Journalist for a day" was an interesting experience, but I think not a job I would want to do on a regular basis. The level of concentration and attention to detail meant that it was difficult to enjoy and appreciate the game. I spent at least 10 minutes in the second half trying to work out who Wath Brow had taken off in a double substitution because Chris Warren hadn't announced this important information. While doing that I was also busy keeping the penalty count, making notes and watching the match.

So the next time a match report in *League Express* or the *Rugby Leaguer* seems to have missed some minor detail, or does not cover the match in great subtlety, I won't be too hard on the harassed reporter. I'll stick to the more placid occupation of writing Rugby League history and occasional magazine and fanzine articles and leave match reporting at the final whistle to real journalists.

Peter Lush

Sponsoring Dominic Peters

For any Londoner older than 25, becoming a Rugby League supporter means being a convert. Unlike in the northern heartlands, where babes in arms are introduced to the game at a very young age, for Londoners before 1980, that wasn't possible. So our supporters have come to Rugby League from a variety of backgrounds.

170

Beverly Maderson, the London Broncos Supporters Club secretary's first experience of Rugby was the other code. "I watched Rugby Union years ago because my boyfriend at the time played for an old boys club. But women weren't expected to know anything about the game. It was male dominated. One of the great things I like about Rugby League is the number of women who watch the game and how easy it is to join in a discussion about it and have people listen to you."

Beverly's first live Rugby League match was the Broncos against Wigan at Brentford Football Club in 1995. "I had seen Martin Offiah play Union and had watched him in Rugby League live on television. So I wanted to see him play. Also, I had talked to some of the Asian pupils in my class at school about Ikram Butt, so I wanted to watch him. I had shown them photos of Ikram Butt to encourage them to play sport - using him as a role model. Later when I started following the Broncos I got to know him. His wife is a teacher like me. One of the things that impressed me as well about Rugby League was the number of black players involved, with no fuss, not like football. At the Brentford game I was talking to a man in a brown coat - who I later found out was club director Barry Maranta - and pointed to a poster of Martin Offiah. 'We should buy him' I said - and the next season he did. What brilliant service from the club! I also said buy Shaun Edwards and he did. But I was disappointed that he didn't sign Tawera Nikau who I think is wonderful."

Live Rugby League made an immediate impression. "I could not believe this game. I was so excited. We had seats quite high up so you could see the way Wigan built up play".

Her next outing was to Twickenham. "I went with my husband to Bath vs. Wigan. I wanted to see if Rugby Union had changed in 20 years. It hadn't! The Bath supporters were nearly all men. The Wigan supporters were men, women and children, having a laugh and a good day out. The Bath men were muttering about not bringing 'sprogs' to games. I saw the Wigan coach arrive and as the players got off Shaun Edwards said hello to a Wigan supporter he knew, greeted her by name. That impressed me. I thought 'she matters'. This is the sport for me."

At the game she met a woman from Warrington who had also brought her husband to the game. She knew more about Rugby Union than the men from Bath. I talked to her - we swapped seats at half time so I could sit next to her. And the Rugby Union guys were shaken rigid. They had expected Wigan to be slaughtered like Bath had been at League".

Beverly then started going to the Broncos matches at Charlton. "I got hooked. I remember the St Helens game. It was such a brilliant game, even though we lost. And it was all so friendly. I like how Rugby League carries on after the game finishes. After we played Bradford I remember Robbie Paul talking to [veteran Broncos' supporter] Harry Stammers for the whole evening. Also I was able to talk to players like Sonny Nickle and Steve McNamara. That's all part of the culture of Rugby League."

The last home game that season against Castleford was the first step to sponsoring a player. "We missed the last train and had to get a mini-cab back. As we were going, a young man signed my shirt. It was Dominic Peters - he had just been told he was being given a contract by the Broncos. He was so enthusiastic and I was so pleased for him. He was the first London boy we had signed." Matt Salter was already an established Rugby Union player when he joined the club. Dominic Peters was the first young player to come through the Academy system.

"So the next season I got a season ticket for The Stoop and was told I could sponsor a player. So I sponsored Dominic. I got his shirt at the end of the season and still wear it to matches. And I still sponsor him. I had a picture taken with him and I've met his parents. It's been great seeing him develop as a player. He's got bigger! And he's 'one of ours' - a Londoner playing for our club. The children at school play touch rugby and I want to take Dominic there to coach them."

Dominic Peters (Photo: Peter Lush)

Beverly then became secretary of the Supporters Club. "I think London has a reputation for being friendly to other supporters. If I see our supporters in the bar on their own I try to introduce them to people. I talk to the other team's supporters at the games and make them welcome. I commiserated with the Castleford supporters after the semi-final. I've made friends with people from lots of other clubs. We go to the Lancashire Supporters Clubs Federation Dinner every year. But there I think I offended Alex Murphy - I didn't know who he was."

She thinks that the club now have a good relationship with the Supporters Club. "The club understand more now what our role is. Tony Rea invites myself and other officers from the Supporters' Club to meetings and asks our opinions. Also, they usually have a representative at our meetings."

One of her best memories is the Wembley Cup Final. "I'd never been to Wembley. The bus trip to some of the grounds we had played at in London was great - my pupils at school made banners and flags for it. And we were up earlier than the Leeds supporters - to decorate the bus."

Beverly had her 'fifteen minutes of fame' when she was in the audience of a sports programme just before Wembley, compared by Eamon Holmes. "I had questions ready for Martin Offiah and had been told I would be asking a question. Then Eamon started asking me questions. I was trying to explain the difference between Rugby League and football. I never got to ask my question. But my pupils at school were all impressed that I was on television, although I found it a bit embarrassing.".

Rugby League is now definitely her top sport. "Every player is equally important in Rugby League, not like football or Union. And there is more scoring. And it's a sport that everyone can enjoy."

Beverly Maderson was interviewed by Peter Lush in January 2000

An Australian in London

Despite being a club that has had more than a few Australian players over the years, from the Craven Cottage years to the present day the club has attracted relatively few Australian supporters. One high profile supporter was Douglas McCllelland, the Australian High Commissioner who was club president in the late 1980s and early 1990s. However, despite the efforts of various club managements to attract them, London based Aussies have never followed the club in great numbers.

However, one Australian supporter who has stuck by the club over the years is Paul Mansfield. He says that: "At any given time there are around 100,000 Antipodeans in Europe. But remember that until recently Rugby League was the main sport in only two of the Australian states and that many of the people who travel to the UK are not Rugby League people. The other three football codes (Australian Rules, soccer and Rugby Union) are also well supported. English club Rugby League does not get a lot of exposure in Australia. The young people who come to Europe do not come here to watch Rugby League. They are more likely to spend their weekends in Amsterdam."

Paul has followed the club in its various guises since arriving in London in 1985. "I came for a three month holiday and to get engaged to a lady I had met in Australia who was from London. I'm still here." As with many of the Australians involved in the club, Paul is from Queensland. His interest in Rugby League started when he first attended matches as a five year old with his father. He comes from the Nambour district, the same district as former Australian Rugby League captain Mal Meninga. Paul first played Rugby League as an eight year old, and remembers Mal Meninga's father playing for the Maroochydore Central team at the same time that Paul was playing for their under-13 side. Paul recalls: "I was invited to play at under-18 level for Souths in Brisbane in the mid-1970s. Souths were in the Brisbane league and Ross Strudwick was playing for Brisbane Valleys in the same competition. I progressed to the reserve grade, equivalent to the Broncos' alliance side, but then my playing career was cut short by a serious car accident."

Paul then moved to Parramatta, where he became a friend of Ray Higgs, a former Nambour District player and legend at Parramatta. It was a good time to be there as Parramatta were in one of their best periods, coached first of all by the famous Jack Gibson, and then by John Monie, in his first major coaching role.

So having arrived in London, Paul first watched Fulham in September 1985 at Chiswick. "I knew [Fulham player] Don Duffy to say hello to, as he had been at Parramatta. He introduced me to the other players and to

Tim Lamb. I felt he was a very good, hardworking director and I was disappointed that he did not continue in that capacity after 1990. My friendship with Tim has lasted to this day. It was impossible not to be impressed by the efforts the hard-core of families put in voluntarily to keep the club running. The Lambs, the Closes, the Snares, the Barlows, the Bandeys, Barry and Gwen Warren all worked hard to make it succeed. I came from a small country club at Nambour District Rugby League. The same sort of people follow Rugby League everywhere. The banter was the same, it reminded me of country Rugby League in Queensland or new South Wales."

Paul gradually got more involved. "Tim encouraged me to attend training and go on away trips on the players' coach. I used to sit in on some of the club meetings in an advisory capacity. Later on, Tim would show me lists of Australian players and ask what I thought of them. I remember saying that Glenn Mansfield [no relation] had been Rookie of the Year at Parramatta and a replacement in a Grand Final. But his career hadn't developed. I thought he could do a good job for Fulham."

Paul welcomed the moves in the club at that time to base the team in the south in 1986. He knew many of the Australian players who joined the club from the Brisbane Valleys and Brisbane Brothers teams. However, he felt that changing coach mid-season was wrong and regretted Bev Risman's departure from the club in the autumn of 1988, and the short time that Phil Sullivan was given as coach in February 1989, when his temporary appointment was not extended.

Paul had not met Ross Strudwick before he arrived at Fulham in 1989. "I remember him as a high profile player and coach in Brisbane. Maybe he wanted to change the club too fast. We never gained anything from the move to Crystal Palace, although there were good training facilities there. Chiswick always had a better feel to it than Crystal Palace. Ross wanted me to help with managing the A team, but work commitments did not allow me to do it. But he is still a close friend and I stay with him when I go to Queensland."

Another coach who Paul holds in high regard and got to know well is Tony Currie, the club's coach from 1996 to 1998. "Tony had been the defensive coach at Brisbane Broncos, which means working on tackling and tackling practice. But he had an impressive playing record and Barry

Maranta knew him well. I felt his man management was very good. He was a good thinker about the game and wasn't threatened by other people's ideas. I used to help with the player match statistics for Tony, by assisting Tim Lamb and the late Bob Evans."

Another area Paul became involved in from 1994 to 1997 was helping first Glen Workman, then Dave Rotheram and finally Kevin Langer who were coaching the club's A team during that period.

One of Paul's best memories of watching the club over the years is Frank Feighan's try against Sheffield in 1986. The club had been on the verge of collapse and the supporters were relieved to see a Fulham team playing. Sheffield won the game easily, but Paul says "Frank scored a length of the field try. There was euphoria when he scored. It gave everyone a huge lift. It was a strange try and a strange situation." Frank was one of Paul's favourite players at the club, others being Glenn Mansfield, who he saw as a "big asset" and Julian O'Neill, who played a few games for the Broncos at the start of the Centenary season. "In my opinion Julian was the most gifted player we have had, with the exception of Shaun Edwards. On his day he was a real match winner. But people said he was a 'rebel without a pause' and the club let him go. Shaun Edwards and Martin Offiah have both contributed to making us a 'bigger' club. Of the current players, Karle Hammond was an exceptionally good signing" Paul recalls the match against Canberra in the World Club Challenge as a highlight, but believes that: "the concept of the World Club Challenge should have been developed further. It gave the sport a higher profile nationally. At least the top two teams from each country should play off. Such a tournament would get a lot of coverage."

When the Broncos joined the Super League, Paul struck up a close relationship with the Burgess family in Wigan. Preferring Wigan to St Helens, where he has cousins (Paul's grandmother was a St Helens lass), Paul recalls: "My Wigan friends were up in arms about the prospect of losing their hallowed Central Park. They were disillusioned with the Wigan administration and as a small protest Joan and Ronnie Burgess asked me for some Broncos posters, car stickers etc. and passed on some useful advice, which I gave to Tony Currie for game plans. Their grandson, Sean Mason, was bravely elected as mascot for the Broncos against Wigan at Central Park. Sky television's Eddie Hemmings

176

announced as the teams ran out: 'And now the London Broncos, led out by Sean Mason. He's from Wigan, but he is an ardent Broncos' supporter', much to the delight of his grandparents and a lot of other Wiganers at the time."

Paul also contributes a regular column to the *London Calling!* fanzine. "It's just an opportunity to express some personal opinions. I try to keep people up to date on former players and coaches, and to have a bit of a laugh. That's what it's all about."

Paul Mansfield was interviewed by Peter Lush in March 2000

On the line

Who would have thought that Rugby League would play such a huge part in the life of a lad born and brought up in Central London? When my dad Barry took my mum, sister and myself down to Craven Cottage on 21 December 1980 to watch Fulham beat Hunslet 15-5, I'd never heard of the game. "Come on," dad said, "it's got to be better than what Fulham F.C. are serving up at the moment." And it was. It was ten times better. We were hooked! I was six years old then and 289 games later, meticulously recorded in my logbook, I am still hooked. In April 1999 though, I moved to York to get married and start a new career. It was a move I thought I would never make, from the home of Rugby League (in my eyes) to the north, where my team is "just a bunch of second rate Aussies".

Strange then that I should now live in the city where I had one of my proudest and certainly my strangest Rugby League experience. I could probably fill a book of my own Rugby League memories from the 20 years of being an avid Fulham/London fan. From scrubbing the balls clean as a ball-boy at the Polytechnic Stadium, Chiswick, to watching long-time supporter Harry Stammers dance on a table at Workington after a 13-12 win. From scraping snow off the pitch at Crystal Palace before the Halifax cup game to buying three programmes at Bramley because the programme sellers were from a women's modelling agency. I was also one of the original "Hole in the Wall" gang of five that started *London Calling!* the London Rugby League fanzine, despite the stresses of a university degree course. All this adds up to a wonderful youth.

But it was a December day in 1993 that provided me with an unforgettable experience. In October, I had passed the British Rugby League Referees Association entrance exam, after a course with my Dad, an already qualified referee. I had been a touch judge for his games in the London Amateur Rugby League hundreds of times, but nothing prepared me for what I was going to be asked to do on 12 December 1993.

It was the Regal Trophy Fourth Round and London Crusaders had been drawn away to York. I had just started at university and I dragged Mark, a friend of mine, who had expressed nothing but a mere interest in Rugby League, down to Victoria Station for 8.15am to get on the supporter's coach. "It'll be a great excuse for a good days drinking" he said. I couldn't agree more. It was bright, sunny and freezing cold, a lovely day for Rugby League but, as the beer flowed, the clouds gathered. By the time we reached Leicester it had started to sleet. "Not to worry, they never get snow in York, it's in a vale," I calmly stated. But then what does a bloke from the south know! By the time we reached the York ring road and went round it a couple of times looking for the exit, there was thick snow everywhere. "Now we're in trouble", I said. 200 miles only for it to be called off we thought. "There's always a visit to the Minster" remarked Crusaders fan Alex Ferguson. "They don't serve beer there," came a comical reply from the front of the coach.

Once we were tucked safely in the warm, cosy bar of Ryedale Stadium, looking out over a snow-covered pitch, Rugby League became a distant memory. The beer continued to flow and by 2.00pm, I was half cut. Just when I was resigned to a day of continued drinking, Crusaders club secretary Neil Robinson walks into the bar and said to Gwen Warren, "Paul's passed his referees exam, hasn't he?" This sounded ominous. Then Neil walks up to me and said, "Fancy running a line today mate?" In this weather? He had to be joking. "David Campbell is stuck in Leeds because of the snow and is going to be late. His two touch judges are in the car with him. We need officials to start the game" Neil added. Well I thought, I can't let the Crusaders down now! David Asquith, a professional grade referee, had arrived to watch the game and agreed to referee it. Stuart Evans from York was the intended fourth official and was to be in charge of a line. Yours truly was selected from a panel of one to be the second touch judge, much to the joy of my mate Mark and the other 40 or so

Crusaders fans. So off I went, escorted to the dressing rooms, where Mr Asquith, who had been on the receiving end of many of my tirades over the years, was seated. I was warmly welcomed and introduced to Stuart Evans. Thankfully they were both well prepared and hastily put together a set of kit for me. I might add that it included a set of woolly gloves.

Another pitch inspection was made, followed by David Asquith banging furiously on the two dressing room doors. "Get your boys out there Sammy [Stewart]!" he shouted. And thus, 20 minutes later, I found myself standing in the tunnel looking out into the gloom with thick snow driving down leaving inches of it on the pitch, and I was about to run out behind my heroes. It was then that we got word that referee and touch judges were still in Leeds and heading back to Widnes. I was going to do the whole game!

I have never been so cold in all my life. At the centre circle and I was doing anything to keep warm. Bending, stretching, running on the spot in front of around 750 people. We shook hands with the skippers, tossed the coin and then I found myself at the London dead ball line ready for kick-off, nervous as anything. However, the ice was broken (excuse the pun) when as I prepared for the start Abi Ekoku standing less than five yards away turned to me, looked away and then immediately looked back and said: "what the hell are you doing here?" I then realised that I'd spent far too much time in Barnet Copthall's bar after matches.

The game started bang on time in front of 741 hardy souls. Crusaders got off to a flyer and scored a couple of early tries. Good stuff I thought, but while remaining neutral of course. Just minutes later, quick hands saw Ekoku flying down the wing. Where's the touchline I thought, and I tried to make out a faint line in the snow, marked by my own boot marks. Up went my flag, he had to be yards in touch and a couple of "you've got to be kidding mate" remarks went up. Oh well, we were 12-0 up.

It didn't matter. Crusaders cruised it 42-10, amazing when you consider that several players including South African Mark Johnson had never even seen snow let alone played in it. I had to run the gauntlet of several songs and chants aimed at me by my very own friends, such as, "I've seen more meat on a chicken's legs," and "Where's Paul gone, he's probably hidden behind the corner flag," in reference to my slim build.

It was a great experience. I soon forgot the cold and enjoyed being a part of a professional Rugby League game. I learnt a lot on that day, including appreciating the difficulties of officiating a game of such speed and intensity. At half-time both David and Stuart remarked how London's game plan was to use dummy runners to the point of almost obstructing the defence, and that we should all be aware of it. The slightest hint of an obstruction would be penalised, said David. Never, I thought to myself, but didn't make a comment. You learn a lot when you're in that situation and I will never forget it.

The journey home was a great one. The beer flowed again, I could bask in the limelight and I couldn't wait to get home and tell Dad all about it. At the same time though I was disappointed for Dad. He'd travelled hundreds of miles over the years refereeing at places like Milton Keynes, Bexleyheath, Streatham Celtic and Peckham Pumas. It should have been him out there enjoying officiating a professional game involving London. But between all us Taylors we've got some fantastic memories and long may London Rugby League continue.

So from now on I'll support London from York, the scene of a treasured Rugby League memory, and support them just as avidly. When London went up the Wembley steps, my sister Clare burst into tears. "It's not fair, I wanted us to win so badly," she exclaimed. I turned to her, put my arm around her and said: "We were there at Fulham, at Chiswick, at Charlton, at Crystal Palace and we were there at Barnet. Clare we've come a long way and it's all been worth it. You should be proud of them. Enjoy." And she smiled.

Paul Taylor

Bus trip to Wembley

One unique event linked to the Broncos' 1999 Rugby League Challenge Cup Final appearance at Wembley was a bus trip to the game organised by the Supporters' Club. The trip was unique because it visited some of the club's past homes on the way to Wembley's twin towers and no other club's supporters had ever done such a trip before.

The club has played at so many grounds in London that not all of them could be included in the trip. It was decided that The Valley in south east

London and Copthall Stadium in north London were too far to travel if the group were to arrive in time for kick-off at Wembley.

The original idea for the trip came from former Supporters' Club treasurer Gwen Warren and was taken up enthusiastically by other supporters. The first problem was finding an open-top bus to hire for the day. Not many companies these days have them for hire. Other problems arose: one company thought that the Supporters' Club was part of the Virgin business empire and wanted £2,000 for the day. Finally, a bus was found at a suitable price and the trip was on.

The next task was decorating the bus. Supporters' Club travel organiser Sylvia Waite recalls: "everyone blowing up balloons by the score" for this special trip and finding handbells, rattles and whistles to make a noise. A silver cup was proudly fixed on to the front of the bus.

One of the ironies of the day, typical of the diverse nature of London Rugby League's supporters is that Sylvia and her husband, Supporters' Club chairman Michael, were raised in Leeds and their first experience of Rugby League was as supporters of the Headingley based club.

One worry for a travel organiser is the bus turning up on time - especially on Cup Final day. Sylvia remembers "waiting at Victoria coach station for the bus to turn up. I had to ring the company on my mobile phone to see where it was."

It arrived and the supporters set off for the club's first - and much loved - home, Fulham Football Club's Craven Cottage, where Fulham Rugby League Club was born in 1980. Historic photos were taken, but the supporters had become thirsty and it had been agreed to stop at The Golden Lion pub, a regular supporters' meeting place in the club's Craven Cottage days. Sylvia recalls that: "When we were on the bus we suddenly realised that we did not know if the pub would be open. So the mobile phone came to the rescue again, with an urgent call to directory enquiries for the number and then a call to the landlord, who opened up specially for us, and made 30 thirsty Rugby League supporters welcome. On the way to the pub we saw Gwen's mum who lives in Fulham and was waiting for us to pass by."

From Craven Cottage, the bus headed off to The Stoop, passing the Polytechnic Stadium at Chiswick on the way, the club's home from 1985

Bus trip to Wembley (Photo: Barry & Gwen Warren)

to 1990. Michael and Sylvia remember: "We waved at Chiswick and then battled through the traffic to The Stoop. The players' coach was leaving just as we arrived. We gave them a cheer - that was quite emotional, seeing them leave for Wembley." More supporters were collected at The Stoop and the bus then headed for Wembley. "People waved as we went by, even if they were not quite sure who we were. We had lunch on the bus. Then we got to Wembley." Michael recalls: "Coming up to Wembley was scary and exciting. Sylvia and I were born and raised in Leeds and now our team were playing Leeds in the Challenge Cup Final. It was indescribable. But there were no divided loyalties - we wanted London to win. People waved as we drove up to the stadium. Before we got there we saw the Leeds supporters outside the pubs around Wembley." Sadly, the match did not go the Broncos' way and Sylvia remembers: "it was very quiet on the way back to Victoria."

The Supporters' Club had attempted to use the trip to help publicise the club's first Challenge Cup Final appearance. Michael remembers: "We were on Talk Radio with a Leeds supporter, before we set off. They heard down the phone the noise our supporters were making." A dozen supporters were also in the audience on ITV's *Sports Show* a couple of days before the final, when Martin Offiah was on the panel. Michael and

Sylvia recall: "We met in a pub and decided what we wanted to say. But unfortunately the discussion on the programme got onto winter or summer Rugby League. A good chance to publicise the club was not fully used."

Michael's first memory of Rugby League is watching Leeds in 1947, taken to the game by his father who had followed the club since the 1920s. He remembers the frustration of working on Saturdays in his father's shop at the age of 14 and being able to hear the cheers from the matches. He started taking Sylvia to matches when they met and she continued to follow Leeds when Michael went away to university in Edinburgh in 1962, going to matches with Michael's sister. Sylvia recalls: "We went to away matches sometimes, on Wallace Arnold coaches. It cost four shillings and sixpence. (That's 22 pence in today's money.)"

In 1966, they moved to York and went to matches there. They remember: "We took our daughter Caroline to York matches when she was a baby." Caroline is now one of the organisers of the Junior Broncos. But then they moved again and lost touch with Rugby League. "From 1970 to 1991 we were living in the Midlands or in Essex - Rugby League wastelands. We would go to Headingley on Boxing Day if we were in Leeds for Christmas. We didn't even realise there was a London team until we drove past a sign for the club."

Their first game in London was the Crusaders against Featherstone in the Challenge Cup in 1994. Michael remembers: "Sylvia decided to take me to the match as a birthday treat." Sylvia rang the club to find out the match details: "I spoke to Neil Robinson. He was so friendly on the phone. I wanted to know the kick-off time. He was almost saying 'what time can you come?'."

That was a good time to start supporting the club. "We didn't go to away games at first. But then we joined the Supporters' Club, went to a presentation night at the end of the season and got to know people. The trip to Paris in 1996 was very good. It's a great shame they are no longer in Super League." Michael became vice-chair of the supporters' club in 1997. "I expected to be in the background. I helped draft a new constitution for the supporters' club." But the next year most of the long-serving committee members resigned and Michael found himself elected as chair. "I originally saw it as keeping the seat warm for someone with more time and ideas. But I have just been elected [February 2000] to serve for another year." At the same time as Michael became chair, Sylvia took on the onerous task of organising the Supporters' Club away travel. "I book the buses, organise tickets for some games, phone people if the pick up times change and keep lists of people who are coming with us. For a big game, such as the Challenge Cup semi-final, I liaise with the police about parking and other arrangements."

Despite their Leeds origins, they are now very committed to the Broncos and enjoy their involvement with the club and the Supporters' Club. A few years ago they went back to their native Yorkshire to watch the Broncos at Doncaster. Sylvia remembers being called a "cockney git" by one of the home supporters. Her response is not recorded!

Michael and Sylvia Waite were interviewed by Peter Lush in February 2000

Thank You, London Broncos

My introduction to Rugby League was during a home-based honeymoon in Hull in September, 1960. The marriage lasted some ten years; my love affair with Rugby League is lifelong. In 1979, financial circumstances forced me to move to Banbury, in Oxfordshire, leaving the city I shall always think of as home, even though I was born and bred in Warwickshire.

In Banbury, all games on TV were watched avidly but, with no Rugby League papers available and no-one else I knew who was into the game, I felt rather cut off from the world of Rugby League. I took the *Today* newspaper, because of their support of London Crusaders and sometimes wondered how and if I would ever get to see them. However, as a single mother of three and also looking after guide dog puppies who couldn't be left, any hope of a visit remained a dream. Wigan became my TV team, not just because they were on TV often, but because I liked their style.

When I broke my leg, I plucked up the courage to write to the Wigan club. They sent a signed photo and also let me know that the *Rugby Leaguer* was still in print, so I ordered it from a local newsagents and felt less isolated. My younger daughter, Maggie, who lives in Bristol, was engaged to an ex-Bath Rugby Union player at the time and said they were going to the cross-code match at Twickenham in May 1996. A fair bit of wheedling got me an invitation to tag along. It brought home to me how very much I missed the colour and excitement of real matches. My enthusiasm encouraged Maggie to arrange for us to see the Broncos play Wigan at the Valley, where I had the extra thrill of sitting in front of one of my all-time favourite players, Joe Lydon. Eddie and Stevo from SKY television also said hello.

Little Leo Dynevor made an impression darting about, but Tony Martin had a real off day. It's good to see him doing so well now in Australia. The bonus was seeing Maggie - it was easier for us to meet in London than for me to go to Bristol. She enjoyed matches too, but couldn't spare the time to go often.

Maggie had lived in Richmond in west London for a while and when the Broncos moved to Twickenham, thought she knew how to travel to The Stoop. However, the match against Castleford in 1997 there was the only time I've ever been late for a game and the only time I've arrived in a taxi! Going home, we walked for miles on a red-lined road, with no buses in sight. It nearly finished me and my newly mended, but crooked, leg.

I was really hooked on live games again and had seen for myself that Rugby League grounds were friendly and safe so started to attend matches on my own. Having read about football horrors, I'd no idea if Rugby League was in the same predicament or not.

Unfortunately, 1998 wasn't a good year for travel by rail from Banbury, because track work meant journeys were partly by bus. As I get travel sick on buses but still went to games, you can tell how much I love Rugby League. Journeys took longer, too, and evening matches weren't possible. My children did "allow" me to go and see the Broncos' evening match versus Wigan, but I had to promise to leave at half time, alas. Half a match is better than none.

In 1999 Chiltern trains had a normal timetable from spring, so I risked some evening matches, arriving home once at 1.30am. It still meant a minimum three-hour journey each way from Banbury. I'm proud of attending 13 Broncos matches that year, plus Wembley. There are those in my family who think I should be sitting safely and sedately at home, doing my cross- stitch sewing and nursing one of the six cats, because I have emphysema, total deafness and more, but even they have to admit the excitement of going to Broncos' matches seems good medicine.

An elderly, lone female in a Wigan shirt isn't the average Broncos supporter, I know. I can't yet call myself a Broncos "fan", as old loyalties to Hull Kingston Rovers and Wigan are strong and new loyalties can't be forced. However, I have strong support for the Broncos' survival as a successful team: it's in my own interests for them to do so and I'm 100 per cent grateful to the club for giving me the opportunity to see live Rugby League. How else could I have seen my Australian team, Cronulla, actually there in front of me, or the emotional 'reunion' with my beloved Hull KR, after 30 years, at the 1998 Challenge Cup tie?

I wish more Rugby League exiles in the south, or even the midlands, would come and enjoy Broncos matches, not just when their own team plays. I've always felt welcome and at home at the Broncos, even wearing the Wigan shirt and with the communication problems because I'm deaf. I've just ordered a season ticket for the first time and found myself telling my other daughter, Cathy, that "we" had signed two Wigan players, so I'm becoming more of a 'Londoner' than I was. I've had some great days out in London before evening matches, too. At first, I attended just to see Rugby League and support the clubs I'd seen in the 1960s. Now I find that I enjoy the whole match day atmosphere and experience. Thank you London Broncos.

Beth Williams

Towers of London

I have split loyalties in Rugby League, Loyalty to the club I learnt the game through watching and loyalty to my hometown team. The two are respectively Wigan and London Broncos, Crusaders, Fulham; call them what you will. I was born in Beckenham, a good 40/20 kick away from Crystal Palace and lived in the Rugby League desert of the south-east until work commitments sent me north to Wigan. It was there that I discovered the game in the flesh. Previously, I had only seen the game on TV and it was only through watching it live that the toughness, honesty and passion of the sport shone through. I adopted Wigan as my team.

186

This decision coincided with the mid-eighties when the club were on the brink of unprecedented glories. I have followed them ever since. But these words are about the London club, my hometown heroes, and my memories of their meetings with my adopted heroes.

The bare facts are that the teams have clashed on 21 occasions since that historic day at Craven Cottage in September 1980. The northerners have taken the spoils on 16 occasions, London on four. There was one famous (or infamous depending upon your perspective) draw, but I'll come to that later.

In the years before 1985, meetings were frequent as London, in their first incarnation as Fulham, yo-yoed between the First and Second Divisions. League honours were shared in 1980-81 and 1983-84 while Fulham's Lancashire Cup win in 1982 has been their sole knockout triumph. My first sight of them was in 1985 in a Lancashire Cup tie at Central Park. I remember little of the game apart from a try on his Wigan debut by Gary Henley-Smith, which was pictured in the next match programme. I don't know why that memory above all others should stand out, but it does. Henley-Smith went on to become one of the dozen or so players to play both for Wigan and in the capital when he moved south just three months later.

In the latter half of the decade, Fulham took up residence in the Second Division and the only chance of them meeting Wigan was due to the vagaries of the cup draw. The more confined geographical nature of the Lancashire Cup in which Fulham competed meant that meetings in that competition were more likely. That said, it was four years until the next encounter at Hendon in 1989. I was back south convalescing from an accident at the time and saw brief pictures of the game on local TV, which goes some way to showing what a big event the game was.

The club had a new name and a new home when I next saw them. The London Crusaders were now based at the Crystal Palace National Sports Centre. I was able to get a seat in the cavernous bowl of the stadium and dragged a couple of friends from their home in Dulwich to see the game. Had I not done so, they would not have known that the match was taking place despite living a mere 10 minutes' walk away from the ground. With 1,890 others, we saw the *Today* sponsored Crusaders go down by 38-10 to a Wigan side on its way to a semi-final defeat at the hands of St Helens in the penultimate Lancashire County Cup.

In 1993-94, the Crusaders finished third in the league a point behind Doncaster. They were able to put the disappointment of being denied promotion by the width of a goalpost (John Gallagher's attempt bouncing away in the drawn game against Workington) behind them to battle through to their first major final. At Old Trafford London were to meet Workington, another of the League's outpost clubs, in the Divisional Premiership Final. I went along to watch Crusaders' Kiwi scrum-half Mark Riley (who was having an outstanding season) and Wigan Academy hooker Phil Cantillon who was playing in the curtain raiser. By a twist of fate, both were injured very early on in their respective games. South African winger Mark Johnson's three tries were not enough to win the game for the Crusaders but they enabled him to finish top try scorer for the season in the game with 43 touchdowns.

By 1994, the club was on its knees financially. Fortunately, help was at hand. The knight in shining armour riding to their rescue to save Rugby League in the capital wore the maroon and gold of the Brisbane Broncos. And they did not bring just a financial lifeline; but also a new name. The London Broncos ended the 1994-95 season in fourth place but were elevated to the Centenary Championship and Super League in the great upheaval of April 1995. This season also saw the club wear a dark maroon jersey with gold, white and red stripes, probably my personal favourite of all their strips.

Now meetings with Wigan would be more frequent. A new home at Charlton's reclaimed and refurbished Valley ground saw London host top-flight football for the first time in over 10 years in the centenary season. However, the Broncos played just four of their 12 home games at their new home. Matches were spread as far apart as Brentford, Barnet Copthall and Harlequins' Stoop Memorial Ground in the shadow of Twickenham Rugby Union stadium. Wigan scored an easy league double in the Centenary season of 1995-96 as London prepared for the serious stuff of Super League. The home match was staged at Brentford and saw Martin Offiah (then a Wigan player) score his 400th career try.

At Central Park in 1996, the Broncos secured the draw that would ultimately end Wigan's run as champions and hand the inaugural Super League title to their bitter rivals, St Helens. On a dull June Sunday, Terry

Matterson's conversion of a try by Graham Strutton tied the scores at 18-all. There were cries of "cheat" over the Broncos' delaying tactics but realistically, the champions were not good enough to overcome them and their crown began to slip. While feeling disappointment at the lost point, I also felt that the Broncos had arrived. The draw effectively cost Wigan the inaugural Super League title - and we knew it at the time. The rain fell and Wigan's domination of the game was over.

The Broncos' first hurrah was in 1997. They finished second to the runaway Bradford Bulls in a season that set them up as creditable title challengers. Wins over Canberra and the Bulls at their new home at The Stoop were topped off with a comprehensive 38-12 win over the newly named Wigan Warriors who were not enjoying a vintage season under Eric Hughes. Shaun Edwards and Martin Offiah put one over their old team-mates that day with a try apiece in the slaughter.

In the semi-final the following year, the clubs met for the first time in the Challenge Cup. The Broncos' Wembley hopes were put on hold for 12 months after a crushing 38-8 defeat at Huddersfield. It was this game and the following year's semi-final against Castleford that showed the RFL seemed unwilling or unable to give the Broncos a fair crack of the whip. A more suitable neutral venue would surely have been Northampton, or perhaps in 1999, Central Park or a Midlands alternative would have been a more logical choice rather than Headingley. Still, in the second match, the Broncos battled through to the last "old Wembley" final in a thrilling game. But there the dream died. An hour's competitiveness was blown away by the Leeds Rhinos' power in the last 20 minutes. I have been fortunate enough to see the Broncos in two major finals (and Wigan in 26). Still the abiding memory is of Terry Matterson's sideline conversion to take a point and the 1996 Super League title from Wigan. Can you hate your hometown team for that? London have been linked with Wigan since that historic first game 20 years ago at Craven Cottage. Then, 9,554 fans and curious onlookers embarked on a journey that was to take the Londoners to Old Trafford and Wembley, to Brisbane, Sydney and Canberra by way of Chiswick, Hendon, Brentford and Charlton all in the name of Rugby League. It has been some journey.

Chris Wilson

London Broncos and the "global vision"

I've never really understood the north/south divide. I understand that there is something intrinsically northern about Doncaster or Hull or Warrington, but I can't work out why that causes division. And I don't understand why that means good players won't come down to play for the Broncos.

I'm writing this in December 1999 in a hotel in Helsinki on a Japanese laptop I bought in Sydney. I was working in Sydney for a company based in Chicago for whom I wrote about European football. I was in Finland for a few days on my way back to live in England after five years in Australia. I'd come via Tokyo and Kyoto. As I get older it seems that most of my friends are also working in this bizarre way; it would have been impossible to imagine this scenario even five years ago.

Sydney being a Rugby League city it was easy enough to follow the exploits of the London Broncos in the papers. In fact there is probably more about them in the *Sydney Morning Herald* than there is in the *Evening Standard*.

Now that I'm back I find myself searching the margins for League news in a way I never did in Newtown, New South Wales, where the newspapers, let alone television and radio, give sport and world news equal space.

I am neither southerner nor northerner. I was born in the Midlands. My dad is from York, and my mother from Portsmouth. I've lived my adult life in London, so maybe now I'm a Londoner, like many immigrants before me. I would rather, for instance, be stuck in the Groucho club with Blur, than suffer Liam and Noel at the Dry Bar. I'd rather share a bottle of Merrydown with Martin Offiah than Shaun Edwards (who probably doesn't drink anyway). Mind you I never miss *Coronation Street*.

Until the centenary season, when I started to attend matches on a regular basis, I rarely got to see Fulham/Crusaders/Broncos play. I was working at weekends, or spending time with girlfriends, or watching Leyton Orient play football.

I think I arrived at the same sort of time as Australian scrum-half Leo Dynevor, my all time favourite Bronco, and the man that cemented my relationship with the club. Perhaps I had thought there was no place for me in this masculine northern world. Somehow, Leo, cunning and innovative, raised in an Aboriginal mission north-west of Brisbane, made me feel that there was a place in League for all of us: that the game could be both cosmo- and metro-politan.

I later followed Leo to Sydney, where, alongside former Bronco Evan Cochrane, he played his best football. In Newcastle's Premiership winning season he neatly eclipsed Andrew and Matthew Johns, probably the best halfback pairing of the current era. I also saw him play his worst football, admittedly in a Western Suburbs side rather short of ideas.

While in Sydney I saw probably the best London Broncos side of their second decade. On a cold Canterbury night (their ground Belmore has all the warmth, welcome and bonhomie of Hull's Boulevard), I watched the Broncos take it to the Bulldogs and lose, but not by much.

The night was memorable for realising quite how English I was. Living in Australia for several years I'd started to wonder if I was English at all. Although I was one of only four or five "Londoners" in the stadium, and being a republican I refused to sing the national anthem, I was somehow spotted by the repellent and spotty youths on the Terry Lamb Hill. They moved closer. I moved further away. The words "Pommy bastard" were aimed in my direction, ironically by Lebanese Australians who probably had to put up with comments on their ethnicity every day of their lives. I wasn't much comforted by the thought. If anything it made me feel worse.

One end of Belmore is a rather northern looking shed which serves to keep the rain off and looks rather like a bus stop, albeit a large one. As two or three cops were standing there drinking coffee out of paper cups and laughing at Martin Offiah, I went and stood near them. I stayed there for the rest of the game, and even managed to make supportive noises when the Broncos did something half-useful. The Clearasil-free zone edged closer, and I angled towards the exit, using the cops as a shield. This went on for most of the first half, and during the second I sneaked into the main stand and sat behind a large Union flag with Fulham RLFC written across the middle. It made me feel more secure. I left before the end. I didn't want to be stuck at Belmore station with the Lakemba phalange breathing down my neck.

The year before I'd been in Paris for another Broncos' defeat. Having a friend who lived in the city, we'd arranged for free accommodation (a square of bedsit floor) and tickets. Fans travelling from London had to pay

for their entry, but the Super League authorities were so desperate for PSG to work that they gave free tickets to any French fan who had booked in advance. Charlety Stadium, especially when only a third full, is a very different experience to Belmore. The wide-open spaces, and the running track make it feel a bit removed. There was plenty of noise from the faithful and the newly converted, and a Paris win in the last few minutes made them even more verbose. But still the feeling was that nobody was ever going to get truly passionate about a team of average Australians. God knows it took us long enough.

It was Bastille Day, and we went dancing. In France, on this national holiday, the fire stations open up for dancing, and serve warm cheap red wine to teenagers, sailors on shore leave being pursued by "models", and depressed Rugby League fans. We danced for a few hours, watched the fireworks over the Eiffel Tower and then walked home through the little side streets. I thought for a moment that maybe the world-wide Super League vision might work after all. But it was only for an evening.

At the game I'd had to explain to our French hosts that there are two types of rugby. Over the years I've explained this to friends in California, Melbourne and London; always adding that ours is the better code. The passion for the game I have seen in Sydney, in the north of England, at Carpentras in France, was really not transferable. Except in London. The fact that Fulham survived, and evolved into the Broncos is testament to extraordinary courage and commitment. Will the Melbourne Storm be around in 20 years? But at least we not joined the likes of Gateshead, Perth, Hunter Mariners, or Paris St Germain. If there's any "global-vision" left in Super League, it's in London.

Craig Wilson

Harry Stammers is one of London's best known supporters.
Top: With friends from Swinton at the Divisional Premiership final
at Old Trafford in 1994.
Bottom: In action at The Stoop
(Both photos: Barry & Gwen Warren)

Broncos player Bernie "Tiger" Carroll with an admiring Gwen Warren
(Photo: Barry & Gwen Warren)

Cold day up north. Barry Warren is in the centre
(Photo: Barry & Gwen Warren)

5. The Key Matches

London Broncos 38 Canberra Raiders 18 - a famous victory
(Photo: David Stevens)

Fulham 24 Wigan 5
Second Division
14 September 1980 at Craven Cottage

It has now passed into Rugby League history, an event so cataclysmic for the sport that judging by the London and national press reaction at the time the millennium had come 20 years early.

It now seems that it was all predestined, but it was not so. The Wigan side of that day had beaten Widnes, the First Division runners-up, the previous Wednesday in the Lancashire Cup and were red-hot favourites to win the Second Division. Also, the Fulham side had never played together and winger Adrian Cambriani had never even played the sport!

On the other hand the hullabaloo around the game certainly helped to knock Wigan off their game and lifted the new Fulham team. The crowd was boosted by free tickets to Fulham FC season ticket holders and hordes of free tickets given to schoolchildren. But it was the press response that knocked everyone sideways. Reporters seemed to fall into three categories: the supporters, the knockers and those who just didn't know what to make of it. The match was even covered by the BBC's football programme *Match of the Day*. To help new fans understand the game a commentary was given during the game by Keith Macklin. Before the game guest of honour Labour politician Lord Peart met the players, while musical accompaniment was the London Girl Irish pipers.

Fulham versus Wigan - the first match (Photo: Tim Wood)

The novice crowd soon warmed to the action, but were confused by an early disqualified try and subsequent penalty into chanting "5-0". In those days a try was only worth three points. But they were soon into the swing of things cheering as Ian van Bellen made his characteristic charges straight at the opposition. With Tony Karalius dominating the scrums, the Londoners were well on top and good work by Mal Aspey saw Cambriani score at the corner.

A good kick in first-half injury time by Iain MacCorquodale saw Cambriani snatch a second try, although player-coach Reg Bowden looked decidedly offside, and Fulham had a 10-0 half-time lead.

The second half was more of the same with substitute Neil Tuffs scoring in the 61st and 65th minutes as Fulham ran riot. David Allen scored the fifth try in the 70th minute and not to be outdone David Eckersley scored a drop goal at his third attempt. Although Wigan scored a last minute try by Bernard Coyle, it was to be the Londoners' day. For the record Karalius won the scrums 16-8 and Wigan won the penalties 15-8. Fulham left to a standing ovation and a lap of honour around the pitch. For once in sport the game had matched the pre-match hype. It was a small miracle as the side had only been put together in six weeks for a figure of some £165,000. But the gamble succeeded and the London press was all over the club. Admittedly the crowd was boosted by the curious and the freebies but, as the attendances that season were to show, it was no fluke for the club. The atmosphere and élan of this day was to provide the impetus for Fulham to scale the heights in Rugby League and to provide a lasting memory for all who were lucky to be there.

Fulham: Risman, Cambriani, Aspey, Noonan, MacCorquodale, Eckersley, Bowden, van Bellen, Karalius, Lester, Gourley, Allen, Hull. Subs: Wood, Tuffs. Tries: Cambriani (2), Tuffs (2), Allen. Goals: MacCorquodale (4). Drop goal: Eckersley.

Wigan: Fairbairn, Ramsdale, Willicombe, Davies, Hornby, Coyle, Flowers, Townend, Pendlebury, Smith, Clough, Hollingsworth, Boyd. Subs: Bolton, Melling.
Try: Coyle. Goal: Fairbairn.

Dave Farrar

Fulham 5 Wakefield Trinity 9
Challenge Cup Round 1
15 February 1981 at Craven Cottage

15,013. Even if you take into consideration the 6,000 who came from Yorkshire, this was (and still is) the best home gate for a London club this side of the 1930s. But another way to look at it was that it was a great missed opportunity, an opportunity arguably not grasped until 18 years later the Broncos saw off Castleford in 1999 to reach Wembley.

This was the high point of the Fulham period. Fulham were a Second Division outfit, tense and hopeful against one of the First Division giants of the game in the latter days of their pomp. Three of the Fulham players had been in the Widnes team that had beaten Wakefield in the 1979 Cup Final. The Rugby League Challenge Cup has great presence, and this tie had all the ingredients for an upset, but sadly it was not to be and all that was left was a memory of a momentous occasion.

The first half was keen but the First Division visitors settled earliest and it was Allan Agar who dropped a goal to give Trinity confidence followed by a try from winger Keith Smith saw the Yorkshire side 4-0 ahead at half time. Early in the second half Fulham went close with efforts from half-back Eckersley and full-back Chris Ganley, but Fulham's hearts were broken when a Mal Aspey pass was intercepted for Agar to set up the international David Topliss, who interchanged with Steve Diamond to put winger Andrew Fletcher in at the corner. Fulham had a mountain to climb, but got back into the game late on with a well worked move that saw Chris Eckersley put loose forward David Hull over and Iain MacCorquodale converted. The home crowd roared the Cottagers on in the last period and Fulham responded by battering the visitors' line, but could not beat the clock. Reg Bowden wrote that: "A club in its first season had given one of the best teams in the country the fright of its life".

Because Fulham had set themselves the target of promotion in the first season this was not seen as a major set-back. However, looking back, it was at least Fulham's high point in terms of attendance and who knows what impact a win and a cup run would have had on the those Londoners in the packed terraces who were still becoming acquainted with the game in that inaugural season.

Fulham: Ganley, Cambriani, Aspey, Noonan, MacCorquodale, Eckersley, Bowden, Beverley, Karalius, van Bellen, Gourley, Allen, Hull. Subs: Risman, Wood.
Try: Hull. Goal: MacCorquodale.

Wakefield Trinity: Box, Fletcher, Day, Smith, Juliff, Topliss, Agar, Murray, McCurrie, Bratt, Thompson, Rayne, Lampkowski. Subs: Diamond, Kelly.
Tries: Smith, Fletcher. Goal: Diamond. Drop goal: Agar.

Dave Farrar

Fulham 5 Australia 22
Tour match
14 November 1982 at Craven Cottage

Second Division Fulham versus the "Invincibles", described as "world beaters" in one match preview and widely considered to be the greatest Rugby team of either code to play the sport. It was not as one sided as the Fulham faithful feared, because on paper for a side that had only conceded four tries prior to the match on an unbeaten tour, would surely rout Second Division opposition.

Fulham had done everything they could to promote the match, going as far as advertising on television, surely another London first. There was even a voucher promotion in the *Evening Standard,* where participants got a free can of beer! As it was the weather was both wet and cold and the expected 15,000 crowd shrunk to 10,432. However, this was still a decent turnout in a season when the next best would be half that.

The Australian side was resplendent with such names as Steve Ella, Gene Miles, Wally Lewis, Steve Mortimer and Les Boyd was never going to roll over on a glue pot pitch. The Londoners briefly led their illustrious opponents when Steve Diamond kicked a third minute penalty. And Fulham were only six points behind at half time, despite losing loose forward Joe Doherty with a badly gashed leg after 30 minutes. However, Reg Bowden's pre-match prediction that Fulham could win was proved over-optimistic.

The house was brought down in the 63rd minute when a Diamond kick was chased by Hussain M'Barki. Australian full-back Ella's dive on the ball was botched and the Fulham winger became only the fifth man to score against the 1982 tourists. After that the Aussies cut loose and ended up with 22 points, including a try by John Ribot who would later play a big role in the Broncos' takeover and the Super League set-up in the 1990s. Fulham supporters were happy that the team had done better than most of the northern outfits and more important had earned the Aussies' respect and helped put Fulham on the Rugby League world map.

Fulham: Eckersley, Cambriani, Allen, Diamond, M'Barki, Crossley, Bowden, Beverley, Dalgreen, Gourley, Herdman, Souto, Doherty. Subs: Tuffs, Lester
Try: M'Barki. Goal: Diamond

Australia: Ella, Anderson, Miles, Lewis, Ribot, Murray, Mortimer, McKinnon, Brown, Boyd, McCabe, Muggleton. Subs: Conescu, Kenny.
Tries: Murray, Ella, McCabe, Muggleton, McKinnon, Ribot. Goals: Lewis, Ella.

Dave Farrar

Fulham versus Australia (Photo: Barry Taylor)

Huddersfield 14 Fulham 8
Second Division
16 March 1986 at Fartown

This was the match that should never have happened. Club owners Roy and Barbara Close had decided that they could no longer sustain losses of £2,500 a week and had announced that Fulham RLFC was to close. While sponsor Richard Lawton and club secretary John Rathbone were trying to find backers to keep the club alive, the players and manager Roy Lester decided to play this match for free to keep Fulham going and buy time for the club to be saved.

Londoner Frank Feighan's comment that he would "walk up the M1 to play Huddersfield if I had to" exemplified the spirit at the time. Sadly Australian scrum-half Mike Davis refused to play and soon left the club to join Leigh. But on-loan Warrington prop Mal Yates did play - his only game for the club.

The *Rugby Leaguer's* front page headline for Huw Richards's story on the crisis summed up the prevailing mood: "For the Love of Fulham".

Despite renaming their Fartown ground "Arena 84" and adopting the nickname "The Barracudas", Huddersfield were in the doldrums at this time. Only 406 people came to what was believed to be Fulham's last stand. The players arrived, as Huw Richards recalled, in a "battered black minibus". Supporters cheered team manager Roy Lester as he walked into the bar. Former Craven Cottage hero Ian van Bellen, who lived in Huddersfield and made his name with the Fartowners, joined the Fulham supporters who had idolised him in the club's historic first season.

The *Huddersfield* BARRACUDAS
Rugby League Football Club
on ARENA'84 Huddersfield HD2 2SD

Sunday, 16th March, 1986 at 3-30 p.m.
Versus
Fulham

Slalom Lager
RUGBY LEAGUE
SECOND DIVISION
CHAMPIONSHIP

MATCH
PROGRAMME
20p

Season 1985/6

An unfamiliar looking team played in the Huddersfield mud, with Don Duffy at full-back and Adrian Cambriani in the second-row. Fulham's only try came from Frank Feighan and Chris Wilkinson kicked a couple of goals. Around 150 Fulham supporters had been at what most believed was the end of nearly six years of professional Rugby League in London. After the collapse of development area teams in South Wales and Southend, Fulham failing to finish the season would have been a devastating blow to Rugby League's hopes of ever building outside the sport's heartlands.

Attempts to stage the following week's home game, against Hunslet collapsed. But then Paul Faires, former Chairman of Kent Invicta, bought the Closes' shares and the show was on the road again. New ideas came in, with half-time entertainment from fire-eaters and disco music at the matches. A new nickname, the Bears, was also suggested. All very similar to ideas that Super League would use ten years on.

The season finished late into May, with double headers on Fridays and Sundays being staged to complete all the home matches. Paul Faires's regime did not last, and after another closure threat, Tim Lamb and Richard Lawton took over as directors that summer with the Closes' support. But the spirit of survival that later sustained the club in the second half of the 1980s had been shown in that muddy afternoon at Huddersfield.

The events around this game are described by Stephen Froggatt in more detail in Part 4 of this book.

Huddersfield: Bostock, Cramp, Leathley, Thomas, Campbell, Johnson, Marshall, J.Johnson, Wroe, Charlton, Boothroyd, Platt, Senior. Subs: Edwards, Kenworthy.
Tries: Marshall, Senior, Cramp. Goal: Platt

Fulham: Duffy, Henley-Smith, Jones, Barrow, Feighan, Wilkinson, Green, Mordell, Garner, Glover, Platt, Cambriani, Kinsey. Subs: Dainty, Yates.
Try: Feighan. Goals: Wilkinson (2)

Peter Lush

Fulham 4 Papua New Guinea 12
Tour match
1 November 1987 at Chiswick

Papua New Guinea's first tour of Great Britain against professional opposition ended with their second victory - a 12-4 win against Second Division Fulham. For the London club, this match was a rare highlight in a season of struggle in the sport's lower flight.

Over 1,200 supporters were at Chiswick to see the teams presented to Neil Kinnock M.P., the Labour leader of the opposition. In their previous match, the Kumuls had lost 28-4 to a strong Yorkshire side, but they were too good for Fulham. They took the lead when Mathias Kitimun scored from Dairi Kovae's pass. Huw Rees reduced the deficit before half-time with a penalty, to make the score 4-2 to the tourists, but a defensive error saw Clement Mou score a second try and substitute Bobby Ako scored a third. Colin Fenn kicked a penalty for Fulham, who could not score a try despite having a great deal of second half possession.

However, the match did achieve some welcome positive publicity for the club. After the match the club staged a dinner for the tourists. Director Richard Lawton recalls: "I remember the Papua New Guinea game very well, which I think was the high point of my involvement. I particularly remember sitting at the dinner afterwards, listening to the Papuans singing their South Sea songs. It was a magic evening".

Fulham: Lawrie, Feighan, Rees, Gillan, Cambriani, Guyett, Murphy, Hutchinson, Taylor, Miller, Grimoldby, Manning, O'Riley. Subs: Kelly, Fenn. Goals: Rees, Fenn.

Papua New Guinea: Kitimun, Saea, Kovae, Kamiak, Krewanty, Atoi, Lapan, Gaius, Matmillo, Lomutopa, Waketsi, Gispe, Kouoru. Subs: Mou, Ako. Tries: Kitimun, Ako, Mou.

Peter Lush

Fulham versus Papua New Guinea 1987
Top: The teams meet Neil Kinnock M.P., Leader of the Opposition
Bottom: The post-match dinner
Photos: Stephen Froggatt

The 1991 tour of the Soviet Union

There has been much about Rugby League in London that is slightly surreal. In sport, truth is usually stranger - and more interesting - than fiction. So the fact that the final official match for Fulham RLFC took place in Leningrad against Ryedale-York was just another event in a 20-year journey through Rugby League. By the start of the next season the club had been renamed London Crusaders.

Originally, Leigh and Ryedale-York were to tour the Soviet Union in the autumn of 1990. But the Rugby League changed the date to May 1991, when the League season had started in the Soviet Union. By then, Leigh had financial problems, so Fulham were invited to take their place, despite the usual money problems of their own. The trip was helped financially by the players playing for free - and most regard it as one of the highlights of their careers. Two marked the occasion by having "USSR" and a hammer and sickle shaved on the back of their heads. And there is no doubt that the venues of Alma-Ata, Leningrad (soon to revert to its original St Petersburg) and Moscow were a welcome change from Fulham's usual coach trips to all points north of Watford.

Roy Close remembers being given the itinerary for the trip. "We flew to Moscow then onto Alma-Ata. Before going I looked it up on the map. We turned two more pages from Moscow. It was next to Tibet and China...a bloody long way."

Fulham and Ryedale-York played an honourable 20-all-draw, then each team played the All Stars of Asia, Fulham winning 6-4 and Ryedale York winning 22-4. Roy Close recalls: "It was our first experience of a stadium in Russia - it was a huge concrete bowl. There was no cover except for the boardroom, which was lined with marble and hardwood. There was loads of food and that horrible Russian champagne. All the local communist officials were in there - they didn't go outside. At the end of the game there was still food and drink left. So I invited one of the interpreters to come in. When I suggested this there was a look of fear on her face. 'That's not for the likes of me' she said. But otherwise Alma-Ata seemed a nice place".

The group then flew to Leningrad. Roy Close remembers the Aeroflot flight well. "The Russians on the plane were passing vodka around.

Everyone was getting sloshed. There didn't seem to be any safety precautions."

Barry and Gwen Warren also have vivid memories of that flight. "A pilot staggered onto the plane, very drunk. We were relieved when he sat down and fell asleep, as we thought he was going to fly the plane".

The teams played another match in Leningrad, Fulham winning 18-12, with Greg Pearce kicking five goals - in front of around 1,000 people - in a stadium that held 100,000. Barry and Gwen remember jugglers and dancing bears at the reception for the party.

The next stop was Moscow, where everyone stayed in the 4,000-room Cosmos hotel. The two teams combined into a Great Britain Select, including six of Fulham's Australians - fondly remembered by Australian Darryl Pitt who still has his Great Britain shirt from the match. The inexperience of the Soviet Union side, despite being coached by Phil Larder, showed as the Great Britain XIII won 42-10, in front of 3,200 fans including a large contingent from the police and the army.

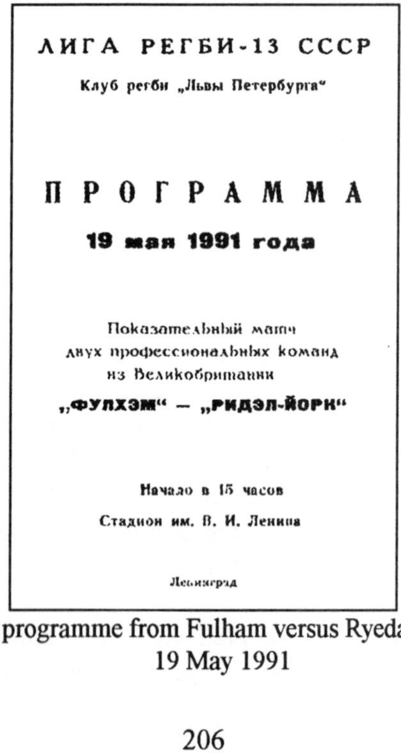

ЛИГА РЕГБИ-13 СССР

Клуб регби „Львы Петербурга"

ПРОГРАММА

19 мая 1991 года

Показательный матч
двух профессиональных команд
из Великобритании

„ФУЛХЭМ" — „РИДЭЛ-ЙОРК"

Начало в 15 часов
Стадион им. В. И. Ленина

Ленинград

The programme from Fulham versus Ryedale-York
19 May 1991

Roy Close recalls the post-match celebrations: "This was the era of *perestroika* and *glasnost*, but things were different from what we were used to at home. We had a meal at the hotel after the game and at around 8pm, as people were finishing, six police came in with unsheathed truncheons. The interpreter was not sure why they had come in. There was no need for them to be there, so we said we would not go until the police left. It was a stand-off, and the police were flummoxed." Later in the bar, when one of the players was playing a guitar and there was some singing, police with truncheons turned up again. Roy's suggestion that people should complain to their Member of Parliament about the police was met with incomprehension - *glasnost* had not spread that far.

Roy remembers it as "a very successful and interesting trip". As Dave Hadfield, one of the few journalists to make the journey said: "It was a remarkable thing that it took place at all".

The following season, three Russian players came to London to have trials with London Crusaders, one playing a couple of first team games. But lack of resources at the club meant they didn't stay. It was a pity because one was reputed to be quicker than Martin Offiah.

Peter Lush

Ryedale-York 20 Fulham 20
16 May 1991 in Alma-Ata

Fulham: A. Render, Leslie, Pitt, Browning, Sada, Dwyer, Holderness, Reinsfield, Callow. Rotheram, Winborn. Lee, Pearce. Subs: Peart, Why, Workman, Scott
Tries: Pitt (2), Pearce, Render. Goals: Pearce (2)

Ryedale-York: Sullivan, Kettlestring, Smith, G. Pryce, Pinkney, Dobson, Maxwell, Horton. Hayes, Shaw, N. Render. Subs: Laws. Martin, Pallister, Wheatley.
Tries: Sullivan, Kettlestring, G.Pryce, Pinkney. Goals: Sullivan (2)

Fulham 6 All Stars of Asia 4

Ryedale-York 22 All Stars of Asia 4

Ryedale-York 12 Fulham 18
19 May 1991 in Leningrad

Fulham: Dwyer, Leslie, Taylor, Pitt, Peart, Browning, Rotheram; Reinsfield, Workman, Scott, Callow, Lee, Pearce. Subs: Winborn, Holderness, Why, Sada.
Tries: Reinsfield, Dwyer. Goals: Pearce (5)

Ryedale York: Sullivan, Kettlestring, S. Pryce, Smith, Wheatley, Dobson, Maxwell, Horton, Hayes, G. Pryce, Laws. N. Render. Subs: Pallister, Wilby, Martin, Shaw.
Try: S. Pryce. Goals: Sullivan (4)

Great Britain Select 42 Soviet Union 10
23 May 1991 in Moscow

Great Britain Select: Sullivan (RY), Kettlestring (RY), Taylor (F), Pitt (F), Smith (RY), Browning (F) Rotheram (F), Dobson (RY), Hayes (RY), Horton (RY), Lee (F), G. Pryce (RY), Pearce (F). Subs: Pinkney (RY), Maxwell (RY), Dwyer (F), Workman (F), N. Render (RY).
Tries: Sullivan, Kettlestring, Dobson, Horton, Pearce, Pinkney, Dwyer. Goals: Pearce (4), Sullivan(3),

Soviet Union: Belaev, Pisconov, Dyatlov, Nichaev, Olar, Parshow, Kartsov, Zarnba, Ossachie, Strach, Lysov, Senin, Sokolov. Subs: Sycophsky, Sharcoff, Tarran, Gloticov.
Tries: Nichaev, Pisconov. Goal: Parshow.

London Crusaders 30 Wakefield Trinity 0
Regal Trophy Round 1
8 November 1992 at Crystal Palace National Sports Centre

This was the game London were never meant to win. The Crusaders were given a 26-point start before the game by most "informed" pundits, and Trinity were fully expected to put on a dazzling display to humble their lower-league opponents. Fate however decreed that events would take a different course and the match entered London Rugby League folklore. The small group of die-hards who braved a sullen winter's afternoon were richly entertained as coach Ross Strudwick pulled off a masterstroke.

Even now, several years down the line, I can hardly believe they did it and I was there! The event, as seen again through the heavily-biased video commissioned by Wakefield, with a Wakefield commentator, seemed to pass in a dream: a dream of another time and another place, as London sounded a loud wake-up call to all their (many) doubters in the north with this result. When you support an outpost club you need all the credibility you can get and this had credibility in spades. Incidentally, it was to be almost seven years since these two teams were to meet again, with Wakefield taking revenge by 40-8.

Early London pressure gave Wakefield little time to settle and with Chris Smith's kicking, the Crusaders started to chalk up points at a steady rate, Strudwick's particular forté was defence and it was this factor that completely disrupted the visitors' attacking patterns with sometimes three men completing one tackle - just to make sure - London established a dominating spirit and the Yorkshiremen were completely at sea, rarely reaching London's half on more than a handful of occasions all game.

London's attacking flair bamboozled the Wakefield defence and it was the arrival of Crusaders' prop Dave King which proved the decisive moment. With King battering a clueless defence, the ball was thrown around with Darryl Pitt taking his chance to nip through a gap out wide to touchdown. Wakefield were finding it difficult to mount a coherent attack and, as the light faded, their mood darkening with the setting sun. They had it all to do if a shock was not to be forthcoming. Half-time arrived and suddenly all bets were off, with the Crusaders 10-0 up.

London restarted brightly and the play became intense as both sides battled to retain their shape and make the passes go to hand as much as possible, Debutant scrum-half Mark Riley had not long arrived in the country from New Zealand but showed that there were no flies on him as he broke away to feed winger Shane Buckley to cross the whitewash against the sound of an ecstatic home support. Riley went on to become one of the finest scrum-halves London have ever had. A mercurial turn of speed, a wicked side-step and brilliant vision for moves, made him a transfer target for several clubs while in Britain.

The Crusaders upped the pressure, spinning the ball from one side to the other as Wakefield struggled to keep their resolve. Again it was King who stepped forward to stretch the lead, hopping out of a tackle to cross in the corner. With it all over bar the shouting, London proved their mettle again with Scott Roskell taking a fine interception to race away and pile on the agony. Wakefield's travelling contingent began to walk to their cars and coaches, thoroughly disgusted with their team's poor performance.

The Londoners, so long the underdogs, had the final word. Capitalising on an inept piece of defensive handling, Darryl Pitt was on hand to take the interception and bring down the curtain on a job well done, Cries of "London! London!" rang around the Palace's vast stand as the hooter ended Wakefield's embarrassment. London fans and players applauded each other and looked forward to another giant-killing in the next round. It didn't happen: the team lost to Leigh in the next Regal Trophy match.

A friend happened to go to Wakefield the next day on business and reported to me that there was "a tangible air of gloom over the town".

London Crusaders: Fisher, Blackman, Roskell, Pitt, Buckley, Halafihi, Riley, King, Workman, Rotheram, Gilbert, Smith, Rosolen. Subs: Mulkerin, Holderness.
Tries: Pitt (2), Buckley, King, Roskell. Goals: Smith (5)

Wakefield Trinity: Spencer, Mason, Benson, Eden, Wilson, Wright, Bagnall, Webster, Bell, Clancy, Price, Fritz, Slater. Subs: Conway, Goddard.

Al Ferrier

London Crusaders 22 Workington Town 30
Second Division Premiership Final
22 May 1994 at Old Trafford

This was the last - and inevitably dramatic - stand of Tony Gordon's marvellous 1993-4 London Crusaders side. The Brisbane Broncos had recently taken over the club, which while ensuring its survival, also saw Tony Gordon's departure as the Broncos decided to bring in a new coach.

The Crusaders had narrowly missed out on promotion that season, the decisive match being a 20-20 draw with Workington at Copthall. The previous week, in the Premiership play-off semi-final, the Crusaders had won at newly promoted Doncaster, much to the surprise and annoyance of their supporters who had been anticipating a day out at Old Trafford. As it was, more than 600 London fans managed to get to Old Trafford for a

1p.m. kick-off. As always for London's big matches up north, there were hundreds - if not thousands - of the opposition supporters there.

This was a London squad stretched to the limit. Losing hooker Scott Carter after six minutes was bad enough, but when star scrum-half Mark Riley was also injured after 13 minutes it was clear the Crusaders were in trouble. His replacement was second row forward Geoff Luxon, a hard-working if inexperienced player, but hardly a proper replacement for Mark Riley. This was a quality Workington side, with Great Britain international Des Drummond on the wing, Dean Marwood at scrum-half, former Widnes star Phil McKenzie at hooker and James Pickering in the front row.

Not surprisingly, Workington dominated the first half. After Mark Johnson had given Crusaders the lead, scoring from a Sam Stewart cross kick, Workington scored five tries, the last four in 23 minutes to establish a 24-6 half-time lead.

Fortunately the half-time break allowed the Londoners the opportunity to reorganise and the second half was a much more even contest. Mark Johnson scored two more tries from Andre Stoop passes to complete his hat-trick and finish as the League's top try scorer for the season. Logan Campbell added a third, but a Stuart Cocker try eight minutes from time gave Workington an eight point lead, and the Crusaders could not come

Presentations at Old Trafford: Sam Stewart, John Gallagher and Dave Rotheram (Photo: David Stevens)

211

back. Workington deserved their victory, but if two key Crusaders' players had not been injured in the first 13 minutes the result might have been very different.

London Crusaders: Stoop, Gallagher, Roskell, Campbell, Johnson, McIvor, M.Riley, Whiteley, Carter, Rotheram, Rosolen, Stewart, Ramsey. Subs: Smith and Luxon.
Tries: Johnson (3), Campbell. Goals: Gallagher (3).

Workington Town: Mulligan, Drummond, Kay, Burns, Cocker, Kitchin, Marwood, Pickering, McKenzie, Armstrong, Hepi, Oglanby, Byrne. Subs: P.Riley & Penrice.
Tries: Byrne, Kay, Cocker (2), Drummond, Mulligan. Goals: Marwood (3).

Peter Lush

London Broncos 26 Leeds 12
Stones Bitter Championship
17 September 1995 at Brentford Football Club

Being a supporter is often a miserable business. Most teams don't win any trophies, more often than not your team loses, and even if they win, they don't play very well. Mid-table mediocrity is often our lot. But occasionally, just occasionally, there is a match, a victory, which in years to come, you can look back on and say "I was there". London Rugby League fans up to 1995 had a few (but only a few) occasions like this. A grim struggle was often our lot. But 17 September 1995, at the unlikely venue of Brentford Football Club's Griffin Park, was such an occasion.

Live on Sky Television, a respectable crowd, and one of the big names of Rugby League as the opposition. The start of a new era, or a heroic defeat? The excuses were ready; the home players were still jet-lagged, they'll need time to learn to play as a team. Every tipster backed the Broncos to lose, some by 20 points.

Early on, a Julian O'Neill penalty gave London a 2-0 lead. We were winning, and we hadn't been nilled. But then, a Leeds try. And another, this time converted. This Leeds team had put 60 past Halifax, who had scored 50 against us. A 50-point defeat to come? A Leeds penalty put

London 2-12 down, but the Broncos were just keeping in the game.

Another Julian O'Neill penalty followed, to cut the lead to 8 points, He took an age over each kick, adding to the tension. Sky might have had to rearrange their broadcasting schedules if London were awarded many more penalties. And just before half-time, Evan Cochrane created an opening for Leo Dynevor, an old Crusaders hero just returned, and vastly improved, to crash over. O'Neill converted and it was 10-12 at the break.

Then the Broncos stormed ahead. Keeping the ball alive on the last tackle, an opening was created in the left-hand corner, and Chris McKenna scored. O'Neill missed the kick, but now London were ahead. Another excellent move sent Ikram Butt free to score in the corner after 63 minutes. O'Neill converted and went on to add two more goals, and a drop goal. New stand off Ben Walker added a drop goal and a 26-12 victory was secured. The hooter ended the gripping tension and the unbelievable had become reality! Leeds trudged off, weary and defeated in the rain, nilled in the second half.

This was a well-deserved victory, the Broncos played open attractive rugby, sometimes on their own line. Justin Bryant's courage in coming out of the blood bin three times showed the Broncos' spirit, but every player made a magnificent contribution. The best crowd since the Craven Cottage days of 1982 lapped it all up. And as if to prove the opening paragraph of this report, this performance inspired myself and Dave Farrar to trek up to Oldham the following Wednesday. Lightning, unfortunately, does not strike twice, and London lost. But when we beat Leeds…I was there.

London Broncos: O'Neill, Butt, Cochrane, McKenna, Vincent, Walker, Dynevor, Mestrov, O'Donnell, Shaw, Rosolen, Bryant, Gill. Subs: Langer, Bawden, Green, Pitt.
Tries: Butt, McKenna, Dynevor. Goals: O'Neill (6). Drop-goals: O'Neill, Walker.

Leeds: Cook, Fallon, Hassan, Innes, Cummins, Kemp, Gibbons, Harmon, Lowes, Faimalo, Morley, Mann, Forshaw. Subs: Shaw, Golden, Field, Fozzard.
Tries: Innes, Fallon. Goals: Cook (2).

Peter Lush
Based on a report originally published in *London Calling!*

London Broncos 38 Paris St Germain 22
Super League
4 April 1996 at The Valley

After all the controversy surrounding its creation, Super League finally arrived in London. And this match seemed to vindicate the dream and the hype that supporters had been promised. There were 9,638 supporters, the biggest crowd for the club since the first season at Craven Cottage, saw a thrilling clash of two teams representing capital cities. They were queuing round the ground to get in, admittedly many with free vouchers from national newspapers, but still keen and enthusiastic to come and support Rugby League in London. And Sky Television was also there, big screen and all. The match was taking place on Thursday evening just before the Easter weekend, a notoriously bad day for travelling in London. Despite this, thousands had turned up.

And people were not disappointed. New Broncos' coach, Tony Currie, shocked by some of the defensive lapses, afterwards famously said the Broncos had been "crap". But for the fans, this was a magic night. Both stands on the sides of the pitch were full. Supporters new to the game and long-established London Rugby League followers combined to make a great atmosphere as the chant of "London, London" was heard throughout the game.

London Broncos versus Paris at The Valley
(Photo: Barry & Gwen Warren)

214

The game started badly for the Broncos, prop and pack leader Gavin Allen breaking his arm in the first minute and being taken to hospital. Nerves were showing for the Broncos early on, as Patrick Entat ran the show for the French team, fresh from their victory against Sheffield the previous week.

But it was centre Keiron Meyer who put the Broncos ahead after 18 minutes, taking a Tony Mestrov pass. Paris pegged the Londoners back with a penalty before Duncan McRae burst through from midfield, beat two people and scored. It was 10-2 when full-back Greg Barwick converted. Arnaud Cervello then replied in the corner for Paris, but Patrick Torreilles missed the conversion, and so after half an hour's hectic action the Broncos led 10-6. McRae then sent Tollett in at the corner to score, with Barwick converting, so the Broncos went in 16-6 ahead at half-time.

Again, the Broncos defence let them down as Ian Turner scored for Paris after 49 minutes. Torreilles converted to pull the Londoners' lead back to 16-12. But five minutes later, scrum-half Leo Dynevor sent in McRae for his second try. Barwick converted to restore a 10 point lead for the Broncos. But Paris were still not finished, as Pascal Bomati scored, with Torreilles converting to make it 22-18 after 57 minutes.

Then a piece of Leo Dynevor magic won the game for the Broncos. On the sixth tackle he chipped through, gathered the ball and scored by the posts. Barwick converted, so with 15 minutes left it was 28-18. Then winger Junior Paul picked up a loose ball from a Barwick chip through to score. It was 32-18, and surely the Broncos were safe now. With six minutes left, Tollett added his second try, Dynevor converting. 38-18 before Jean-Luc Ramondou scored in the last minute to make the final score 38-22 to the victorious Broncos.

Terry Matterson and Tony Rea had played a key role in holding together a Broncos side that was still coming together after the truncated Centenary season. The Broncos developed from this win to finally finish fourth. Paris struggled, but managed to avoid relegation, a key victory being over London in the return match. Although there were some good matches during the rest of that season at Charlton, none equalled the evening that Super League started in London.

London Broncos: Barwick, Paul, Meyer, Tollett, Carroll, McRae, Dynevor, Bawden, Rea, Allen, Shaw, Pitt, Matterson. Subs: Mestrov, Bryant, Keating, Smith.
Tries: McRae (2), Tollett (2), Meyer, Dynevor, Paul. Goals: Barwick(4), Dynevor.

Paris St Germain: Lucchese, Bomati, Turner, Chamorin, Cervello, Brown, Entat, Kacala, Torreilles, Utoikananu, Adams, Cabestany, Pech. Subs: Regis-Pastres, Ramondou, Devecchi, Wulf.
Tries: Cervello, Turner, Bomati, Ramondou. Goals: Torreilles (3).

Peter Lush

London Broncos 38 Canberra Raiders 18
World Club Championship
21 July 1997 at The Stoop

For British Rugby League, it is fair to say that the inaugural, and so far only 1997 World Club Championship was a disaster. Maybe at test level the British could be competitive with the Australians on a good day but, at club level, their game was clearly well ahead of the British scene.

But for the London Broncos, the tournament was one of the highlights of the momentous 1997 season. This best ever London Broncos team, who were to finish runners-up in Super League, had an additional incentive - a lot of the club's Australian players felt they had something to prove against the Australians. The draw had hardly been favourable - Brisbane, Canterbury and, in a clash of the capital cities, Canberra Raiders.

In the first series of matches in Australia, the Broncos had given Brisbane a fright before running out of steam and losing 42-22. At Canterbury a 34-18 defeat was a respectable result. But between these two matches the wheels had fallen off at Canberra, with a 66-20 defeat. Compared to the other British clubs in this tournament, except for the Canberra defeat, these were very respectable results.

The World Club Championship matches attracted great interest in London, and 7,819 fans for the visit of Canberra gave The Stoop a great atmosphere. But when Scott Roskell was sin-binned after two minutes for holding down in the tackle, the Raiders took advantage of his absence to run in two tries. A third score by Jason Burnham gave the Raiders a 14-0 lead and another slaughter of a British team looked on the cards.

But Tony Currie brought scrum-half Shaun Edwards off the bench after 20 minutes and the game started to move in the Broncos favour. Two tries from Terry Matterson and three Greg Barwick goals made the half-time score 14-all. And, importantly, Australian international captain Laurie Daley was sin-binned a couple of minutes before half time.

Two minutes into the second half, Terry Matterson set up a try for Peter Gill and the Broncos were in the lead.

From then there was no looking back. Further scores from Tulsen Tollett, Greg Barwick and Scott Roskell, with a further four Barwick goals gave the Broncos a 38-18 victory, Luke Priddis's try being the Raiders only second-half score.

Neil Fissler in *League Express* described the Broncos as "Splendid, magnificent, awesome, breathtaking, glorious, stunning, brilliant". Fair comment really.

The Broncos couldn't quite reach these heights again. 9,846 fans saw Brisbane win 34-16 at The Stoop and five days later Canterbury won 44-22. However, the victory over Canberra meant that the Broncos qualified for the quarter-finals.

But in that game Cronulla won 40-16 in the final match of the season at The Stoop to knock the Broncos out. It was the last stand of the wonderful 1997 team.

London Broncos: Mardon, Roskell, Barwick, Martin, Offiah, Tollett, Beazley, Mestrov, Matterson, Bawden, Dunford, Rosolen, Gill. Subs: Edwards, Hamilton, Howard, Krause.
Tries: Matterson (2), Gill, Tollett, Barwick, Roskell. Goals: Barwick (7).

Canberra Raiders: Nagas, Boyle, Wiki, Croker, Fulivai, Daley, Stuart, Davico, Priddis, Pongia, Furner, Kennedy, Burnham. Subs: Westley, McFadden, Woodford, Nadruku.
Tries: Boyle (2), Burnham, Priddis. Goal: Furner:

Peter Lush

London Broncos 33 Castleford Tigers 27
Challenge Cup semi-final 1999
27 March 1999 at Headingley

Has there ever been a better semi-final? Has more emotion, hope and possible despair ever been packed into 15 minutes of Rugby League than in the last quarter of an hour of this game?

There were 7,561 at a supposedly neutral Headingley. 7,000 from Castleford, the rest from London. The London fans' chant: "You're supposed to be at home" when the Castleford masses were silenced as another Broncos try was scored was a telling comment on the venue.

Headingley is a slightly strange place at this time of year. Before the game, having arrived early as usual, I was sitting in the cricket ground on the Western Terrace, looking at the cricket pitch, eating my chicken burger, watching the crowds come in - mainly Castleford supporters, but a few from London. The usual variety of London shirts, which showed what a changeable existence the club had endured; and then there was long-standing London fan Cliffie waving a Fulham flag.

Last time I had been at Headingley was in August 1998, when I had watched Yorkshire versus Lancashire at cricket before going to the Broncos match at Leeds on the other side of the stand in the evening. That was a disastrous defeat. What would today's visit bring?

Inside the ground, most London fans were in the seats, with the terraces taken over by the masses of Castleford fans. They even had three mascots - compared to a solitary Buck.

Karle Hammond's try gave London the lead, converted by Brett Warton. Stuart Cummings's decisions in the first half, in the opinion of the London supporters, seemed to be one sided, although on such occasions they often do, particularly when Martin Offiah believed he had caught the ball in goal, threw it to Shaun Edwards to take a 20 metre tap kick, only for a penalty for offside to be given in front of the posts. The decision was shown to be correct on television replays, but it did not seem fair at the time. However, an excellent try by Martin Offiah, and a dive over from a play the ball by Robbie Beazley and it was 14-2. But then Castleford fought back, was their weight advantage in the pack starting to tell? By half-time the Broncos were hanging on at 14-12.

A Robbie Beazley drop goal extended the lead, then Shaun Edwards took a pass from Brett Warton to score under the posts. Warton converted, 21-12 with 25 minutes left. One more try and surely London would be safe.

But Castleford fought back again. Two tries in six minutes, neither converted, and there was only one point in it, 21-20, with that agonising final 15 minutes to come. With eight minutes left, Castleford took the lead for the first time in the match. This time Danny Orr converted, so London were 26-21 behind. Then Peter Gill dummied through and scored. Warton converted again. Castleford's only lead in the match had lasted four minutes. Four minutes to go, 27-26 to the Broncos.

From the kick-off, Warton unluckily had a foot in touch while trying to catch the ball. From the scrum, Castleford set up a drop goal. It was 27-all with two minutes left. Was extra time to come?

From the kick-off London won possession. With the Broncos' fans screaming for a drop goal, Hammond's attempt was charged down. But the Broncos retained possession and, instead of trying for another drop goal, Robbie Beazley put in man-of-the-match Steele Retchless who dived triumphantly over the line. Brett Warton converted, the hooter sounded and it was all over at 33-27.

Eleven tries, six goals and two drop goals, with the Broncos scoring six tries. To be fair, as much as one can in a semi-final, neither side deserved to lose. This was Rugby League drama at its best, and for London it wiped out the memory of the 1998 semi-final massacre by Wigan at Huddersfield.

This victory was especially a reward for people who have followed the club from the beginning; those who watched second division Rugby League in the rain at Chiswick in the 1980s or contemplated the wide open spaces of Crystal Palace in the early 1990s. Some supporters - me included - were close to tears at the end of the game.

A Wembley cup final appearance would finally show people that Rugby League was alive and kicking in London. Maybe even the most hardened died-in-the-wool northerner would realise that development out of the heartlands was essential for the future of our game. In 1929, at the first Wembley final, Dewsbury made their cup final debut. How fitting that the last final at the old stadium would see a team from the capital make their cup final debut.

Whatever happened at Wembley, this was London's day. Having had desperate disappointments in (mainly football) semi-finals in the past, it was a day I would never forget.

Castleford Tigers: Flowers, Gay, Eagar, Maloney, Rogers, Orr, Davis, Sykes, Raper, Sampson, Tonks, Fritz, Vowles. Subs: Pickering, Lynch, Tallec, Wells. Tries: Gay (2), Eagar (2), Rogers. Goals: Orr (3). Drop goal: Orr.

London Broncos: Tollett, Warton, Fleming, Timu, Offiah, Hammond, Edwards, Retchless, Beazley, Millard, Simpson, Peters, Gill. Subs: Ryan, Toshack, Callaway, Salter.
Tries: Hammond, Offiah, Beazley, Edwards, Gill, Retchless. Goals: Warton (4). Drop goal: Beazley.

Peter Lush
Based on a report originally published in *London Calling!*

Leeds Rhinos 52 London Broncos 16
Challenge Cup Final
2 May 1999 at Wembley Stadium

Being there, at the end of the day, was not quite enough. The last 20 minutes of the last Challenge Cup Final in the old Wembley Stadium confirmed Broncos' fans fears - that their injury hit team was not strong enough to compete at the very top level.

But being there was still something beyond our wildest dreams even a few years ago. Coming out of the station at Wembley, seeing all the support for the club, I took some photos just to make sure I was not dreaming and would not wake up soon.

A group of us had seats at the tunnel end. One of my friends is a Rugby Union fan, who we had been trying to convince for years to come and watch a League match in London. It took Wembley to get him there. Another is a lifelong Hunslet fan, who naturally was supporting London. We saw Richard Branson walking towards the tunnel, in apparently controversial attire of jeans and an open neck shirt, shunning the formality of the occasion. And we saw London's props, Grant Young and Darren Bradstreet, both injured, in suits, at the edge of the pitch. They would be missed. However, Shaun Edwards had decided he could play despite having a broken thumb and would lead the Broncos.

After the formalities, it all started so well. After five minutes, Martin Offiah scored - his fifth Wembley cup final try - to give the Broncos the lead. He had gathered John Timu's kick through, and there was an agonising wait as the video referee decided if the try stood. It did and Smyth converted. Soon Robbie Simpson scored from a Karle Hammond pass, and it was 10-0. Then Leeds fought back, and by half-time were 12-10 ahead. The danger signs were there, particularly as Martin Offiah went off with a dead leg at half-time. But then Greg Fleming scored, Smyth converted and the Broncos were 16-12 ahead.

It didn't last. With 20 minutes to go Leeds were 20-16 in front and in a mad moment of optimism, I said "we can still do this - they're walking". But as the Broncos under-strength team tired, the tries flowed in, with Leroy Rivett taking advantage of Offiah's absence through injury to score a cup final record of four tries and take the Lance Todd Trophy.

The score of 52-16 was a cup final record for us of the wrong type. It was the biggest ever margin of victory and was probably a bit of an injustice for a weakened Broncos team who never stopped trying, but finally ran out of steam. But we had still had our day at Wembley, a reward for both players and supporters who had kept Rugby League in London alive over the years.

Leeds Rhinos: Harris, Rivett, Blackmore, Godden, Cummins, Powell, Sheridan, McDermott, Newton, Fleary, Morley, Farrell, Glanville. Subs: St. Hilaire, Jackson, Hay, Mathiou.
Tries: Rivett (4), Godden, McDermott, St.Hilaire, Harris, Cummins. Goals: Harris (8).

London Broncos: Tollett, Smyth, Fleming, Timu, Offiah, Hammond, Edwards, Retchless, Beazley, Salter, Millard, Simpson, Gill. Subs: Toshack, Callaway, Ryan, Air.
Tries: Offiah, Simpson, Fleming. Goals: Smyth (2).

Peter Lush

Wembley memories

London day out! Sandra, Dave,
Rachel and Glyn (Photo: Peter Lush)

The Virgin gorilla.
The Broncos had
so many injuries he nearly
played in the pack.
(Photo: Barry & Gwen Warren)

Richard Branson at Wembley (Photo: Peter Lush)

The teams line up before the match (Photo: Peter Lush)

The score Broncos' fans will remember. An early 10-0 lead.
(Photo: Peter Lush)

Match action from Wembley - Tulsen Tollett with the ball
(Photo: Peter Lush)

Shaun Edwards receiving his medal (Photo: Peter Lush)

Shaun Edwards and Martin Offiah leave the pitch after the final
(Photo: Peter Lush)

Two special matches from the 1990s

Doncaster versus London Crusaders. Division Premiership semi-final 1994
(Photo: Barry & Gwen Warren)

Roy Waudby presents the Alliance Second Division trophy to
Broncos A team skipper Chris Smith in 1996 (Photo: Barry & Gwen Warren)

6. The Grounds

Permanent homes

Occasional homes

NB This chapter does not include grounds used when a cup match was switched to an opponent's home or played at a neutral ground because weather problems.

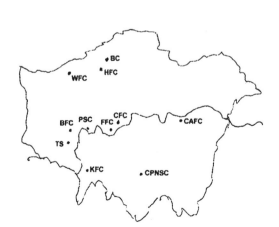

Key:
FFC: Fulham Football Club
CPNSC: Crystal Palace National Sports Centre
PSC: Polytechnic Stadium, Chiswick
BC: Barnet Copthall Stadium
CAFC: The Valley
TS: The Stoop
CFC: Stamford Bridge
WFC: Wealdstone FC
HFC: Hendon Football Club
BFC: Brentford Football Club
KFC: Kingstonian FC

Permanent homes

Craven Cottage
1980 to 1984

The home of Fulham Football Club and to many supporters from the club's early years still the club's spiritual home. Fulham Football Club bought the site in 1894, having previously shared a ground off Putney High Street with the Wasps Rugby Union club.

In 1911, the ground staged an England versus Australia Rugby League test match, the Australians winning 11-6 in front of a crowd of 6,000 on a Wednesday afternoon.

The ground is in a middle class residential area and during the first season, the club had to contend with local residents trying to use the Sunday observance laws to stop the club playing.

Craven Cottage is on the banks of the river Thames. It currently has two stands - the original one on Stevenage Road, which was designed by the famous architect Archibald Leitch, and the modern cantilever Eric Miller stand on the river side. There is terracing behind both goals.

The famous Cottage is in the corner by the Stevenage Road stand. The original cottage was built in 1780 and burnt down in 1888. The author Edward Bulwer-Lytton wrote *The Last Days of Pompeii* there. The current cottage was built at the same time as the Stevenage Road stand.

The future of the ground was uncertain for much of the 1980s and 1990s, with the threat of redevelopment hanging over it. But there are now plans to redevelop it as a modern football stadium. It will be interesting to see if the rebuilding manages to retain the charm and character of the original ground.

Fulham's most famous match at Craven Cottage was the first game against Wigan. But the record crowd for a London club Rugby League match since the Second World War was against Wakefield Trinity in the Challenge Cup. The last match at Craven Cottage was on 25 April 1984 when just 1,146 supporters saw a 25-13 victory over Widnes.

Craven Cottage record:
Played 68 Won 41 Drawn 3 Lost 24. Percentage success: 62.5%

Fulham versus Wigan 14 September 1980. The Eric Miller stand
is on the right of the picture. (Photo: Tim Wood)

Fulham 21 York 13 17 April 1983
The players on the balcony of the Cottage celebrating the win that
gave Fulham the Second Division Championship. (Photo: Barry Taylor)

Crystal Palace National Sports Centre
1984 - 1985 and 1990 to 1993

Following the traumatic events in the summer of 1984, when the club nearly died, the new owners, Roy and Barbara Close, had to find a new home quickly, as Craven Cottage was no longer available for the Rugby league team. In those days Rugby Union was still 'amateur' and their grounds were not available to professional Rugby League clubs.

Crystal Palace offered good training facilities and 16,500 seats. The move was intended to be for a one season trial, but from February 1985 onwards, the cub were looking for new venues. The journey from west London by public transport was not easy and the cavernous stadium lacked any atmosphere.

In the club's second spell there, supporters were allowed to stand by the advertising hoardings by the pitch. But it made little difference to the atmosphere. The club actually lost a layer of supporters when it returned there in 1990, people who had not liked it before, found the journey difficult and a poor view when they got there. The club had some unusual companions at Crystal Palace - included in the complex were a small zoo and model car racing.

Crystal Palace record:
Played: 60 Won: 38 Drawn: 2 Lost: 20 Percentage success: 65%.

The wide open spaces of Crystal Palace: London Crusaders versus
Sheffield Eagles (Photo: Peter Lush)

The Polytechnic Stadium, Chiswick
1985 - 1990

It is ironic that the ground that had the most basic facilities of all the club's permanent home grounds is the most fondly remembered by the clubs' supporters from that time. The club was run by volunteers and came the closest it has ever been to being a community club.

The club played one match at Chiswick in March 1985 when it had become apparent that Crystal Palace was not a suitable home. The Stadium is owned by the University of Westminster (formerly the Polytechnic of Central London).

When Fulham moved there in the summer of 1985, except for the changing rooms, the facilities had not been used for many years. Supporters worked to renovate the stand, turnstiles and toilets to make it fit to stage professional Rugby League. Later, caravans arrived for a club shop and a burger bar.

The main stand has two tiers and offered some protection from the weather. But the rest of the ground was open to the elements and could be a bleak place on a winter afternoon watching a team who often struggled. One other attraction was a model railway that ran behind the main stand.
The ground was also not very accessible by public transport, being a 15 minute walk from Chiswick station or a bus ride from Hammersmith.

The ground had no floodlights and winter matches kicked off at 2.15pm or 2.30pm. One cup replay was held on a midweek afternoon. The ground had potential for development, but the club could never reach along term agreement with the trustees that could have secured Sports Council grants to improve the facilities. In 1990, the club decided to move back to Crystal Palace. The stadium is now used by the Polytechnic Football Club.

The Polytechnic Stadium record:
Played: 85 Won: 40 Drawn: 5 Lost: 40 Percentage success: 50%.

For further memories of the club's time at Chiswick, see Stephen Froggatt's The Fulham Maintenance Crew in Part 4.

Photo of The Polytechnic Stadium overleaf by Stephen Froggatt

232

Moving into Chiswick....

Moving out... to Crystal Palace in 1990

Photo: Stephen Froggatt

Barnet Copthall Stadium
1993 to 1995

In the spring of 1993, the club's ownership changed hands again, with Richard and Samantha Bartram becoming owners. In the summer, they moved the club to Barnet Copthall Stadium, situated in Mill Hill in suburban north London.

The stadium was built primarily as an athletics stadium. The main stand seats around 800 people and there is open terracing on the other side of the ground. The elevation of the stand gave a far better view for supporters than Crystal Palace.

The stadium is not particularly well served by public transport, so the club organised buses from Mill Hill East underground station to bring supporters to the ground. One transport advantage was that the stadium is very near the M1 motorway, giving easy access from the north.

When the Broncos took over in 1994, they kept the club at Copthall for the 1994-5 season, but realised that it did not have the potential for staging Super League matches. A couple of matches were played there during in the autumn of the nomadic 1995-6 centenary season. The club installed extra seating for those matches. The Stadium was in the news in 1999 when Barnet Football Club tried to move there, but were refused planning permission on appeal.

Barnet Copthall Stadium record:
Played: 35 Won: 28 Drawn: 2   Lost: 5 Percentage success: 83%

LONDON CRUSADERS
RUGBY LEAGUE CLUB

at

BARNET COPTHALL STADIUM
Great North Way, NW4 (A41)
(Junction 2 off the M1, Southbound)

STONES BITTER SECOND DIVISION

Friday 27th August 1993
v BATLEY - kick off 8pm

 Friday 10th September 1993
v DONCASTER - kick off 7.30pm

Sunday 26th September 1993
v DEWSBURY - kick off 3pm

Sunday 10th October 1993
v RYEDALE YORK - kick off 3pm

Special matchday bus service from
Mill Hill East tube station to and from stadium

Ticket enquiries and information
please call: 081 203 4211

"SUPPORT PROFESSIONAL
RUGBY LEAGUE IN LONDON"

The main stand at Copthall (Photo: Peter Lush)

235

The Valley
1995-6, 1996 and 2000

The club played four low key matches at Charlton Football Club's The Valley in the 1995-6 centenary season. It was then decided to make The Valley the club's new home for the 1996 Super League campaign. The season got off to a magnificent start with over 9,000 supporters seeing a victory over Paris St Germain in the first game, and long queues around the ground to get in.

After that very positive start, attendances varied and at the end of the season the club decided that they could gain more support back in west London. This meant a move to The Stoop in Twickenham to try to attract supporters in a strong Rugby Union area. But after three years at The Stoop, the club decided that The Valley was a better venue for Rugby League and crossed London again.

The club now has training facilities at Charlton Park RFC, a couple of miles from The Valley and is doing a great deal of work in the community to win new supporters.

The Valley has been Charlton Football Club's home since 1919. However, there was a break from 1985 to 1992 when internal problems forced the club into exile at Crystal Palace's Selhurst Park and then half a season at West Ham United FC's Upton Park. The campaign for a return to The Valley included the club's supporters standing candidates in the 1990 local elections to persuade the Council to give planning permission.

For the 2000 season the Broncos are using the modernised main stand and one seating area behind the goal. The overall capacity of the ground is now around 20,000.

The Valley now offers very good facilities for supporters. There is much more of a sense of partnership with their landlords than there ever was at The Stoop. The only danger for the club at The Valley is that Charlton playing Premiership football could overshadow Rugby League.

The Valley record: (to end 1996 season)
Played: 15 Won: 9 Drawn: 0 Lost: 6 Percentage success: 60%

Back to The Valley: London Broncos versus Huddersfield-Sheffield
Giants in March 2000. Top: The main stand.
Bottom: Mat Toshack about to score for the Broncos. (Photos: Peter Lush)

The Stoop
1995-6 and 1997 to 1999

Rugby Union going "open" in the summer of 1995 opened the way for professional Rugby League matches to be played at Rugby Union grounds. The club played four matches at Harlequins RFC's The Stoop Memorial Ground (to give it its full title) in November in the 1995-6 centenary season while the club decided on a permanent new home.

Supporters who had never been to a first-class Union ground before were shocked at how poor the facilities were. The main stand which had around 1,000 seats, open seating on the opposite side and nothing behind the goals. And the Twickenham Stadium dominating the skyline - the home of the Rugby Union establishment.

The club decided after that season that The Valley was to be its new home. But after spending the 1996 season in south-east London, it was decided that maybe more support could be won in the club's traditional area of south-west London. By now The Stoop had undergone major redevelopment, with a new covered east stand and open seating behind both goals. The open layout of the ground was also good for match day activities and facilities.

At first the move was successful, with crowds nearing capacity for the World Club Challenge games. These games had a tremendous atmosphere as the Broncos challenged major Australian teams. But over the next two seasons the crowds declined along with the team's fortunes on the pitch and the club decided to return to The Valley. The club had also faced opposition from local residents and the local council and was forced to play some matches under temporary floodlights as the planning permission for the east stand prevented use of the permanent floodlights on Sunday nights. One match against Warrington was reminiscent of the early days of floodlight matches with dark patches on the pitch.

The Stoop record:
Played: 50 Won: 29 Drawn: 3 Lost: 18 Percentage success: 61%

Match day at The Stoop.
Top: The East Stand.
Bottom: Junior Broncos in action - face painting.
(Photos: Peter Lush)

Occasional homes

Naughton Park - Widnes RLFC

Towards the end of the 1982-3 season, the pitch at Craven Cottage was experiencing major drainage problems. As the football team were pressing for promotion, the board decided to switch some Rugby League matches from Craven Cottage to other grounds. To the disgust of the club's supporters, two were played at Widnes RLFC on April 12 and April 14. Both were won easily, but it was a further sign of the declining relationship between the Football and Rugby League clubs at Fulham.

Naughton Park record:
Played: 2 Won: 2
Percentage success: 100%

```
          F U L H A M   v.   S W I N T O N
          ------------------------------------

          Venue:  Naughton Park, Widnes
          Date:  12th April, 1983

   As Cardiff have refused to play this game tonight,
   we have, at short notice, re-arranged the match
   with Swinton, to whom we are deeply grateful.  We
   regret any inconvenience caused but you will
   appreciate that this was outside Fulham's control.

                      TEAM SHEET
   FULHAM                      SWINTON
   GANLEY, Chris        1      HUNTER, Paul
   CAMBRIANI, Adrian    2      SUTTON, David
   ALLEN, David         3      WILSON, Denny
   DIAMOND, Steve       4      TURNER, Steve
   BAYLISS, Steve       5      CRAWSHAW, Carl
   CROSSLEY, John       6      GORTON, John
   BOWDEN, Reg          7      MERCER, Colin
   BEVERLEY, Harry      8      WALSH, Steve
   DOHERTY, Joe         9      HITCHENS, Gary
   GOURLEY, Tony       10      CLARKE, Terry
   HERDMAN, Martin     11      ROWBOTTOM, Mark
   SOUTO, Peter        12      HIGHTON, Tommy
   KINSEY, Tony        13      PIERCE, Daryle
   M'BARKI, Hussein    14      HAZELDENE, Mike
   WOOD, John          15      PEERS, Mike

                      OFFICIALS
            Referee:  Mr. J. McDonald
        Touch Judges:  Mr. J. W. Fairhurst
                       Mr. J. E. Lloyd
```

The team sheet for the Fulham versus Swinton match.

Stamford Bridge - Chelsea Football Club

Another temporary venue at the end of the 1982-3 season was just down the road - Chelsea Football Club's Stamford Bridge ground. Fulham versus Cardiff Blue Dragons on 6 May 1983 was the third Rugby League match played at the ground. In 1908, New Zealand had defeated Great Britain in a test match and in 1952 a British Empire XIII had defeated New Zealand. Fulham lost an ill-tempered match 14-20.

Stamford Bridge record:
Played: 1 Won: 0 Drawn: 0 Lost: 1 Percentage success: 0

Lower Mead - Wealdstone Football Club

At the end of the 1984-5 season, the club played three matches at Wealdstone Football Club's Lower Mead ground. Although the venue was adequate for the club's crowds at that time, there was limited seating and there were also questions over the long term future of the ground. It was eventually sold for a supermarket development. Completely different from Crystal Palace, supporters were so close to the action that they could hear the players swear at each other when a move went wrong!

Lower Mead record:
Played: 3 Won: 1 Drawn: 1 Lost: 1
Percentage success: 50%

Fulham versus Bramley teamsheet

Fulham vs. Bramley at Wealdstone. Chris Wilkinson
being tackled. (Photo: Barry Taylor)

241

Claremont Road - Hendon Football Club

When Fulham were drawn against illustrious Wigan in the Lancashire Cup in the 1989-90 season, the club moved the match to Hendon Football Club's Claremont Road ground so that the game could be played in the evening. 3,200 supporters saw Fulham fight all the way against the all-conquering northern giants, eventually losing 4-32.

The club returned to Claremont Road as an occasional venue in the 1993-4 and 1994-5 seasons, when Copthall Stadium was unavailable. The ground was fine for this purpose, but would not have been able to stage Super League matches, only having a small stand and limited facilities.

Claremont Road record:
Played: 8 Won: 5 Drawn: 0 Lost: 3 62.5%

Griffin Park - Brentford Football Club

The club's first home match in top-flight Rugby League for over 10 years was staged at the unlikely venue of Brentford Football Club's Griffin Park ground. Although this victory against Leeds in September 1995 (See chapter 5) and the later match against Wigan in the centenary season were both well supported, the ground did not have enough corporate facilities to stage Super League matches and the relationship between the two clubs apparently did not work well. But there was support for both matches from Brentford football supporters and the ground had a compact feel that gave it a good atmosphere.

Griffin Park record:
Played: 2 Won: 1 Drawn: 0 Lost: 1 Percentage success: 50%

Welford Road - Leicester Tigers RFC

The club moved the home match against the Bradford Bulls in 1999 to Leicester to help "spread the word" for Rugby League at Super League's request. Augmented by a large following of Bulls' fans, the match also attracted a reasonable number of locals in a crowd of over 8,000.

But the ground authorities were used to Leicester's crowds which are mainly members and there was a 45 minute delay in the kick off as supporters queued to buy tickets outside. A curtain raiser saw the Leicester Phoenix amateur Rugby League team play Coventry Bears in a friendly match.

The staging of the match at one of Rugby Union's best venues was a further sign of the more cordial relationship between the codes. The experiment is to be repeated, this time at a weekend, to the relief of Broncos supporters who had to run for the last train to get home after the delayed kick off. The Broncos lost narrowly to the Bulls, a considerable improvement on a disastrous defeat at Bradford a few weeks before.

Welford Road record: (to end 1999 season)
Played: 1 Won: 0 Drawn: 0 Lost: 1 Percentage success: 0%

Kingsmeadow Stadium - Kingstonian Football Club

The club moved back to The Valley for the start of the 2000 season, but the new home ground was not available for the Challenge Cup matches. Thus, two matches were staged at Kingsmeadow Stadium, Kingstonian Football Club's ground. It was the eleventh venue used by the club in the capital. The ground was adequate for the two matches staged there, but would struggle with a large crowd. The Broncos beat Cumbrian Amateurs Wath Brow Hornets, but then lost in the next round to Salford City Reds.

Kingsmeadow Stadium record: (to end March 2000)
Played: 2 Won: 1 Drawn: 0 Lost: 1 Percentage success: 50%

London Broncos versus Bradford Bulls at Welford Road
July 1999 (Photo: Peter Lush)

London Broncos versus Salford City Reds
at Kingsmeadow Stadium February 2000 (Photo: Peter Lush)

7. Club Records and International Appearances

All records to the end of the 1999 season, except Shaun Edwards's playing record to retirement in April 2000.

Honours

Challenge Cup Finalists 1999
Challenge Cup semi-finalists 1998
Super League Runners-up 1997
Alliance Second Division
Champions 1995-6

Second Division Premiership
Runners-up 1993-4
Second Division Champions 1982-3
Lancashire Cup semi finalists 1928-3
Promoted (third) from Second
Division 1980-1

Team records

Biggest victory:	82-0 versus Highfield, 12 November 1995
Highest score:	82-0 versus Highfield, 12 November 1995
Biggest defeat:	6-72 versus Whitehaven (a) 14 September 1986
Most points conceded:	12-74 versus Bradford(a) June 1999

Highest attendance

Craven Cottage:	15,013 versus Wakefield Trinity 15 February 1981
Crystal Palace:	2,700 versus Wigan 15 September 1991
Chiswick:	1,665 versus Bradford Northern 11 February 1990
Copthall:	1,818 versus Bradford Northern 19 December 1993
Hendon FC:	3, 200 versus Wigan 27 September 1989
The Valley:	10,014 versus Wigan 17 August 1986
The Stoop:	9,846 versus Brisbane Broncos 27 July 1997

International appearances

Great Britain:
John Dalgreen vs. Australia 1982.
Tulsen Tollett tour to Papua New
Guinea & New Zealand 1996
Matthew Salter Academy tour to
New Zealand 1996
England:
John Wood vs. France 1982 (not
recognised as international match)
Ireland:
Rob Smyth 1999 vs. Wales &

Scotland
Shaun Edwards 1998 vs. France
Gavin Gordon 1997 vs. France
Scotland:
Scott Cram 1999 vs. Wales &
Ireland
Andrew Duncan 1997 vs. France
Iain Higgins 1997 vs. France
Nick Mardon 1997 vs. France
Darren Shaw 1996 vs. Ireland

South Africa:
Mark Johnson 1994 Sydney Sevens
Wales:
David Bishop 1992 vs. England &
France
Adrian Cambriani vs. France &

England twice in 1981
Martin Herdman vs. England twice
in 1981, vs. Australia in 1982.
Karle Hammond 1999 vs. Ireland &
Scotland

Individual records

Most tries in a match:

5: Martin Offiah versus Whitehaven (h)	14 March 1999
4: Mark Riley versus Highfield (h)	17 October 1993
Mark Johnson versus Highfield (a)	1 April 1994
Scott Roskell versus Bramley (a)	19 March 1995
Evan Cochrane versus Sheffield (a)	27 September 1995
Paul Hauff versus Workington (h)	1 October 1995
Shane Vincent versus Highfield (h)	12 November 1995
Greg Barwick versus Castleford (h)	25 August 1996
Karle Hammond versus Halifax (h)	23 July 1999

Most goals in a match: 11

Steve Guyett versus Huddersfield (h)	23 October 1988
Greg Pearce versus Runcorn (h)	26 August 1990
Terry Matterson versus Workington (h)	21 April 1996

Most points in a match:

28: Greg Barwick versus Castleford (h)	25 August 1996
26: Terry Matterson versus Workington (h)	21 April 1996
24: John Gallagher versus Bramley (h)	27 March 1994

Most tries in a season:	Mark Johnson 1993-4: 43
Most goals in a season:	John Gallagher 1993-4: 159
Most appearances:	Steve Rosolen (1992-1998): 171 (158+13 as sub)
Most tries:	Scott Roskell (1992-1997): 86
Most goals:	Steve Diamond (1981-1984): 305 + 4 drop goals
Most points:	Steve Diamond (1981-1984): 691

Appearances:

(Over 50 including as substitute. Shown as full appearances + substitute appearances. Where this is not shown all appearances were full)

Steve Rosolen	171 (158+13)	Chris Wilkinson	73 (69+4)
Hussain M'Barki	163 (148+15)	Sam Stewart	72 (70+2)
Tony Kinsey	156 (131+25)	Peter Souto	71 (51+20)
Darryl Pitt	154 (100+54)	Russell Bawden	71 (44+27)
Dave Rotheram	150 (114+36)	Mike Hutchinson	65 (61+4)
Scott Roskell	144 (136+8)	John Wood	65 (57+8)
Tony Gourley	131 (125+6)	Shane Buckley	63
Adrian Cambriani	121 (119+2)	Chris Ganley	60 (55+5)
Reg Bowden	120 (116+4)	Neil Tuffs	60 (48+12)
Kieron Murphy	119 (105+14)	Justin Bryant	60 (42+18)
Charlie Jones	116 (94+22)	John Dalgreen	58
Peter Gill	115 (108+7)	Huw Rees	58 (51+7)
Russ Bridge	113 (109+4)	Colin Fenn	58 (50+8)
Steve Diamond	109	Matt Salter	58 (17+41)
David Allen	108 (102+6)	Kevin Langer	57 (43+14)
Steve Mills	108 (100+8)	Ian Mellors	57 (41+16)
Harry Beverley	106 (104+2)	Steele Retchless	56 (54+2)
Joe Doherty	104 (93+11)	Russell Browning	55 (51+4)
Dave Gillan	101 (97+4)	Matt Toshack	55 (40+15)
Tulsen Tollett	95 (91+4)	Adrian Spencer	55 (13+42)
Mark Riley	94 (89+5)	John Timu	53 (52+1)
Chris Smith	94 (74+20)	Chris Ryan	53 (48+5)
David Eckersley	93 (85+8)	Don Duffy	52
Martin Herdman	92 (71+21)	Shaun Edwards	52 (42+10)
John Crossley	91 (88+3)	John Gallagher	51
Chris Smith	90 (72+18)	David Hull	50 (49+1)
Sean Hoare	90 (61+29)	Greg Pearce	50 (47+3)
Mick Taylor	87 (84+3)	Nick Grimoldby	50 (45+5)
Robbie Beazley	81 (66+15)	Roy Leslie	50 (41+9)
Tony Mestrov	80 (78+2)	Leo Dynevor	50 (37+13)
Terry Matterson	74	Matt Dunford	50 (21+29)
Mark Johnson	73		

Try scorers:

(30 and over)

Scott Roskell	86	Mark Johnson	66
Hussain M'Barki	74	Mark Riley	62

Darryl Pitt	52	Martin Offiah	36
Steve Mills	50	Dave Allen	34
John Crossley	48	Shane Buckley	33
Adrian Cambriani	42	Steve Rosolen	31
Dave Gillan	38		

Goal scorers:
(100 and over)

Steve Diamond	305 + 4 dg	Greg Barwick	138 + 2 dg
John Gallagher	196 + 2 dg	Greg Pearce	121
Chris Smith	153	Terry Matterson	116 + 6 dg
Chris Wilkinson	141 + 13 dg	Colin Fenn	107

Drop goal scorers:
(10 and over)

| David Eckersley | 17 | Tony Kinsey | 10 |
| Chris Wilkinson | 13 | | |

Point scorers:
(150 and over)

Steve Diamond	691	Mark Johnson	264
John Gallagher	470	Darryl Pitt	255
Greg Barwick	370	Mark Riley	249
Chris Wilkinson	363	Colin Fenn	218
Scott Roskell	344	Mark Riley	217
Chris Smith	334	Steve Mills	199
Terry Matterson	330	Tulsen Tollett	191
Steve Guyett	289	Iain MacCorquodale	171
Greg Pearce	274	Dave Gillan	152
Hussain M'Barki	265	John Crossley	150

First team Manager / Coach

Reg Bowden:	July 1980 to June 1984
Roy Lester:	August 1984 to April 1986
Bill Goodwin:	April 1986 to July 1987
Bev Risman:	July 1987 to October 1988
Bill Goodwin:	October 1988 to January 1989
Phil Sullivan:	January 1989 to February 1989
Bill Goodwin:	February 1989 to May 1989
Ross Strudwick:	July 1989 to February 1993

Tony Gordon:	March 1993 to May 1994
Gary Greinke:	July 1994 to January 1996
Tony Currie:	January 1996 to October 1998
Dan Stains:	November 1998 to June 1999
Tony Rea and Les Kiss:	June 1999 to September 1999
John Monie:	October 1999 to present

Notes: Reg Bowden was player-coach

Top try and goal scorers season by season

Tries		**Goals**		**Drop Goals**	
1980-1					
Mal Aspey	16	Iain MacCorquodale	75	David Eckersley	10
Adrian Cambriani	13	David Eckersley	5		
1981-2					
John Crossley	15	Steve Diamond	92	John Dalgreen	2
Hussain M'Barki	8			David Eckersley	2
1982-3					
John Crossley	27	Steve Diamond	136	David Eckersley	4
Hussain M'Barki	23				
1983-4					
Hussain M'Barki	17	Steve Diamond	77	Tony Kinsey	9
Trevor Stockley	10			Steve Diamond	3
1984-5					
Mike Davis	17	Chris Wilkinson	63	Chris Wilkinson	7
Steve Mills	17	Paul Rochford	14		
1985-6					
Steve Mills	11	Chris Wilkinson	72	Alan Platt	4
Adrian Cambriani	10	Alan Platt	27	Russ Gibson	2
Chris Wilkinson	10				
1986-7					
Steve Mills	12	Colin Fenn	65	Kieron Murphy	3
Kieron Murphy	8	Huw Rees	7	Chris Wilkinson	3
Huw Rees	8				
1987-8					
Dave Gillan	9	Colin Fenn	40	Nick Grimoldby	3
		Steve Guyett	19		
1988-9					
Dave Gillan	14	Steve Guyett	65	Brian Brown	5
		Jeff Coutts	11		

1989-0

Brett Daunt	12	Greg Pearce	47	Brett Daunt	3
Mick Taylor	12	Steve Guyett	33		
Hussain M'Barki	11				

1990-91

Darryl Pitt	10	Greg Pearce	74	Craig Grauf	2
		Tim Dwyer	27		

1991-2

Shane Buckley	17	Chris Smith	78	None	
Darryl Pitt	12	Darryl Pitt	11		

1992-3

Shane Buckley	16	Chris Smith	61	Paul Fisher	1
Mark Riley	12	Darryl Pitt	12	Mark Riley	1

1993-4

Mark Johnson	43	John Gallagher	157	John Gallagher	2
Mark Riley	30				
Scott Roskell	21				
John Gallagher	17				

1994-5

Scott Roskell	24	John Gallagher	39	Craig Green	2
Mark Johnson	19				
Darryl Pitt	14				

1995-96

Paul Hauff	13	Terry Matterson	21	Ben Walker	3
Leo Dynevor	9	Leo Dynevor	20		

1996

Greg Barwick	16	Greg Barwick	53	Greg Barwick	2
Tulsen Tollett	10	Terry Matterson	25		

1997

Scott Roskell	19	Greg Barwick	85	Terry Matterson	2
Martin Offiah	13	Terry Matterson	38		
Shaun Edwards	13				

1998

Chris Ryan	12	Terry Matterson	32	Terry Matterson	4

1999

Greg Fleming	26	Brett Warton	59	Glen Air	1
Karle Hammond	20	Rob Smyth	28	Robbie Beazley	1
Martin Offiah	13	Tulsen Tollett	24	Karle Hammond	1

League Record 1980-81 to 1999
Won 283 Drawn 22 Lost 250

League positions & summary of results season by season

Season	Division	Place	Played	Won	Draw	Lost	Points	For	Against
1980-1	Two	3rd	28	20	0	8	40	447	237
1981-2	One	13th	30	9	1	20	19	365	539
1982-3	Two	1st	32	27	1	4	55	699	294
1983-4	One	13th	30	9	1	20	19	401	694
1984-5	Two	8th	28	17	1	10	35	528	519
1985-6	Two	9th	34	16	1	17	33	679	709
1986-7	Two	12th	28	8	2	18	18	461	632
1987-8	Two	17th	28	10	0	18	20	382	559
1988-9	Two	15th	28	10	0	18	20	464	650
1989-0	Two	8th	28	16	2	10	34	496	488
1990-1	Two	7th	28	17	2	9	36	450	338
1991-2	Two	4th	28	14	0	14	28	428	483
1992-3	Two	5th	28	12	2	14	26	534	562
1993-4	Two	3rd	30	21	2	7	44	842	522
1994-5	Two	4th	30	20	1	9	41	732	480
1995-6	SBC	10th	20	7	0	13	14	466	585
1996	SL	4th	22	12	1	9	25	611	462
1997	SL	2nd	22	15	3	4	33	616	418
1998	SL	7th	23	10	0	13	20	415	476
1999	SL	8th	30	13	2	15	28	644	708

SBC: Stones Bitter Championship
SL: Super League

	Played	Won	Draw	Lost	Points	For	Against
First Division/SBC/SL:	177	75	8	94	158	3518	3882
Second Division:	378	208	14	156	430	7142	6473

League matches against other clubs

Barrow:	W: 6	D: 0	L: 4	Cardiff:	W: 1	D: 0	L: 1
Batley:	W: 13	D: 0	L: 7	Carlisle:	W: 13	D: 1	L: 6
Blackpool:	W: 6	D: 0	L: 4	Castleford:	W: 5	D: 2	L: 7
Bramley:	W: 18	D: 1	L: 7	Chorley:	W: 4	D: 0	L: 0
Bradford N/Bulls:	W: 4	D: 0	L: 11	Dewsbury:	W: 11	D: 1	L: 6
Bridgend:	W: 2	D: 0	L: 0	Doncaster:	W: 10	D: 1	L: 5

251

Team	W	D	L	Team	W	D	L
Featherstone:	W: 2	D: 0	L: 8	Rochdale:	W: 12	D: 0	L: 14
Gateshead:	W: 1	D: 1	L: 0	St Helens	W: 1	D: 1	L: 12
Halifax:	W: 3	D: 2	L: 5	Salford:	W: 7	D: 0	L: 5
Huddersfield:	W: 18	D: 2	L: 9	Sheffield:	W: 12	D: 0	L: 12
Hull:	W: 6	D: 0	L: 4	Southend:	W: 2	D: 0	L: 0
Hull KR:	W: 1	D: 0	L: 7	Springfield:	W: 1	D: 0	L: 1
Hunslet:	W: 8	D: 1	L: 5	Swinton:	W: 10	D: 1	L: 7
Highfield: *	W: 15	D: 0	L: 5	Trafford:	W: 3	D: 0	L: 1
Keighley:	W: 10	D: 0	L: 6	Wakefield:	W: 6	D: 0	L: 8
Leeds:	W: 4	D: 1	L: 10	Warrington:	W: 6	D: 0	L: 8
Leigh:	W: 4	D: 1	L: 9	Widnes:	W: 2	D: 0	L: 2
Mansfield:	W: 3	D: 0	L: 5	Whitehaven:	W: 13	D: 2	L: 9
Nottingham:	W: 2	D: 0	L: 0	Wigan:	W: 3	D: 1	L: 12
Oldham:	W: 9	D: 1	L: 8	Workington:	W: 11	D: 1	L: 6
Paris SG:	W: 3	D: 0	L: 1	York:	W: 13	D: 0	L: 13

* Also includes Huyton and Runcorn Highfield

Challenge Cup Results

Season	Rnd	Opponent	Date	H/A	Result
1980-1	1	Wakefield	15.2.81	H	5-9
1981-2	1	Hunslet	14.2.82	H	14-4
	2	Hull	28.2.82	H	5-11
1982-3	1	Rochdale	16.2.83	A	24-4
	2	Bradford	27.2.83	H	4-11
1983-4	P	Swinton	29.1.84	H	14-4
	1	Whitehaven	12.2.84	A	17-10
	2	Widnes	26.2.84	H	10-12
1984-5	1	Halifax	10.2.85	H	4-17
1985-6	1	Barrow	26.2.86	H *	14-26
1986-7	P	Kells	22.1.87	A	4-4
	R	Kells	27.1.87	H	22-14
	1	Halifax	1.2.87	H	10-38
1987-8	1	Mansfield	31.1.88	H	4-16
1988-9	1	Bradford N.	29.1.89	H	10-28
1989-0	P	Doncaster	14.1.90	H	23-16
	1	York	28.1.90	H	14-14
	R	York	31.1.90	A	16-12
	2	Bradford N.	11.2.90	H	2-20
1990-1	1	Halifax	17.2.91	A	6-46
1991-2	1	Highfield	2.2.92	A	12-12
	R	Highfield	4.2.92	H	24-10
	2	Workington	9.2.92	A	2-9
1992-3	1	Oldham	31.1.93	A	6-34
1993-4	3	Shaw Cross	16.1.94	H	40-14
	4	Featherstone	30.1.94	H	14-28
1994-5	3	Ellenborough	22.1.94	H	30-10
	4	Hull KR	12.1.95	H	20-26
1995-96	4	Dewsbury	31.1.96	A	10-12
1997	4	Lancashire L	9.2.97	A	48-5
	5	Bradford B	22.2.97	H	12-34
1998	4	Batley	15.2.98	A	44-20
	5	Halifax	1.3.98	H	21-18
	6	Hull KR	15.3.98	H	46-18
	SF	Wigan	29.3.98	N(1)	8-38
1999	4	Doncaster	14.2.99	H	64-0
	5	Hull KR	28.2.99	A	6-0
	6	Whitehaven	14.3.99	H	54-6
	SF	Castleford	27.3.99	N(2)	33-27
	F	Leeds	1.5.99	W	16-52

* At Wigan N(1) Huddersfield N(2) Leeds W: Wembley

Won: 18 D: 3 Lost: 19

John Player and Regal Trophy Results

Season	Rnd	Opponent	Date	H/A	Result
1980-1	1	Leeds	23.11.80	H	9-3
	2	Leigh	7.12.80	A	9-17
1981-2	1	Warrington	17.10.81	A	15-24
1982-3	1	St Helens	27.11.82	A	5-17
1983-4	1	Featherstone	6.11.83	A	10-12
1984-5	1	Hull	18.11.84	H	14-36
1985-6	1	Warrington	24.11.85	H	13-20
1986-7	1	Castleford	30.11.86	H	24-34
1987-8	P	Oldham	8.11.87	A	8-36
1988-9	P	Bramley	6.11.88	A	10-56
1989-0	1	Halifax	3.12.89	H	18-32
1990-1	1	Castleford	2.12.90	H	8-14
1991-2	1	Oldham	17.11.91	A	10-16
1992-3	1	Wakefield	8.11.92	H	30-0
	2	Leigh	6.12.92	A	6-16
1993-4	1	St Esteve	31.10.93	H	48-16
	2	Featherstone	14.11.93	H	26-12
	3	Ryedale-York	12.12.93	A	42-10
	4	Bradford N	19.12.93	H	10-22
1994-5	2	Hemel H	27.11.94	H	34-16
	3	Salford	4.12.94	A	14-16
1995-6	2	Highfield	12.11.95	H*	82-0
	3	Halifax	25.11.95	H**	18-22

* Copthall ** The Stoop

Won: 7 D: 0 Lost: 16

Lancashire Cup Results

Season	Rnd	Opponent	Date	H/A	Result
1980-1			Did not enter		
1981-2	1	Swinton	16.8.81	H	32-15
	2	Salford	23.8.81	A	3-19
1982-3	1	Swinton	5.9.82	H	20-8
	2	Wigan	15.9.82	A	15-4
	SF	Warrington	30.9.82	W	8-17
1983-4	1	Salford	4.9.83	A	15-16
1984-5	1	Swinton	16.9.84	H*	18-25
1985-6	1	Wigan	15.9.85	A	13-24
1986-7	1	Whitehaven	14.9.86	A	6-72
1987-8	1	Salford	13.9.87	A	4-58
1988-9	1	Rochdale	18.9.88	A	14-25
1989-0	1	Workington	17.9.89	A	30-24
	2	Wigan	27.9.89	H**	4-34
1990-1	1	Runcorn	H 26.8.90		50-0
	2	Leigh	2.9.90	A	8-40
1991-2	1	Wigan	15.9.91	H	10-38

* At Swinton ** Hendon FC W: Wigan

Won: 5 Draw: 0 Lost: 11

Divisional Premiership Results

Season	Rnd	Opponent	Date	H/A	Result
1990-1	1	Halifax	21.4.91	A	24-42
1991-2	2	Huddersfield	26.4.92	H	14-4
	SF	Oldham	10.5.92	A	14-22
1993-4	1	Keighley	8.5.94	H	66-12
	SF	Doncaster	15.5.94	A	16-6
	F	Workington	22.5.94	OT	22-30
1994-5	1	Whitehaven	8.5.95	H	28-1
	SF	Keighley	14.5.95	A	4-38

OT: Old Trafford

Won: 4 Draw: 0 Lost: 4

Premiership Results

Season	Round	Opponent	Date	Home or away	Result
1996	SF	St Helens	1.9.96	A	14-25
1997	QF	Sheffield	14.9.97	H	16-58

Won: 0 Draw: 0 Lost: 2

World Club Challenge Results

1997 season

Brisbane Broncos	6.6.97	A	22-42	
Canberra Raiders	15.6.97	A	20-66	
Canterbury Bulldogs	23.6.97	A	18-34	
Canberra Raiders	21.7.97	H	38-18	
Brisbane Broncos	27.7.97	H	16-34	
Canterbury Bulldogs	1.8.97	H	22-44	
Cronulla Sharks	5.10.97	H	16-40	(Quarter final)

Results season-by-season

Key:

Home matches in **bold**
Only official matches are included
D1: First Division
D2: Second Division
SBC: Stones Bitter Championship
SL: Super League
CC: Challenge Cup
JPT: John Player Trophy
WCC: World Club Challenge

RT: Regal Trophy
LC: Lancashire Cup
DivP: Divisional Premiership
P: Premiership
Tour: Tour match
Rounds of cup competitions are shown
numerically. P: Preliminary round

1980-1			
Wigan	**D2**	**14.9.80**	**24-5**
Keighley	D2	21.9.80	13-24
Swinton	**D2**	**28.9.80**	**25-11**
Blackpool	D2	5.10.80	15-2
Huddersfield	**D2**	**12.10.80**	**30-7**
Doncaster	D2	19.10.80	28-16
York	**D2**	**26.10.80**	**23-5**
Bramley	**D2**	**9.11.80**	**10-7**
Dewsbury	D2	16.11.80	9-7
Leeds	**JPT1**	**23.11.80**	**9-3**
Wigan	D2	30.11.80	2-15
Leigh	JPT2	7.12.80	9-17
Hunslet	**D2**	**21.12.80**	**19-5**
Batley	**D2**	**28.12.80**	**15-5**
Whitehaven	D2	4.1.81	0-6
Rochdale	**D2**	**11.1.81**	**8-24**
Bramley	D2	18.1.81	21-11
Huyton	**D2**	**25.1.81**	**25-4**
Hunslet	D2	1.2.81	12-11
Swinton	D2	8.2.81	9-13
Wakefield T	**CC1**	**15.2.81**	**5-9**
Blackpool	**D2**	**1.3.81**	**8-0**
Keighley	**D2**	**8.3.81**	**24-3**
Huyton	D2	15.3.81	19-3
Dewsbury	**D2**	**22.3.81**	**16-4**
York	D2	29.3.81	10-15
Whitehaven	**D2**	**5.4.81**	**15-0**
Batley	D2	12.4.81	8-10
Rochdale	D2	16.4.81	19-5
Huddersfield	D2	19.4.81	3-8
Doncaster	**D2**	**20.4.81**	**37-11**

1981-2			
Salford	LC 2	23.8.81	3-19
Whitehaven	D1	15.11.81	10-2
Wigan	**D1**	**22.11.81**	**14-15**
Warrington	D1	29.11.81	8-16
Castleford	**D1**	**6.12.81**	**7-19**
Leigh	D1	3.1.82	11-18
Wakefield	**D1**	**24.1.82**	**13-12**
Widnes	D1	27.1.82	12-33
Castleford	D1	31.1.82	14-26
Barrow	**D1**	**7.2.82**	**5-18**
Hunslet	**CC1**	**14.2.82**	**14-4**

Hull KR	D1	17.2.82	3-20
Hull KR	**D1**	**21.2.82**	**10-31**
Hull	**CC2**	**28.2.82**	**5-11**
Bradford N	**D1**	**7.3.82**	**5-15**
Whitehaven	**D1**	**14.3.82**	**25-14**
Wakefield	D1	17.3.82	13-18
St Helens	**D1**	**21.3.82**	**2-17**
Featherstone	D1	28.3.82	10-35
Leigh	**D1**	**4.4.82**	**11-10**
York	D1	9.4.82	22-13
Wigan	D1	12.4.82	4-19
Hull	**D1**	**18.4.82**	**17-12**
Leeds	**D1**	**25.4.82**	**20-24**
Bradford N	D1	28.4.82	5-8

1982-3			
Doncaster	**D2**	**22.8.82**	**30-10**
Bramley	**D2**	**25.8.82**	**10-2**
Hunslet	D2	29.8.82	26-15
Swinton	**LC1**	**5.9.82**	**20-8**
Rochdale	D2	10.9.82	20-5
Wigan	LC2	15.9.82	15-4
Wakefield	**D2**	**19.9.82**	**18-12**
Salford	D2	26.9.82	26-13
Warrington	LCSF*	30.9.82	8-17
Dewsbury	**D2**	**3.10.82**	**23-18**
Cardiff	D2	10.10.82	15-10
Blackpool	**D2**	**17.10.82**	**8-15**
Swinton	D2	24.10.82	23-7
Whitehaven	**D2**	**31.10.82**	**18-0**
Dewsbury	D2	7.11.82	13-7
Australia	**Tour**	**14.11.82**	**5-22**
Rochdale	**D2**	**21.11.82**	**14-13**
St Helens	JPT1	27.11.82	5-17
Huyton	D2	5.12.82	50-5
Batley	**D2**	**19.12.82**	**36-10**
York	D2	2.1.83	18-7
Huddersfield	D2	9.1.83	22-7
Huyton	**D2**	**16.1.83**	**41-2**
Blackpool	D2	23.1.83	28-5
Doncaster	D2	30.1.83	10-4
Salford	**D2**	**6.2.83**	**17-9**
Rochdale	CC1	16.2.83	24-4
Bramley	**D2**	**20.2.83**	**12-18**
Bradford N	**CC2**	**27.2.83**	**4-11**

255

Hunslet	**D2**	**6.3.83**	**25-25**
Whitehaven	D2	13.3.83	6-0
Wakefield	D2	20.3.83	25-15
Keighley	**D2**	**3.4.83**	**29-0**
Batley	D2	10.4.83	21-5
Swinton	**D2****	**12.4.83**	**34-2**
Huddersfield	**D2****	**14.4.83**	**35-3**
York	**D2**	**17.4.83**	**21-13**
Keighley	D2	24.4.83	11-17
Cardiff	**D2*****	**6.5.83**	**14-20**

• Wigan ** Widnes
*** Chelsea FC

1983-4

Wakefield	D1	21.8.83	14-18
Leigh	D1	24.8.83	8-22
Featherstone	**D1**	**28.8.83**	**21-11**
Salford	LC1	4.9.83	15-16
Whitehaven	**D1**	**11.9.83**	**24-6**
Oldham	D1	18.9.83	12-30
Hull	**D1**	**25.9.83**	**29-24**
Warrington	D1	2.10.83	9-29
St Helens	D1	9.10.83	14-18
Leeds	**D1**	**16.10.83**	**10-44**
Wakefield	**D1**	**22.10.83**	**16-14**
Bradford N	D1	30.10.83	2-21
Featherstone	JPT1	6.11.83	10-12
Hull KR	D1	13.11.83	10-42
Oldham	**D1**	**20.11.83**	**21-4**
Castleford	**D1**	**4.12.83**	**6-6**
Hull	D1	11.12.83	11-36
Bradford N	**D1**	**18.12.83**	**6-16**
Leeds	D1	26.12.83	6-30
Salford	D1	2.1.84	6-4
Hull KR	**D1**	**8.1.84**	**18-38**
St Helens	**D1**	**22.1.84**	**0-30**
Swinton	**CCP**	**29.1.84**	**14-4**
Castleford	D1	5.2.84	7-26
Whitehaven	CC1	12.2.84	17-10
Wigan	**D1**	**19.2.84**	**22-10**
Widnes	**CC2**	**26.2.84**	**10-12**
Whitehaven	D1	4.3.84	0-18
Wigan	D1	18.3.84	18-38
Widnes	D1	21.3.84	16-14
Leigh	**D1**	**25.3.84**	**12-24**

Salford	**D1**	**8.4.84**	**10-12**
Warrington	**D1**	**15.4.84**	**32-58**
Featherstone	D1	22.4.84	18-38
Widnes	**D1**	**25.4.84**	**25-13**

1984-5

Sheffield	D2	9.9.84	18-14
Swinton	**LC1***	**16.9.84**	**18-25**
Swinton	D2	23.9.84	10-31
Runcorn	D2	30.9.84	16-22
Carlisle	**D2**	**6.10.84**	**18-47**
Huddersfield	**D2**	**13.10.84**	**26-8**
Whitehaven	D2	21.10.84	18-28
Blackpool	**D2**	**28.10.84**	**4-8**
York	**D2**	**4.11.84**	**22-20**
Salford	D2	9.11.84	12-28
Hull	**JPT1**	**18.11.84**	**14-36**
Wakefield	**D2**	**25.11.84**	**13-12**
Bramley	D2	9.12.84	12-11
Salford	**D2**	**16.12.84**	**13-19**
Southend	D2	1.1.85	16-14
Huddersfield	D2	3.2.85	24-8
Halifax	**CC1**	**10.2.85**	**4-17**
Blackpool	D2	3.3.85	22-25
Bridgend	**D2**	**8.3.85**	**23-8**
Rochdale	**D2**	**10.3.85**	**19-16**
Wakefield	D2	17.3.85	12-34
Rochdale	D2	20.3.85	25-0
Runcorn	**D2****	**24.3.85**	**17-16**
York	D2	31.3.85	20-36
Southend	**D2**	**5.4.85**	**24-17**
Bridgend	D2	8.4.85	32-8
Whitehaven	**D2*****	**14.4.85**	**10-10**
Carlisle	D2	17.4.85	14-10
Sheffield	**D2**	**21.4.85**	**40-30**
Bramley	**D2 *****	**28.4.85**	**22-20**
Swinton	**D2*****	**3.5.85**	**19-26**

*At Swinton
**Chiswick
***Wealdstone FC

1985-6

Blackpool	**D2**	**1.9.85**	**6-2**
Doncaster	D2	8.9.85	14-11
Wigan	LC1	15.9.85	13-24

Wakefield	D2	18.9.85	10-18
Batley	**D2**	**22.9.85**	**22-41**
Bramley	D2	29.9.85	42-24
Whitehaven	**D2**	**6.10.85**	**21-17**
Rochdale	D2	13.10.85	6-12
Wakefield	**D2**	**20.10.85**	**4-18**
Barrow	D2	27.10.85	8-40
Leigh	D2	3.11.85	13-42
Bramley	**D2**	**10.11.85**	**18-20**
Workington	D2	17.11.85	28-24
Warrington	**JPT1**	**24.11.85**	**13-20**
Sheffield	**D2**	**8.12.85**	**28-21**
Carlisle	D2	15.12.85	14-13
Runcorn	**D2**	**22.12.85**	**44-2**
Leigh	**D2**	**5.1.86**	**18-22**
Keighley	D2	12.1.86	6-18
Workington	**D2**	**19.1.86**	**36-8**
Rochdale	**D2**	**26.1.86**	**26-12**
Barrow	**CC1***	**26.2.86**	**14-26**
Blackpool	D2	2.3.86	22-12
Whitehaven	D2	9.3.86	8-18
Huddersfield	D2	16.3.86	8-14
Doncaster	**D2**	**6.4.86**	**12-14**
Runcorn	D2	16.4.86	8-26
Sheffield	D2	20.4.86	12-23
Hunslet	D2	23.4.86	20-14
Huddersfield	**D2**	**27.4.86**	**26-26**
Carlisle	**D2**	**2.5.86**	**22-41**
Barrow	**D2**	**5.5.86**	**18-50**
Mansfield	D2	7.5.86	42-16
Mansfield	**D2**	**10.5.86**	**43-20**
Batley	D2	11.5.86	13-28
Hunslet	**D2**	**16.5.86**	**34-28**
Keighley	**D2**	**18.5.86**	**27-14**

* At Wigan

1986-7

Whitehaven	LC1	14.9.86	6-72
Sheffield	**D2**	**21.9.86**	**14-68**
Mansfield	D2	28.9.86	18-32
Keighley	**D2**	**5.10.86**	**44-12**
Rochdale	D2	12.10.86	12-20
Batley	**D2**	**19.10.86**	**23-24**
Hunslet	**D2**	**2.11.86**	**4-16**
Sheffield	D2	9.11.86	8-17
Dewsbury	**D2**	**16.11.86**	**16-6**
Bramley	D2	23.11.86	10-18
Castleford	**JPT1**	**30.11.86**	**24-34**
Dewsbury	D2	7.12.86	26-30
Blackpool	**D2**	**14.12.86**	**30-12**
York	**D2**	**21.12.86**	**18-16**
Swinton	D2	26.12.86	10-50
Huddersfield	**D2**	**4.1.87**	**12-18**
Kells	CCP	22.1.87	4-4
Huddersfield	D2	25.1.87	24-16
Kells	**CCPR**	**27.1.87**	**22-14**
Halifax	**CC1**	**1.2.87**	**10-38**
Blackpool	D2	8.2.87	28-48
Bramley	**D2**	**15.2.87**	**24-20**
Swinton	**D2**	**22.2.87**	**15-15**
York	D2	1.3.87	19-21
Runcorn	**D2**	**8.3.87**	**19-2**
Hunslet	D2	15.3.87	4-30
Whitehaven	**D2**	**22.3.87**	**8-8**
Whitehaven	D2	29.3.87	14-32
Keighley	D2	4.4.87	9-22
Batley	D2	5.4.87	15-8
Mansfield	**D2**	**12.4.87**	**12-20**
Rochdale	**D2**	**17.4.87**	**16-33**
Runcorn	D2	20.4.87	9-18

1987-8

Sheffield	**D2**	**30.8.87**	**12-20**
Runcorn	D2	6.9.87	16-23
Salford	LC1	13.9.87	4-58
Keighley	**D2**	**20.9.87**	**34-6**
Workington	D2	27.9.87	14-22
Doncaster	**D2**	**4.10.87**	**12-17**
Bramley	D2	11.10.87	26-18
Featherstone	**D2**	**18.10.87**	**19-16**
Dewsbury	D2	25.10.87	10-32
Papua NG	**Tour**	**1.11.87**	**4-12**
Oldham	JPTP	8.11.87	8-36
Bramley	**D2**	**15.11.87**	**16-8**
Huddersfield	D2	22.11.87	14-52
Sheffield	D2	29.11.8	6-16
Workington	**D2**	**6.12.87**	**2-12**
Keighley	D2	12.12.87	10-33
Dewsbury	**D2**	**20.12.87**	**24-0**
Mansfield	D2	3.1.88	6-18

Runcorn	D2	10.1.88	22-20
Springfield	D2	17.1.88	0-17
York	**D2**	**24.1.88**	**4-36**
Mansfield	**CC1**	**31.1.88**	**4-16**
Featherstone	D2	7.2.88	0-14
Wakefield	**D2**	**14.2.88**	**12-28**
Huddersfield	**D2**	**6.3.88**	**10-17**
Wakefield	D2	13.3.88	0-32
Batley	D2	20.3.88	34-6
Mansfield	**D2**	**27.3.88**	**6-32**
Batley	**D2**	**1.4.88**	**40-16**
Doncaster	D2	3.4.88	11-6
York	D2	10.4.88	13-34
Springfield	**D2**	**17.4.88**	**9-8**

1988-9

Doncaster	D2	28.8.88	12-25
Sheffield	**D2**	**4.9.88**	**21-20**
Huddersfield	D2	11.9.88	28-16
Rochdale	LC1	18.9.88	14-25
Bramley	**D2**	**25.9.88**	**20-30**
Batley	**D2**	**9.10.88**	**2-22**
Bramley	D2	16.10.88	8-30
Huddersfield	**D2**	**23.10.88**	**61-22**
Runcorn	D2	30.10.88	12-20
Bramley	JPTP	6.11.88	10-56
Mansfield	D2	20.11.88	4-8
York	**D2**	**27.11.88**	**8-22**
Workington	D2	4.12.88	17-16
Hunslet	**D2**	**11.12.88**	**10-16**
Batley	D2	18.12.88	12-31
Rochdale	**D2**	**1.1.89**	**10-20**
Carlisle	D2	8.1.89	10-52
Whitehaven	**D2**	**15.1.89**	**16-32**
Dewsbury	D2	22.1.89	18-16
Bradford N	**CC1**	**29.1.89**	**10-28**
Mansfield	**D2**	**5.2.89**	**26-12**
Dewsbury	**D2**	**12.2.89**	**19-9**
Whitehaven	D2	19.2.89	0-60
Runcorn	**D2**	**26.2.89**	**28-4**
Workington	**D2**	**5.3.89**	**21-19**
York	D2	12.3.89	10-30
Doncaster	**D2**	**24.3.89**	**20-16**

Sheffield	D2	26.3.89	16-24
Carlisle	**D2**	**2.4.89**	**22-26**
Rochdale	D2	6.4.89	12-26
Hunslet	D2	9.4.89	21-26

1989-0

York	**D2**	**3.9.89**	**10-9**
Huddersfield	D2	10.9.89	8-6
Workington	LC1	17.9.89	30-24
Chorley	D2	24.9.89	20-8
Wigan	**LC2***	**27.9.89**	**4-34**
Carlisle	**D2**	**1.10.89**	**50-6**
Whitehaven	D2	8.10.89	14-15
Rochdale	**D2**	**15.10.89**	**4-18**
Bramley	**D2**	**22.10.89**	**16-6**
Hull KR	D2	29.10.89	0-44
Whitehaven	**D2**	**5.11.89**	**24-0**
Bramley	D2	12.11.89	17-0
Oldham	**D2**	**19.11.89**	**10-40**
Batley	D2	26.11.89	12-10
Halifax	**RT1**	**3.12.89**	**18-32**
Hull KR	**D2**	**17.12.89**	**6-60**
Doncaster	D2	31.12.89	8-8
Trafford	**D2**	**7.1.90**	**10-20**
Doncaster	**CCP**	**14.1.90**	**23-16**
Rochdale	D2	17.1.90	8-42
Batley	**D2**	**21.1.90**	**17-14**
Ryedale- York	**CC1**	**28.1.90**	**14-14**
Ryedale-York	CC1R	31.1.90	16-12
Oldham	D2	4.2.90	4-52
Bradford N	**CC2**	**11.2.90**	**2-20**
Nottingham	D2	18.2.90	34-14
Doncaster	**D2**	**25.2.90**	**28-12**
Ryedale-York	D2	4.3.90	14-18
Huddersfield	**D2**	**11.3.90**	**34-10**
Trafford	D2	18.3.90	22-18
Nottingham	**D2**	**25.3.90**	**44-10**
Carlisle	D2	1.4.90	14-2
Dewsbury	**D2**	**8.4.90**	**14-14**
Chorley	**D2**	**13.4.90**	**38-10**
Dewsbury	D2	16.4.90	16-22
Hull KR	DivP1	22.4.90	6-40

* Hendon FC

1990-1			
Runcorn	**LC1**	**26.8.90**	**50-0**
Leigh	LC2	2.9.90	8-40
Workington	D2	9.9.90	4-9
Barrow	**D2**	**16.9.90**	**22-8**
Whitehaven	**D2**	**23.9.90**	**8-30**
Dewsbury	D2	30.9.90	6-16
Bramley	**D2**	**7.10.90**	**20-6**
Keighley	D2	14.10.90	29-22
Runcorn	D2	21.10.90	22-12
Batley	**D2**	**28.10.90**	**14-7**
Trafford	D2	4.11.90	28-27
Ryedale-York	**D2**	**11.11.90**	**4-9**
Swinton	D2	18.11.90	4-13
Dewsbury	**D2**	**25.11.90**	**14-10**
Castleford	**RT1**	**2.12.90**	**8-14**
Doncaster	D2	16.12.90	4-0
Trafford	**D2**	**6.1.91**	**13-6**
Leigh	**D2**	**20.1.91**	**20-23**
Ryedale-York	D2	27.1.91	4-22
Swinton	**D2**	**3.2.91**	**26-10**
Halifax	CC1	17.2.91	6-46
Chorley	D2	24.2.91	36-2
Leigh	D2	27.2.91	12-12
Batley	D2	3.3.91	20-4
Workington	**D2**	**10.3.91**	**6-7**
Barrow	D2	17.3.91	20-8
Whitehaven	D2	24.3.91	20-16
Chorley	**D2**	**29.3.91**	**28-9**
Bramley	D2	1.4.91	8-8
Doncaster	**D2**	**7.4.91**	**6-12**
Keighley	**D2**	**10.4.91**	**28-16**
Runcorn	**D2**	**14.4.91**	**24-14**
Halifax	DivP1	21.4.91	24-42

1991-2			
Workington	D2	1.9.91	8-12
Rochdale	D2	8.9.91	28-26
Wigan	**LC1**	**15.9.91**	**10-38**
Sheffield	**D2**	**22.9.91**	**22-44**
Leigh	**D2**	**29.9.91**	**20-18**
Oldham	**D2**	**6.10.91**	**20-23**
Carlisle	D2	13.10.91	4-12
Ryedale-York	**D2**	**20.10.91**	**20-10**
Workington	D2	27.10.91	10-4

Rochdale	**D2**	**3.11.91**	**14-22**
Sheffield	**D2**	**10.11.91**	**12-29**
Oldham	RT1	17.11.91	10-16
Leigh	**D2**	**24.11.91**	**14-4**
Oldham	D2	8.12.91	10-0
Carlisle	**D2**	**22.12.91**	**12-8**
Leigh	D2	26.12.91	6-13
Ryedale-York	**D2**	**5.1.92**	**18-6**
Rochdale	D2	12.1.92	32-12
Rochdale	**D2**	**19.1.92**	**20-18**
Highfield	CC1	2.2.92	12-12
Highfield	**CC1R**	**4.2.92**	**24-10**
Workington	CC2	9.2.92	2-9
Oldham	**D2**	**16.2.92**	**8-12**
Carlisle	D2	23.2.92	24-28
Sheffield	D2	27.2.92	12-36
Workington	**D2**	**1.3.92**	**28-7**
Ryedale-York	D2	8.3.92	14-8
Oldham	D2	15.3.92	4-16
Carlisle	**D2**	**22.3.92**	**20-15**
Leigh	D2	29.3.92	8-30
Ryedale-York	D2	5.4.92	4-16
Sheffield	D2	12.4.92	4-38
Workington	**D2**	**17.4.92**	**32-16**
Huddersfield	**DivP1**	**26.4.92**	**14-4**
Oldham	DivPSF	10.5.92	14-22

1992-3			
Oldham	D2	30.8.92	12-27
Rochdale	**D2**	**6.9.92**	**30-10**
Carlisle	D2	20.9.92	46-14
Huddersfield	**D2**	**27.9.92**	**46-10**
Bramley	D2	4.10.92	8-30
Swinton	D2	11.10.92	6-16
Featherstone	D2	18.10.92	10-40
Rochdale	**D2**	**25.10.92**	**12-24**
Carlisle	**D2**	**1.11.92**	**18-18**
Wakefield	**RT1**	**8.11.92**	**30-0**
Rochdale	D2	15.11.92	16-25
Swinton	**D2**	**22.11.92**	**20-6**
Huddersfield	D2	29.11.92	14-18
Leigh	RT2	6.12.92	6-16
Bramley	D2	13.12.92	8-16
Featherstone	**D2**	**20.12.92**	**8-30**
Swinton	**D2**	**10.1.93**	**12-6**

259

Bramley	D2	17.1.93	20-0
Featherstone	**D2**	**24.1.93**	**6-32**
Oldham	CC1	31.1.93	6-34
Carlisle	D2	7.2.93	28-14
Featherstone	D2	14.2.93	12-58
Bramley	**D2**	**21.2.93**	**20-12**
Rochdale	D2	24.2.93	18-30
Swinton	D2	7.3.93	24-26
Huddersfield	**D2**	**14.3.93**	**31-17**
Oldham	D2	21.3.93	27-20
Huddersfield	D2	25.3.93	2-17
Carlisle	**D2**	**28.3.93**	**30-8**
Oldham	**D2**	**31.3.93**	**20-20**
Oldham	**D2**	**18.4.93**	**30-18**

1993-4

Batley	**D2**	**27.8.93**	**40-6**
Keighley	D2	5.9.93	17-14
Doncaster	**D2**	**10.9.93**	**38-18**
Huddersfield	D2	19.9.93	10-34
Dewsbury	**D2**	**26.9.93**	**17-42**
Barrow	D2	3.10.93	12-37
Ryedale-York	**D2**	**10.10.93**	**24-20**
Highfield	**D2**	**17.10.93**	**62-6**
Hunslet	**D2**	**24.10.93**	**48-12**
St Esteve	**RT1**	**31.10.93**	**48-16**
Workington	D2	7.11.93	13-12
Featherstone	**RT2**	**14.11.93**	**26-12**
Carlisle	**D2**	**28.11.93**	**38-24**
Bramley	D2	1.12.93	30-18
Whitehaven	D2	5.12.93	16-16
Ryedale-York	RT3	12.12.93	42-10
Bradford N	**RT 4**	**19.12.93**	**10-22**
Swinton	**D2**	**29.12.93**	**22-12**
Rochdale	D2	2.1.94	8-15
Shaw Cross	**CC3**	**16.1.94**	**40-14**
Doncaster	D2	23.1.94	10-20
Featherstone	**CC4**	**30.1.94**	**14-28**
Huddersfield	**D2**	**6.2.94**	**10-24**
Batley	D2	13.2.94	18-29
Keighley	**D2**	**16.2.94**	**13-10**
Dewsbury	D2	20.2.94	30-16
Barrow	**D2**	**27.2.94**	**52-14**
Ryedale York	D2	6.3.94	22-14
Hunslet	D2	13.3.94	46-22

Workington	**D2**	**20.3.94**	**20-20**
Bramley	**D2**	**27.3.94**	**64-0**
Highfield	D2	1.4.94	58-6
Rochdale	**D2**	**4.4.94**	**28-10**
Swinton	D2	12.4.94	20-18
Whitehaven	**D2**	**17.4.94**	**30-21**
Carlisle	D2	24.4.94	26-12
Keighley	**DivP1**	**8.5.94**	**66-12**
Doncaster	DivPSF	15.5.94	16-6
Workington	DivPF *	22.5.94	22-30

- Old Trafford

1994-5

Carlisle	D2	21.8.94	38-16
Hunslet	D2	28.8.94	14-25
Barrow	D2	4.9.94	16-10
Keighley	**D2**	**11.9.94**	**10-30**
Highfield	D2	18.9.94	30-8
Batley	**D2**	**25.9.94**	**30-2**
Swinton	**D2**	**2.10.94**	**40-29**
Dewsbury	D2	9.10.94	8-23
Bramley	**D2**	**16.10.94**	**40-12**
Rochdale	**D2**	**21.10.94**	**12-3**
Ryedale-York	**D2**	**30.10.94**	**10-13**
Carlisle	**D2**	**6.11.94**	**23-16**
Hunslet	**D2**	**13.11.94**	**40-2**
Hemel H	**RT2**	**27.11.94**	**34-16**
Salford	RT3	4.12.94	14-16
Barrow	**D2**	**11.12.94**	**30-6**
Leigh	D2	26.12.94	10-24
Hull KR	D2	8.1.95	4-38
Keighley	D2	11.1.95	25-14
Huddersfield	D2	15.1.95	8-20
Ellenborough	**CC3**	**22.1.95**	**30-10**
Highfield	**D2**	**29.1.95**	**42-4**
Batley	D2	5.2.95	22-10
Hull KR	**CC4**	**12.2.95**	**20-26**
Swinton	D2	19.2.95	38-26
Dewsbury	**D2**	**5.3.95**	**22-16**
Whitehaven	**D2**	**15.3.95**	**18-16**
Bramley	D2	19.3.95	38-6
Ryedale-York	D2	26.3.95	12-25
Hull KR	**D2**	**2.4.95**	**34-22**
Huddersfield	**D2**	**9.4.95**	**24-24**
Leigh	**D2**	**14.4.95**	**60-6**

Rochdale	D2	18.4.95	4-22
Whitehaven	D2	23.4.95	30-12
Whitehaven	**DivP1**	**8.5.95**	**28-1**
Keighley	DivPSF	14.5.95	4-38

1995-6

Warrington	SBC	20.8.95	6-46
Halifax	SBC	23.8. 95	12-50
Bradford B	SBC	3.9.95	16-26
Wigan	SBC	10.9.95	12-50
Leeds	**SBC***	**17.9.95**	**26-12**
Oldham	SBC	20.9.95	8-19
Sheffield E	SBC	24.9.95	42-10
Workington	**SBC****	**1.10.95**	**44-8**
Oldham	SBC***	27.10.95	46-14
St Helens	**SBC******	**1.11.95**	**34-50**
Castleford	SBC	5.11.95	37-8
Highfield	**RT2****	**12.11.95**	**82-0**
Halifax	**SBC******	**15.11.95**	**38-27**
Warrington	**SBC******	**19.11.95**	**10-18**
Halifax	**RT3******	**25.11.95**	**18-22**
Wigan	**SBC***	**3.12.95**	**10-42**
Bradford B	**SBC*****	**10.12.95**	**27-24**
Sheffield	**SBC*****	**17.12.95**	**14-21**
Leeds	SBC	19.12.95	12-30
Workington	SBC	7.1.96	10-32
St Helens	SBC	17.1.96	18-48
Castleford	**SBC*****	**21.1.96**	**44-50**

*Brentford FC **Copthall
***The Valley ****The Stoop

1996

Dewsbury	CC(4)	31.1.96	10-12
Halifax	SL	30.3.96	24-22
Paris St G	**SL**	**4.4.96**	**38-22**
Bradford B	SL	8.4.96	24-31
Sheffield E	SL	14.4.96	18-34
Workington	**SL**	**21.4.96**	**58-0**
Leeds	SL	5.5.96	27-20
St Helens	SL	12.5.96	22-24
Castleford	SL	19.5.96	21-20
Warrington	SL	25.5. 96	24-28
Oldham	**SL**	**2.6.96**	**28-22**
Wigan	SL	9.6.96	18-18
Halifax	**SL**	**16.6.96**	**24-52**

Workington	SL	23.6.96	34-6
Bradford B	**SL**	**29.6.96**	**16-22**
Sheffield E	**SL**	**6.7.96**	**45-8**
Paris St G	SL	13.7.96	18-24
Leeds	**SL**	**21.7.96**	**33-16**
St Helens	**SL**	**27.7.96**	**28-32**
Warrington	**SL**	**4.8.96**	**20-13**
Oldham	SL	11.8.96	22-14
Wigan	**SL**	**17.8.96**	**13-34**
Castleford	**SL**	**25.8.96**	**56-0**
St Helens	PSF	1.9.96	14-25

1997

Lancashire L	CC4	9.2.97	48-5
Bradford B	**CC5**	**22.2.97**	**12-34**
St Helens	**SL**	**16.3.97**	**24-28**
Warrington	SL	21.3.97	38-18
Paris SG	**SL**	**28.3.97**	**28-10**
Oldham	SL	1.4.97	32-22
Bradford B	SL	6.4.97	14-19
Halifax	SL	13.4.97	24-24
Salford	**SL**	**18.4.97**	**48-12**
Leeds	**SL**	**27.4.97**	**40-16**
Wigan	SL	9.5.97	10-38
St Helens	SL	16.5.97	22-22
Warrington	**SL**	**23.5.97**	**30-6**
Paris SG	SL	26.5.97	20-16
Sheffield	**SL**	**30.5.97**	**32-12**
Brisbane	WCC	6.6.97	22-42
Canberra	WCC	15.6.97	20-66
Canterbury	WCC	21.6.97	18-34
Castleford	**SL**	**27.6.97**	**17-10**
Wigan	**SL**	**4.7.97**	**38-12**
Sheffield	SL	13.7.97	50-8
Canberra	**WCC**	**21.7.97**	**38-18**
Brisbane	**WCC**	**27.7.97**	**16-34**
Canterbury	**WCC**	**1.8.97**	**22-44**
Oldham	**SL**	**5.8.97**	**36-28**
Castleford	SL	8.8.97	22-13
Leeds	SL	17.8.97	8-36
Salford	SL	22.8.97	27-16
Halifax	**SL**	**25.8. 97**	**28-28**
Bradford	**SL**	**31.8.97**	**28-24**
Sheffield	**PQF**	**14.9.97**	**16-58**
Cronulla	**WCCQF**	**5.10.97**	**16-40**

1998			
Batley	CC4	15.2.98	44-20
Halifax	**CC5**	**1.3.98**	**21-18**
Hull KR	**CC6**	**15.3.98**	**46-18**
Wigan	CCSF*	29.3.98	8-38
Halifax	**SL**	**5.4.98**	**6-32**
Hull	SL	10.4.98	4-6
Warrington	**SL**	**19.4.98**	**14-4**
Wigan	SL	26.4 98	10-24
Leeds	**SL**	**8.5.98**	**13-14**
Huddersfield	SL	17.5.98	28-20
Salford	**SL**	**24.5-98**	**21-12**
Bradford B	SL	29.5.98	14-17
Sheffield E	**SL**	**7.6.98**	**26-22**
St Helens	SL	14.6.98	6-58
Castleford	**SL**	**21.698**	**16-36**
Halifax	SL	27 6.98	14-34
Hull	**SL**	**5.7.98**	**38-6**
Bradford B	SL**	18.7.98	22-8
Warrington	SL	2.8.98	23-14
Wigan	**SL**	**7.8.98**	**15-18**
Leeds	SL	14.8.98	12-34
Huddersfield	**SL**	**23.8.98**	**20-8**
Salford	SL	30.8.98	20-23
Bradford B	**SL**	**6.9.98**	**34-8**
Sheffield E	SL	11.9.98	19-18
St Helens	**SL**	**18.9.98**	**22-37**
Castleford	SL	27.9.98	18-23

*Huddersfield ** Edinburgh

1999			
Doncaster	**CC4**	**14.2.99**	**64-0**
Hull KR	CC5	28.2.99	6-0
Huddersfield	**SL**	**7.3.99**	**24-18**
Whitehaven	**CC6**	**14.3.99**	**54-6**
Sheffield	SL	20.3.99	26-20
Castleford	CCSF*	27.3.99	33-27
Hull	**SL**	**2.4.99**	**12-10**
Leeds	SL	5.4.99	12-38
St Helens	**SL**	**9.4.99**	**18-34**
Wakefield	SL	18.4.99	8-40
Warrington	SL	24.4.99	18-30
Leeds	CCF**1.5.99		16-52
Halifax	SL	5.5.99	24-26
Castleford	**SL**	**9.5.99**	**12-12**
Salford	SL	16.5.99	14-31
Gateshead	**SL**	**23.5.99**	**18-18**
Wigan	**SL**	**28.5.99**	**12-30**
Huddersfield	SL	6.6.99	21-20
Bradford	SL	9.6.99	12-74
Sheffield	**SL**	**13.6.99**	**44-12**
Hull	SL	20.6.99	47-6
Leeds	**SL**	**26.6.99**	**16-22**
St Helens	SL	4.7.99	24-22
Wigan	SL	7.7.99	4-22
Wakefield	**SL**	**11.7.99**	**36-26**
Warrington	SL	18.7.99	14-28
Halifax	**SL**	**23.7.99**	**48-12**
Bradford	SL***28.7.99		16-19
Castleford	SL	1.8.99	16-52
Salford	**SL**	**7.8.99**	**28-14**
Gateshead	SL	15.8.99	28-22
Huddersfield	SL	22.8.99	40-4
Sheffield	SL	28.8.99	16-20
Hull	**SL**	**5.9.99**	**28-12**
Leeds	SL	10.9.99	8-14

*Leeds **Wembley ***Leicester

262

Player appearances

(All records complete to the end of the 1999 season, except Shaun Edwards - record to April 2000)

Player	A	S	TA	T	G	D	P
Dazi Abdurahman	7	2	9	0	0	0	8
Glen Air	38	4	42	12	0	1	49
David Aitken	19	1	20	5	0	0	20
Bola Aiyede	0	2	2	0	0	0	0
Adrian Alexander	3	0	3	0	0	0	0
David Allen	102	6	108	34	0	0	107
Gavin Allen	10	0	10	0	0	0	0
Ray Allen	5	3	8	3	0	0	12
Des Armitage	1	1	2	0	0	0	0
Mal Aspey	35	6	41	19	0	0	57
Colin Atkinson	40	2	42	6	0	0	24
Tony Bader	1	0	1	0	0	0	0
David Baker	4	0	4	0	0	0	0
Bill Barker	1	0	1	1	0	0	4
Norman Barrow	36	3	39	9	10	0	56
Greg Barwick	37	6	43	23	138	2	370
Russell Bawden	44	27	71	10	0	0	40
Steve Bayliss	41	0	41	21	0	0	71
Robbie Beazley	66	15	81	19	0	1	77
Ben Beevers	8	1	9	0	0	0	0
Gary Berney	6	2	8	2	0	0	8
Roger Best	1	10	11	1	0	0	4
Tony Best	1	0	1	0	0	0	0
Harry Beverley	104	2	106	3	0	0	9
Neil Bibby	20	13	33	3	0	0	12
Mark Birmingham	0	1	1	0	0	0	0
David Bishop	0	1	1	0	0	0	0
Richard Blackman	12	1	13	4	0	0	16
Craig Booth	8	1	9	1	30	0	64
Reg Bowden	116	4	120	14	0	0	42
Karl Bowen	5	1	6	0	0	0	0
Bob Boyce	21	3	24	3	0	0	12
Wayne Boyle	1	0	1	0	0	0	0
Darren Bradstreet	4	0	4	2	0	0	8
Gary Braniff	1	1	2	0	0	0	0
J Breem	0	3	3	0	0	0	0
Phil Briscoe	11	0	11	1	0	0	4
Russ Bridge	109	4	113	12	0	0	48
Brian Brown	6	0	7	1	0	5	9
Jeff Brown	2	0	2	0	0	0	0
Michael Brown	0	2	2	0	0	0	0
Russell Browning	51	4	55	8	0	0	32
George Bryan	18	0	18	3	0	0	12
Justin Bryant	42	18	60	8	0	0	32
Shane Buckley	63	0	63	33	0	0	132
David Bullough	16	1	17	9	0	0	36
Mike Burke	0	1	1	0	0	0	0
Martin Burridge	1	0	1	0	0	0	0
Alan Burrows	1	0	1	0	0	0	0
Peter Bush	3	1	4	0	0	0	0
John Butler	1	1	2	0	0	0	0
Ikram Butt	21	1	22	4	0	0	16
Dean Callaway	17	14	31	8	0	0	32
Steve Callow	5	2	7	0	0	0	0
Logan Campbell	31	1	32	25	0	0	100
Adrian Cambriani	119	2	121	42	0	0	146
Chris Camilleri	6	0	6	0	0	0	0
Bernard Carroll	5	2	7	3	0	0	12
Mark Carroll	19	3	22	1	0	0	4
Scott Carter	31	1	32	6	0	1	21
Peter Cass	4	0	4	0	0	0	0
T Caton	0	1	1	0	0	0	0
Paul Chambers	2	2	4	0	0	0	0
Damien Chapman	9	2	11	4	13	2	44
Ian Chatterton	16	2	19	1	0	0	4
Paul Cheetham	19	4	23	6	0	0	24
Kris Chesney	1	2	3	0	0	0	0
Lachlan Churchill	30	8	38	8	0	0	32
Evan Cochrane	18	1	19	7	0	0	28
Andy Collier	1	0	1	0	0	0	0
J Collis	0	1	1	0	0	0	0
Dominic Cooper	12	6	18	0	0	1	1
Tony Cooper	2	1	3	0	0	0	0
Colin Corcoran	9	8	17	0	0	0	0
Wes Cotton	13	1	14	5	0	0	20
Jeff Coutts	46	1	47	17	21	3	61
Scott Cram	15	0	15	0	0	0	0
Kieran Crompton	0	1	1	0	0	0	0
John Crossley	88	3	91	48	0	0	150
Mark Croston	2	0	2	0	0	0	0
David Cruickshank	12	2	14	3	0	0	12
John Dalgreen	58	0	58	9	0	2	29
Brett Daunt	26	0	26	12	0	3	39
Mike Davis	44	1	45	25	0	1	101
Gary Deaker	26	1	27	5	0	0	20
Martin Dean	1	0	1	0	0	0	0
Alan Dearden	41	2	43	1	0	0	4
Steve Diamond	109	0	109	24	305	4	691
Joe Doherty	93	11	104	13	0	0	42
Sid Domic	18	1	19	8	0	0	32
Roger Draper	0	1	1	0	0	0	0
Matt Dray	37	5	42	5	0	0	20
David Driver	14	1	15	8	0	0	32
Don Duffy	52	0	52	9	0	0	36
Andrew Duncan	4	4	8	3	0	0	12
Darryl Duncan	6	0	6	0	0	0	0
Matt Dunford	21	29	50	4	0	1	17
Keith Durham	0	1	1	0	0	0	0
Joe Dutton	11	1	12	4	0	0	16
Tim Dwyer	21	0	21	3	27	0	66
Leo Dynevor	37	13	50	21	27	0	138
David Eckersley	85	8	93	21	6	17	93

Shaun Edwards	42	10	52	23	1	0	94
Abi Ekoku	27	0	27	15	0	0	60
Nick Elgar	6	0	6	1	0	0	4
Dave Evans	9	1	10	3	0	0	12
Lynn Evans	0	2	2	0	0	0	0
"Butch" Fatnowna	11	3	14	5	0	0	20
Frank Feighan	38	6	44	10	0	0	35
Neil Felton	1	0	1	0	0	0	0
Colin Fenn	50	8	58	1	107	0	218
Paul Fisher	29	0	29	6	3	1	31
John Fiso	1	1	2	0	0	0	0
Brian Flashman	5	0	5	2	0	0	8
Greg Fleming	35	0	35	26	1	0	106
Hugh Francis	8	4	12	2	0	0	8
Mick Francis	3	0	3	0	0	0	0
John Gallagher	51	0	51	19	196	2	470
Chris Ganley	55	5	60	13	0	0	40
Ernie Garland	6	0	6	2	0	0	8
Steve Garner	33	3	36	7	0	0	28
Brett Garside	4	2	6	0	0	0	0
Russ Gibson	13	5	18	5	6	2	34
Bernie Gilbert	18	4	22	2	0	0	8
Peter Gill	108	7	115	25	0	0	100
Dave Gillan	97	4	101	38	0	0	152
Mick Glover	24	0	24	2	0	0	8
Luke Goodwin	9	2	11	3	1	1	15
John Gould	0	1	1	0	0	0	0
Tony Gourley	125	6	131	2	0	0	6
Mike Graham	1	0	1	0	0	0	0
Craig Grauf	29	0	29	7	0	2	30
Craig Green	43	5	48	13	9	2	72
Ken Green	13	13	26	1	0	0	4
John Green	1	0	1	0	0	0	0
Gavin Green	1	0	1	0	0	0	0
Nick Grimoldby	45	5	50	4	3	3	25
Steve Guyett	74	6	80	12	117	3	289
Glen Haggath	18	0	18	3	2	0	16
Nick Halafihi	39	10	49	8	0	0	32
Andrew Hamilton	5	10	15	3	0	0	12
Karle Hammond	33	0	33	20	2	1	85
Chris Hanson	0	1	1	0	0	0	0
Dave Harvey	0	1	1	0	0	0	0
Paul Hauff	13	0	13	13	0	0	52
Ross Heisner	2	0	2	0	0	0	0
Albert Helg	2	2	4	0	0	0	0
Gary Henley-Smith	18	0	18	8	0	0	32
Harold Henney	37	2	39	8	0	1	33
Justin Herbert	0	1	1	0	0	0	0
Martin Herdman	71	21	92	14	0	2	90
Cavill Heugh	31	6	37	4	23	0	62
Darren Higgins	8	7	15	3	0	0	12
"Iain" Higgins	2	7	8	2	0	0	8
Sean Hoare	61	29	90	16	0	0	54
Mark Hodson	1	0	1	0	0	0	0
Darren Hogg	1	1	2	0	0	0	0
Tim Hogg	1	0	1	0	0	0	0
Kevin Holderness	1	5	6	0	0	0	0
Kim Howard	7	7	14	1	0	0	4
Roger Hudson	2	5	7	0	0	0	0
Stefan Hughes	0	5	5	0	0	0	0
David Hull	49	1	50	6	0	0	22
Steve Hulme	1	0	1	0	0	0	0
Brian Hunter	6	0	6	2	0	0	8
Mike Hutchinson	61	4	65	3	0	0	12
Bob Jackson	8	0	8	1	0	0	4
Ed Jennings	1	2	3	0	0	0	0
Scott Jennings	16	1	17	1	2	0	8
Lawrence Johanneson	24	13	37	2	0	0	8
Mark Johnson	73	0	73	66	0	0	264
Nick Johnson	0	1	1	0	0	0	0
Charlie Jones	94	22	116	16	0	0	63
Tony Karalius	20	2	22	2	0	0	6
Noel Keating	36	16	52	2	0	0	8
Shaun Keating	9	4	13	1	0	0	4
Shane Kelly	13	4	17	3	0	0	12
Eric Kennedy	21	0	21	6	0	0	24
Jason Kerapa	5	1	6	2	0	0	8
Ivan Kete	9	3	12	0	0	0	0
Andrew Key	23	3	26	4	0	0	16
Alan Kimaingatau	3	0	3	0	0	0	0
Mick Kimberley	1	0	1	0	0	0	0
Dave King	20	7	27	10	0	0	40
Tony Kinsey	131	25	156	18	0	10	74
Bob Knight	24	0	24	1	0	0	4
M Koehner	10	0	10	0	0	0	0
David Krause	27	3	30	9	0	0	36
Gary Lane	12	0	12	3	0	1	13
Kevin Langer	43	14	57	13	0	0	52
Geordie Lawrie	19	5	24	2	0	0	8
"Leroy" Leapai	2	0	2	0	0	0	0
Mark Lee	26	2	28	7	0	0	28
Roy Leslie	41	9	50	8	0	0	32
Roy Lester	28	19	47	4	0	0	12
Peter Liddell	25	5	30	2	0	0	8
Dave Long	0	1	1	0	0	0	0
Tony Looker	47	1	48	9	0	0	36
Geoff Luxon	1	10	11	1	0	0	4
Iain MacCorqoudale	28	0	28	6	75	3	171
Mark Maguire	14	4	18	7	13	0	54
Warren Mann	6	0	6	2	0	0	8
Kevin Manning	20	5	25	2	0	0	8
Glenn Mansfield	26	0	26	9	0	0	36
Greg Manthey	16	0	16	2	0	0	8
Nick Mardon	23	0	23	4	0	0	16
Tony Martin	34	2	36	10	1	1	43
Santi Masa	9	0	9	2	0	1	9
Luke Massey	19	5	24	2	0	0	8
Ben Matautia	0	1	1	0	0	0	0
Terry Matterson	74	0	74	23	116	6	330
Frank Matthews	17	4	21	4	0	0	16
Ian Matthews	17	4	21	4	0	0	16
John Mayo	6	0	6	0	0	0	0
Hussain M'Barki	148	15	163	74	0	0	265
Red McCabe	18	0	18	8	0	0	32
Ray McCarthy	1	1	2	0	0	0	0
Frank McFadden	2	3	5	0	0	0	0
Dixon McIvor	17	13	30	4	0	0	16
Grant McKenzie	2	0	2	2	0	0	8

Player							
Gerry McMullen	0	1	1	0	0	0	0
Chris McKenna	13	0	13	9	0	0	36
Duncan McRae	14	2	16	6	0	1	25
Colin Meachin	0	1	1	0	0	0	0
Ian Mellors	41	16	57	4	0	0	16
Tony Mestrov	78	2	80	8	0	0	32
Keiran Meyer	9	0	9	2	0	0	8
Darren Michalski	23	14	37	2	0	0	8
Andrew Mighty	25	1	26	7	0	0	28
Shane Millard	30	6	36	3	1	0	14
Craig Miller	29	1	30	4	0	0	16
Wayne Millington	9	0	9	1	0	0	4
Paul Mills	1	0	1	0	0	0	0
Steve Mills	100	8	108	50	3	0	199
John Minto	13	0	13	4	0	0	16
Simon Mitchell	3	2	5	0	0	0	0
Sean Mohr	5	2	7	4	0	0	16
Bob Mordell	5	3	8	0	0	0	0
Graham Moss	2	0	2	0	0	0	0
Danny Mulkerin	40	3	43	2	0	0	8
Kieron Murphy	105	14	119	24	0	3	99
Matt Nable	2	2	4	1	0	0	4
Glen Nissen	18	2	20	4	0	0	16
Mick Noble	15	3	18	3	0	0	12
Tony Noel	1	0	1	0	0	0	0
Derek Noonan	18	0	18	4	0	0	12
Gary O'Brien	3	0	3	2	0	0	8
Pat O'Doherty	18	1	19	7	0	0	28
David O'Donnell	10	2	12	0	0	0	0
Julian O'Neill	3	0	3	0	13	1	27
Paul O'Riley	16	3	19	5	0	0	20
Martin Offiah	45	3	48	36	0	0	144
Ben Olsen	27	3	30	3	0	0	12
Ray Ovens	4	0	4	1	0	0	4
Junior Paul	4	1	5	1	0	0	4
Brian Parkes	5	0	5	0	0	0	0
Greg Pearce	47	2	49	8	121	0	274
Barry Peart	1	1	2	0	0	0	0
Ian Perryment	2	2	4	2	0	0	8
Dominic Peters	19	10	29	5	0	0	20
Darryl Pitt	100	54	154	52	25	1	255
John Plath	15	2	17	4	0	0	16
Alan Platt	27	0	27	5	27	4	78
Billy Platt	2	0	2	0	0	0	0
Jason Pram	2	1	3	0	0	0	0
Greg Pratt	16	0	16	1	0	0	4
Paul Prendergast	1	0	1	0	0	0	0
Carl Radbone	36	2	38	9	4	0	35
Darren Rampling	2	7	9	0	0	0	0
Neville Ramsey	44	0	44	11	0	1	49
Tony Rea	46	1	47	11	0	0	44
Huw Rees	51	7	58	15	12	2	86
Peter Reinsfield	28	6	34	4	0	0	16
Brain Rendell	11	5	16	2	0	0	8
Andrew Render	2	4	6	0	0	1	1
Ian Rex	5	2	7	0	0	0	0
Steele Retchless	54	2	56	4	0	0	16
Mark Riley	89	5	94	62	0	1	249
Andy Rippon	4	0	4	2	7	0	22
John Risman	18	2	20	3	0	0	9
Jason Roach	11	0	11	5	0	0	20
Steve Roberts	5	5	10	0	0	0	0
Karl Robertson	3	2	5	1	0	0	4
Paul Rochford	13	0	13	4	14	0	44
Frank Rolls	2	3	5	0	0	0	0
Scott Roskell	136	8	144	86	0	0	344
Steve Rosolen	158	13	171	31	0	0	124
Adam Ross	0	1	1	0	0	0	0
Troy Rugless	15	0	15	4	0	0	16
Chris Ryan	48	5	53	20	14	0	108
Adam Sada	3	0	3	1	0	0	4
Matt Salter	17	41	58	0	0	0	0
Wayne Sanchez	21	0	21	3	9	0	30
Conrad Scott	13	8	21	0	0	0	0
Gary Scott	1	1	2	0	0	0	0
John Scourfield	10	0	10	7	0	0	28
Mick Seaby	4	2	6	1	0	0	4
Anthony Seibold	22	3	25	3	0	0	12
Andy Shaw	2	2	4	0	0	0	0
Darren Shaw	41	3	44	4	0	0	16
Kevin Simpson	4	5	9	0	0	0	0
Ian Simpson	11	2	13	1	0	0	4
Robbie Simpson	9	9	18	1	0	0	4
Chris Smith	74	20	94	7	153	0	334
Danny Smith	2	1	3	1	0	0	4
Martyn Smith	4	1	5	0	0	0	0
Paul Smith	9	1	10	3	0	0	12
Rob Smyth	32	1	33	10	28	0	96
Ian Snowden	1	0	1	0	0	0	0
Andre Sokolov	1	1	2	0	0	0	0
Peter Souto	51	20	71	9	0	0	28
Adrian Spencer	13	42	55	6	7	0	38
Paul Stevens	14	6	20	2	0	0	8
Sam Stewart	70	2	72	8	0	0	32
John Stockley	3	0	3	1	0	0	4
Trevor Stockley	39	1	40	14	0	0	56
Andre Stoop	15	0	15	9	0	0	36
Harold Stringer	6	0	6	1	0	0	3
Graham Strutton	10	1	11	4	0	0	16
Wayne Sykes	0	2	2	0	0	0	0
Ray Tabern	7	0	7	1	0	0	4
Takura Tawera	15	0	15	0	0	0	0
Craig Taylor	41	0	41	3	0	0	12
Mick Taylor	84	3	87	19	0	0	76
Paul Terry	0	1	1	0	0	0	0
Giles Thomas	2	2	4	0	0	0	0
Victor Timms	8	5	13	3	0	0	12
John Timu	52	1	53	15	0	0	60
Eddie Tinsley	5	3	8	0	0	0	0
Kerrod Toby	2	4	6	0	0	0	0
Ken Tolcher	1	0	1	0	0	0	0
Tulsen Tollett	91	4	95	29	37	1	191
Matt Toshack	40	15	55	11	0	0	44
Glen Townsend	14	7	21	3	0	0	12
Dennis Trembath	1	1	2	0	0	0	0
Trialist (S.African)	3	0	3	0	3	0	6
Neil Tuffs	48	12	60	6	0	2	20
Ian van Bellen	20	2	22	4	0	0	12

Player								Player							
Shane Vincent	7	0	7	5	4	0	28	Chris Wilkinson	69	4	73	17	141	13	363
Ben Walker	15	1	16	6	5	3	37	Bart Williams	5	3	8	1	0	0	4
Jason Walker	17	0	17	6	0	0	24	Brett Williams	26	1	27	1	0	0	4
Paul Walker	15	0	15	1	0	0	4	Doug Winborn	5	6	11	1	0	0	4
Michael Walsh	2	3	5	0	0	0	0	Jason Wing	13	0	13	2	0	0	8
Jimmy Ward	2	2	4	1	0	0	4	Chris Winstanley	24	3	27	3	0	0	12
Brett Warton	18	1	19	3	59	0	130	John Wood	57	8	67	11	0	0	33
Duncan Webster	11	0	11	2	0	0	8	Martin Woodcock	0	1	1	0	0	0	0
Josh White	20	3	23	11	0	1	45	Graham Worgan	2	1	3	0	0	0	0
Peter White	22	1	23	7	0	0	28	Glen Workman	25	17	42	1	0	0	4
Chris Whiteley	28	9	37	0	0	0	0	Rob Wright	7	4	11	0	0	0	0
John Whittaker	1	0	1	0	0	0	0	Andrew Wynyard	16	4	20	3	0	0	12
Adrian Why	0	5	5	0	0	0	0	Mal Yates	0	1	1	0	0	0	0
Ian Wightman	11	3	14	1	0	0	4	Grant Young	29	2	31	4	0	0	16
Tim Wilby	24	4	28	1	0	0	4	Andrew Zillman	37	1	38	2	0	0	8
Bernie Wilkinson	41	4	45	8	0	0	32								

367 players have appeared for the club's first team.

Bibliography

Tony Adams	*Masters of the Game*
Dean Bell	*Ultimate Warrior*
Mike Colman	*Super League - The Inside Story*

Dave Farrar & Peter Lush with Michael O'Hare
Touch and Go - A History of Professional Rugby League in London

Ray French	*100 Great Rugby League Players*
Ray French	*The Match of my Life*
John Gallagher	*The World's Greatest Rugby Player?*
Dave Hadfield	*Playing Away*
Dave Hadfield (ed)	*XIII Winters*
Dave Hadfield (ed)	*XIII Worlds*
Neil Hanson	*Blood, Mud and Glory*
David Lawrenson	*Offiah - A Blaze of Glory*
Mark Newbrook	*A short history of the Southern Amateur Rugby League*
Martin Offiah	*My Autobiography*
Stephen M. Wild	*The Lions of Swinton*
Paul Wilson	*The Best Years of our Lives*

Index

This index only covers people in the text, not statistics or team lists.

267

The Fulham Dream
Rugby League comes to London
By Harold Genders

Harold Genders was the man who in 1979 had the idea of bringing Rugby League to the south and setting up the club at Fulham - the first club outside the sport's heartlands since 1951. Told for the first time, this is the inside story of how he did it - one man's dream becoming reality.

Harold tells the story of:
* Convincing the Fulham football officials that it wasn't a crazy idea to have Rugby League at Craven Cottage;
* Persuading the Rugby League to change its rules to allow the club to join;
* Recruiting the players in eight weeks to play - and beat - Wigan in the first match

All this is covered in the book, with a behind the scenes account of the marvellous first season that saw the team promoted to the First Division. It includes Harold's view of the key matches, controversies and events that saw the team triumph at the end.
The book also includes a full record of the first season, profiles of all the 1980-81 Fulham players and reports of all the matches.
The photos are mainly by the club's official photographer and recall those great days at Craven Cottage.

Every Rugby League fan from London and elsewhere will enjoy this book.

To be published in August 2000 at £6.95.
Special offer for readers of this book - order your copy for £6.00 post free from: London League Publications, PO Box 10441, London E14 0SB
(Cheques payable to London League Publications Ltd, no credit cards).

A new Rugby League magazine, to be published twice a year, with new writing on the game by leading Rugby League writers.

Order a sample copy for £2.00 or subscribe for 4 issues for £7.00 from
London League Publications, PO Box 10441, London E14 0SB.
(Cheques payable to London League Publications, no credit cards)

JOIN THE
Rugby League
Supporters Association

And get *The Greatest Game!* delivered free
Don't just read the headlines... Join the RLSA and help us make them

Our aims:
- To democratically represent the views of our members
- To campaign for supporters' views to be heard at all levels in the game
- To encourage friendship between supporters of all clubs and countries
- To seek to work for the promotion and expansion of rugby league

To join the RLSA, and get TGG! delivered to your door, just complete the following details and send with your payment to the address below. Please make cheques payable to the RLSA.

Yes! I would like to join the RLSA and receive my four issues of TGG! starting from issue no____ . I enclose a cheque / postal order for £6.00

Name:

Address: (Please include your postcode)

Optional information:
Telephone (including STD code)
Email
I follow...
(Please enter your team or tick one of the boxes)
[] The Super League [] The Northern Ford Premiership [] Other

N.B. The RLSA does not release member details to third parties
Post to: RLSA Memberships, 5, Wesley Street, Cutsyke, Castleford WF10 5HQ (photocopy if you do not want to cut the book)

Support the London Broncos?
Why not join the London Broncos
Rugby League Supporters Club?

We offer:
- Travel to away matches
- A regular newsletter
- Regular Meetings
- Social events
- The chance to meet other supporters

For more information and membership details, write to: London Broncos Supporters Club, c/o 30, Richmond Court, Richmond Road, London SW20 0PB or visit our stall in the Millennium Bar before London Broncos home matches.

BOOKS AVAILABLE FROM ROBERT GATE

REDUCED TO £5.00 EACH!:
* *Gone North : Welshmen In Rugby League (Volume 1)*
* *Gone North : Welshmen In Rugby League (Volume 2)*
* *Champions : A Celebration of the Rugby League Championship 1895-1987*
* *The Struggle For The Ashes (1986)*
* *The Struggle For The Ashes II (1996)*

All the above books are profusely illustrated and are available at £5.00 each,
which includes postage (United Kingdom only).
Special offer - all five books for £20.00 (postage included, UK only)

Also still available in limited supply at £11.95 (including postage, UK only):
There Were A Lot More Than That : Odsal 1954

To order, send cheques (payable to RE Gate) to:
RE Gate, Mount Pleasant Cottage, Ripponden Bank, Ripponden,
Sowerby Bridge, Yorkshire HX6 4JL (Tel: 01422 823074)